CORPORATE COUNTRY

CORPORATE COUNTRY

A State Shaped to Suit Technology

William H. Rodgers, Jr.

RODALE PRESS, INC.
Book Division
Emmaus, Pennsylvania 18049

Standard Book Number 0–87857–055–1
Library of Congress Card Number 72–90824

COPYRIGHT © 1973 by William H. Rodgers, Jr.

All rights reserved. No part of this publication may be reproduced or transmitted in any form or by any means, electronic or mechanical, including photocopy, recording, or any information storage and retrieval system.

Photographs by Thomas L. Gettings and Robert Griffith

Printed in the U. S. A.
   B-297
First Printing—March 1973

Printed on Recycled Paper

HC
110
.P55 R6

CONTENTS

INTRODUCTION vi

1. BOTTLES AT LARGE 2

2. NO CRACK IN THE CONCRETE 28

3. SMELTING THE POPULATION 52

4. COUNTRY LIVING 86

5. DDT: DEFENDING THE THRONE 110

6. THE WASHDAY MIRACLE 134

7. ALUMINUM'S ALLOYS 160

8. THE HAZARDS OF WHISTLE-BLOWING . . . 190

9. SILENT NIGHT 214

10. CORPORATE COUNTRY 240

    NOTES 251

    INDEX 289

136162   EMORY & HENRY LIBRARY

INTRODUCTION

It seems to be that the on'y thing to do is to keep polyticians an' businessmen apart. They seem to have a bad infloonce on each other. Whiniver I see an aldherman an' a banker walkin' down the street together I know th' Recordin' Angel will have to ordher another bottle iv ink. *

---

*Finley Peter Dunne, *Dissertations of Mr. Dooley* (New York: Harper & Brothers, 1906), p. 275.

Keeping politicians and businessmen apart is like getting the snake out of the grass. It isn't easy. Penn Central goes into bankruptcy, Lockheed calls on the Congress, ITT visits the White House, and business keeps the pressure on.

Technology brought them together. No technology comes into being, none survives, without an industrial beneficiary and a government sponsor. Cyclamates, the SST, the breeder reactor rise or fall at the whim of the state. Man's discovery of his environment a few years ago put the relationship in life-and-death perspective: Barry Commoner says the post-war technologies and the higher profits they bring are the chief culprits in today's environmental crisis, but he promises improvement if we get rid of $600 billion worth of ecologically faulty capital equipment.[1] Recommending the elimination of one-fourth of the capital equipment in the United States is a spine-chiller for the corporations wedded to those technologies and a spine-tester for the government.

But Commoner doesn't explore another imperative of technology: its endurance. Threatened with a catastrophic loss of existing capital investment and with massive commitments to new and unproductive technologies, corporations have fought back. The power of the government over technology becomes a business risk that must be minimized; technological preservation suddenly rivals technological innovation. Shaping the state to suit the technology calls for action on many fronts using the three techniques of the Corporate Country: political influence, concoction of technical data, propagandist appeals. They superintend the technological defense in the Corporate Country.

The nine chapters that follow reiterate the theme of

state subversion to the ends of defending technology. In all, there is a technology under attack: aluminum and copper smelting, automobiles, jet airplanes, nuclear power, pesticides, detergents, non-returnable containers, the new land development techniques. In all, the sponsors are corporations with well understood goals: live and grow, raise capital, use specialized manpower and, crucially, protect the investment. In all, the defense draws heavily on political influence, biased technical data and propaganda. And in all, law and policy bend to fit the technology with greater assurance than the technology concedes the public need.

Before outlining the three techniques of the Corporate Country, it should be acknowledged that this field has been tilled, though not quite from the view I choose. The Ralph Nader studies are pioneering explorations of the relationship between the state, its corporations and their technology: James Turner on food and drugs, Harrison Wellford on pesticides; John Esposito on air pollution; Marcy Benstock and David Zwick on water pollution. Ralph Nader's *Unsafe At Any Speed* is a paradigm of the Corporate Country. So, too, is Robert Engler's *The Politics of Oil,* Morton Mintz' *By Prescription Only,* Robert Heilbroner's *In The Name of Profit,* and the Mintz and Jerry Cohen book *America, Inc.* John Kenneth Galbraith illumined the imperatives of corporate planning in *The New Industrial State,* and Barry Commoner links those imperatives with worldwide environmental degradation in *The Closing Circle.*

The nine subjects I chose are as much an accident of access as they are a cross section of technological politics. The study of Boise Cascade land developments in California ignores GAC in Florida. The study of the Bonneville Power Administration leaves out the Tennessee Valley Authority. And the study of the incest between the aluminum industry and the Boyce Thompson Institute neglects the steel industry and the Mellon Institute. I have said little about the technology of war, of space, of the earth where the mines snuff out lives and machines thirty stories high chew up the land, of the oceans where the tankers tread heavily on the planet's sources of life. These technologies, too, are driven by the industrial imperatives of growth, survival, a striving for plenary power.

What do I mean by influence? Very simply, the power of decision in all affairs of state. Planning for political contingencies is now a dominant aspect of industrial production and a major preoccupation of the managerial class. Industrial political planning reaches to the far corners of the law's application to technology—the technical or advisory committee, the city council or the White House, the creator of standards, their interpreters and undertakers. The complexities of technology have spawned a goliath state that purports to rule it. Influencing the state often calls for a sophistication far beyond the grass roots campaign: Boise Cascade lobbies by computer, American Smelting & Refining Company quietly moves to capture a technical study that will set the agenda for dozens of public hearings to be.

Political influence begins as a right to petition the government. It shades into bullying, bribery and conflict of interest. It may be only a procedural advantage: the insider's access, staff superiority, the *ex parte* plea, the last word when the decision is in doubt. It is no less important for being so.

Science is commissioned also to the political ends of technological preservation. The techniques include selective release of data, deification of rubbish, arbitrary honing of hypotheses. They are advanced by trade secret agreements, suppression clauses in research contracts, the choice of circumspect consultants who say the right thing. The lawyer's strategy of secrecy helps keep the science under control.

Fragmentation of discipline lends itself to bending science to suit the commercial needs of the technology. Open criticism of industry and its technological insults is frowned upon in many a professional school—forestry, nuclear engineering, aeronautics and astronautics. The petroleum engineering department at the University of California predictably went to work on the Santa Barbara spill not for the state but for the Western Oil & Gas Association. The narrower the research specialty, moreover, the easier to guard against generality in the findings. Questions raised about a technology's adverse effects are invariably inconclusive and deserving further study, more research extending over a longer period of time. There is always a trade-off or a balancing, and no single discipline is said to comprehend the complexities that converge at the top. As the technology grows, the voices qualified to be raised against it are slowly stripped of their credentials.

Propaganda is a technological imperative of two dimensions: it reinforces predictability in sales and growth, and it quiets concern about bad effects. The technique of selling the kilowatt or recreational plot, the pesticide or detergent to the limits and beyond of consumer need is a well recognized hedge against the uncertainty the corporation strives to overcome. *"Stimulating Desire"* is the way it was put by the Association of National Advertisers at the Federal Trade Commission hearing on detergents: "Few, very few of us, even in our own best interests act without a nudge. The nudge . . . can come through dictation as in a controlled economy; or it can occur through the suggestions imparted through advertising." The use of advertising, said the Association, "has made voluntary that which, in the past and even today in the evolving countries of Asia and Africa, could be done only by dictation and compulsion." In the Corporate Country the dictatorship of the advertising budget stands in the stead of the decrees of the Sultan.

The propagandist appeal to the loyal or to the wavering to take up arms in defense of the technology intensifies according to the strength of the attack. Political losses on the issues of DDT [Chap. 5], throw-away containers [Chap. 1], jet engine retrofit [Chap. 9], the 90 per cent emission standard for smelters [Chap. 3], and to a lesser extent the gas tax [Chap. 2] and phosphates in detergents [Chap. 6], were seen in life-and-death terms by the technologies' defenders. The constituencies varied—the electorate, user groups, labor—but the propaganda saturation is ever present.

Public relations campaigns are defended as commendable exercises of free speech, but the needs of technological preservation spill over beyond the First Amendment into the realm of coercion, fraud and criminality. The cynical threats of a shut-down, deliberate public deception, conniving violations of campaign reporting laws are indications the technology is backed into a corner. It should come as no surprise that the public relations artists of the Soap & Detergent Association would stoop to rewriting a government publication on detergents and disseminating it under false auspices [Chap. 6]. For a tobacco industry under fire once found it necessary to hire a sportswriter to refute the suggestion that smoking is a health hazard, to promote his publication in *True* magazine, and, posing as the editors of *True,* to distribute reprints to hundreds of thousands of persons.

The theory of the legal system is that technologies' detractors, like the defenders, will be equally equipped to draw upon the three techniques of the Corporate Country. Out of the clash of competing interests the truth is supposed to emerge; professional extremists will neutralize each other. But if there is no clash or if the clash is one-sided, extremism survives. Corporate planning in defense of technology exploits opportunities to avoid a clash.

Other themes will be found in these pages. They can be summarized as the four imperatives of technological preservation.

Technological Subsidy

The $63 billion in public subsidies uncovered by the Joint Economic Committee of the Congress goes far to explode the myth that the planners and the free marketers still have something to argue about.[2] The state participates, and the question is how much and for whose benefit. The merger between the state and its corporations is seen clearly in cases of direct raids on the treasury—the Lockheed loan, the SST financing. These controversies at least spur debate over whether the public return is worthy of the investment.

Conscription of the public fisc is not always so honorable or so open. The billions in the highway trust fund are immune from the normal appropriation process. Free markets in the aluminum industry were long ago submerged in cradle-to-grave subsidies highlighted by federal dams, give-away power rates, tax concessions and the stockpile.

Favorable tax treatment is a tiresome indicator of corporate power.

The subsidies acutely felt are the social costs of technology. Millions hit by pollution serve with their lives, their peace of mind and their pocketbooks. The statistics on pollution costs or occupational accidents don't begin to tell the story, but they are reminders that technological efficiency demands heavy public contributions. While the giant corporation strives for investments that are ever more risk-free, the general population is increasingly risk-burdened.

Technology is not bad because we pay for it. But because we pay for it, we can ask that it not be bad.

Technological Criminality

Crime in the suites lacks the shock value of crime in the streets. It is not at all an understatement to say that during most of 1970 tens of thousands of corporations committed flagrant and repeated criminal violations of the Rivers and Harbors Act of 1899. There were a handful of fines and a few injunctions, that's about all. By year's end, the President was offering amnesty, calling it a permit program and billing it as a tough crackdown against water polluters. It now becomes more irresponsible for me to make the charge than it was for them to commit the crime. Technological criminality has a vaporous quality.

In the chapters that follow, lawlessness is routine. The occasion may be a direct technological insult—a standard violated, an unauthorized discharge—or a procedural offense stemming from political or propaganda campaigns in defense of technology. One conclusion is that a corporation with a technology under fire violates the law. Cutting corners on quality control, falsifying documents, intimidating inspectors and exceeding standards are accepted techniques for defending the investment though they offend society's recorded code of right and wrong. The lust to control the destiny of the technology brings the need to write the rules.

A second conclusion is that technological crime is not taken seriously. Penalties are non-existent, ludicrously light, secretly recorded or negotiated away. Specialization brings a dilution of the personal culpability long associated with the criminal law. Concurrently with the consolidation of power at the top among those who turn the specialized fragments into policy, there is an erosion of responsibility, for we are prone to forgive the general who loses track of some of the skirmishes. The search for the technological criminal is a whodunit with no ending. Grievous wrongs bring retribution only against the corporation which can't be punished and can't be rehabilitated.

A third conclusion is that a tolerance policy on technological crime is a good measure of political power. Influence slowly whittles down the offense: in its definition if possible and inevitably in its application. If and when the sanction comes, it is a fine, quickly paid, soon forgotten, occasionally deducted. A young Indian man attempts (unsuccessfully) to catch a fish with the wrong kind of net, and he gets six months in jail; a builder of dams errs in design, kills 5 million fish in a single year, and he gets an appropriation to do more research.[3]

Technological Conspiracy

Technology under fire brings another theme—the conspiracy, a joining together for anti-social ends. The commitments to the technologies discussed in the chapters that follow are generally industry-wide—copper and aluminum smelting, the internal combustion and the turbofan engine, the throw-away container. Playing down the effects of sulfur dioxide, fluorides, carbon monoxide—or for that matter tobacco, lead in gasoline, phosphates in detergents—are not the concern of a lonely producer who stands accused but of the entire industry and its technology.

The need to preserve the technology brings the conspiracy. Often there is little to be gained, much to be lost by rapid technological advances in pollution control. The corporate combination moves easily to suppress competition, defend damaging technologies, stifle improvements and preempt governmental conduct. Joint submissions to agencies allege the standards are too tough, joint research proves it. The conspiracies I address go by many names, but the trade association is distinguished for its infamy— the American Mining Congress, the National Soft Drink Association, the Aluminum Association and the Soap & Detergent Association.

Combinations to defend what is bad about technology often grow out of joint ventures to do good. To begin with, industry competitors are close. They are usually oligopolists who have learned to live together: joint advertising, research and development are common. Massive capital commitments require a pooling of resources to build a pipeline or a power plant, to develop a reactor. Some combines are cost justified, a necessity of new technology, often a response to international competition and justifiable under the antitrust laws. But the group is ready to stifle and suppress, instead of innovate, if the negative response serves the communal aims of survival and growth. We should not forget too quickly a conspiracy like the one among auto manufacturers to postpone innovation in air pollution control technology.

Technological Mythology

The technological defense spins its own mythology, and this mythology is turned into law by political influence, made respectable by manufactured science and made palatable through heavy propaganda. The mythology diverts responsibility (and the costs that go with it) from the technology and its design. Auto dealers have been heard to complain that wretched quality control by manufacturers drafts the dealer as an added stage of the assembly line where he must make repairs, uphold warranties and forfeit earnings. Next on this assembly line is the driver, who pays with his life and through his pocketbook.

The theme is discernible if irregular. People must defend themselves from the technology, for the technology cannot be made safe for the people. The law is urged to come down on the driver, not the vehicle; the litterer, not the container; the sprayer, not the pesticide; the housewife, not the detergent. Influence brings forth a law that makes paramount the words on the pesticide label. The user is the object of propaganda about reading the label, and he becomes a statistic in biased research if he does not.

Getting out of the way of the technology is the eternal prescription: if it's noisy in the plant, wear ear plugs; if there's too much lead, go work elsewhere; if you object to living next to the airport, move. Man is adaptable, but designing him to fit the technology seems to forget who created what. A triumph of sorts in clearing the path for technology was won in 1971 by the salmon on the Columbia River who now migrate by trucks courtesy of the Corps of Engineers. The old route preferred by Lewis and Clark is no longer suitable for fish because the dam-building technology neglected to anticipate nitrogen supersaturation.

Technological mythology strives to become public policy. Politics, public relations, data creation are part of it. But there is more. Not only does big business seek to dominate the state, it purports to duplicate the state. Businessmen still acknowledge their obligation to make a profit, but many speak eloquently of their social responsibilities. Government and industry sit down together to work for the public interest. Businessmen beat the state to the punch on many a good deed.

How can such odd behavior be reconciled with Adam Smith's "unseen hand?" Business investments to relieve poverty, ignorance and pollution, states the argument can be defended as long-run profit ventures: what's good for society is good for General Motors. "The highway interest is the public interest" is the confident summary of the Highway Users Federation.

This blurring of the roles of the state and the corporations is tested and found wanting in the chapters that follow. The well motivated business-sponsored Advertising Council becomes the mouthpiece for the frothy propaganda of Keep America Beautiful, the Joint Task Force on Eutrophication gangs up in defense of detergents, the Primary Non-Ferrous Smelting Industry Liaison Committee rips pages out of the government-financed air pollution study. Business is anxious to steal the functions of the state but not its commitments; the talk of the executive belies the pace of his corporation. To those industrialists who profess to see no conflict between the roles of the corporation and the state, I say you have no cause to complain when the public looks to you for an accountability, openness and commitment indistinguishable from the state's. A firm pledge of corporate responsibility is ultimately a paradox coming from the lips of the descendents of Adam Smith.

A conspicuous example of the confounding of the responsibilities of business and government is the National Industrial Pollution Control Council, set up in the Department of Commerce by order of the President in April of 1970.[4] Made up of top executives from the nation's leading industrial enterprises, NIPCC and its thirty-odd sub-councils were charged with giving the administration advice on pollution. Advice was given—in scores of secret meetings at the highest levels recorded only in the skimpiest of minutes. The Corporate Country's three techniques were much in evidence—an informational service explaining how much industry was doing to combat pollution, an advisory group to provide technical input. Of the industries discussed in these pages, at least three—the copper smelting, detergent, and packaging interests—used political influence within NIPCC to gain relief for their respective technologies. Members of the council contributed heavily to the President's reelection compaign, and the man collecting the money was the same man who pushed the contributors' policy preferences when he was Secretary of Commerce—Maurice Stans. Stans summed up the contributions of this industrial fifth column: "You have played an increasingly important role in both government policy-making and in industry leadership. . . . Virtually no major move is made in environmental policy without drawing on your advice and criticism. The rough spots in administration of environmental laws, standards and implementation actions have been easier to spot and smooth out because you are always available to give us help."

Imponderables of international competition, trade balances, capital requirements are said to cement the government-business partnership. My view is that if the corporation and the state need one another, they will have one another. But the relationship should be open and notorious, like a marriage at common law. My prescription for sorting out the responsibilities of the state and the corporations draws on Mr. Dooley who is quoted at the outset of this introduction: insist upon a bright line between the two by holding the state strictly accountable.

Chapter Ten summarizes a number of procedural reforms that contribute to the bright line: a mandatory stiffening of administrative spines, reform of campaign financing, opening up the advisory committee and the trade association. The elimination of secrecy is the consummate need. The state bankrolls and doctors technologies new and old; the industrial client and the corporate patient should not be allowed to hide the symptoms.

I have no doubt that corporations must remain profit-making centers, despite regular pretensions of "higher" purposes. When they act as beneficent corporate states, they are prone to sink to skulduggery, using the opportunity at hand to act as the sovereign to dress up technological defenses. It troubles me not at all to know that our corporations, like our armed forces, are not meant to be all things to all men. Being mean, cutting red tape, firing incompetents or whistleblowers, saving dollars, defending rickety and deadly technology, if there is profit in it, is their job. The state's job is to take care of societal ills. Corporations are meant to be efficient, the government is meant to be humane. There is no perfect harmony in these goals. I prefer a bright line between the two—and a better understanding of who is doing what to take care of social needs.

CORPORATE COUNTRY

1 BOTTLES AT LARGE

Some people have a deep, abiding respect for the natural beauty that was once this country. . . . and some people don't. *

Back in 1958, the beer and soft drink you bought was sold mostly in returnable bottles. Since then, there has been a technological revolution. Today, your beer and soft drink comes mostly in non-returnables. You drink, and you throw the containers away. You throw away enough containers to build seventeen stacks to the moon; stretched end-to-end, they would reach around the earth 165 times.[1] Containers sometimes turn up as litter.

One important group is unprepared to put the blame for litter on containers. "Who is guilty?" asks a colorful brochure of Keep America Beautiful, Inc. The answer: "[L]itter doesn't throw itself away. *People spread litter and only people can prevent it. . . .* All of us—from the vacationing family to the seasonal sportsman—are just as responsible for preserving America's beauty and outdoor resources as the professional conservationist."[2] Litter is a people problem.

So says the leading anti-litter voice in the United States. Far and away the dominant force in the field since its founding in 1953 by the brewers and bottle and can makers, Keep America Beautiful calls itself the National Public Service Organization for the Prevention of Litter. It is supported

---

*A paid advertisement by Keep America Beautiful, in the *Seattle Times*, Aug. 30, 1971, p. E-7, col. 4.

today by 130 corporations, business organizations and labor unions. Its board of directors reads like a list of Who's Who in non-returnable refuse and has included such prominent names as Fred W. Dickson, former president of Coca-Cola, and William F. May, president and chairman of the board of American Can Company. KAB publicity stresses the "three E's" of litter prevention—Education of the public, Enforcement of anti-littering laws and Equipment, notably more trash barrels. *People disseminate litter,* according to KAB's credo, *and only people can prevent it.*

KAB gives wide distribution to its movies, reports, pamphlets, public service ads and model ordinances. Money moves the message. A 1969 ad campaign conducted for KAB by the Advertising Council (a "non-partisan and non-political" group founded and supported by American business to conduct public service campaigns) garnered over $35 million worth of media time and space in contributions from industries (more than twice the 1970 fiscal year budget of the federal Bureau of Solid Waste Management).[3] A hundred or so anti-litter ads were run in such diverse publications as *Field and Stream, Saturday Review, Photoplay* and *Black Careers.*

For elementary school use KAB has produced teachers' manuals and "The Litter Monster," a 15-minute sound and color film dramatizing litter prevention projects being conducted by young people across the country. For teen-agers there are "Keep America Beautiful Projects for Youth Groups," like the YMCA-YWCA, Boy Scouts and Campfire Girls. KAB has a message for everyone: educating, exhorting, seducing with attractively designed trash barrels, threatening with strategically placed warning signs, discovering who is prone to offend and how to relieve the impulse. Statistics are kept on the number of trash barrels available and fines levied.

The KAB truth is endorsed and amplified in many ways by the major industries and groups concerned about the litter problem. The Glass Container Manufacturers Institute widely espouses KAB's "three 'E's'" of litter prevention. *"The answers to the litter problem,"* insists Pepsico President Donald M. Kendall, "are consumer education, provision of adequate means for the proper disposal of potential litter . . . and strict enforcement of anti-littering laws."⁴ The same message comes from the Aluminum Association, the steel industry, the retail grocers, the Chamber of Commerce, the National Council of State Garden Clubs. "Litter is a people problem," says Joe Callis of the Pepsi-Cola Bottling Company, Salis, Maryland. "Litter is a people problem," says the Illinois Soft Drink Association. "Litter is a people problem" reads the marquee in front of a Seattle Safeway store. "Packages do not litter—people do," insists Kaiser Aluminum. The message is taught in the classrooms, preached from the pulpit, endorsed in the board rooms of major corporations.

No persuasive technological myth can exist without its technical trappings. The classic in the litter field is a 1969 study paid for by Keep America Beautiful and contracted under the auspices of the Highway Research Board of the National Academy of Sciences—National Academy of Engineering. Counting items along the roadside in twenty-nine states during winter months was the technique employed in this authoritative and oft-cited "National Study of the Composition of Roadside Litter," which managed to equate a bottle or can with a scrap of newspaper or a dead porcupine. By this deviousness bottles are reduced to "only 6 per cent" of the litter problem, bottles and cans together to "only 22 per cent" of the problem (a more pertinent weight or volume analysis elevates bottle and can culpability to around 50 per cent). Whatever the data, there can be no misunderstanding the conclusion of the study paid for by KAB: *"It would seem that publicity efforts led by Keep America Beautiful, Inc. and the state highway departments continue to offer the most practical approach to the problem of reducing litter."*

Linking the National Academy of Sciences to a policy of preachment is a coup for litter manufacturers whose technology is unaffected by talk. How the Academy can be so used is obscure. Clearly seen is an example of the fraud by hypothesis that becomes an integral part of the technological defense.

Technological mythology looms large and is epitomized by Keep America Beautiful's domination of the pedestrian public issue of litter. Espousing sound psychology (personal responsibility) and sound social objectives (cleaning up litter), KAB's three "E's" solution has become the only way to look at the problem. KAB is the preacher of litterism, the three "E's" its manifesto. The litter myth is socially accepted, legally enforced and professionally supported.

The litter myth is sustained also by corporate common sense. For if people are the problem, packaging policies and sales and promotional practices are not at issue. The KAB ideology becomes a political strategy for defending special interests, instead of a practical program for solving problems. Always of questionable utility, its function is now blatantly defensive—it diverts hostile energies away from damaging inquiries.

For despite constant reminders by KAB that "Litter is a People Problem," some people are beginning to get the radical notion that they could cope with their problem a little bit better if the temptation were not so great. Among the hostilities directed at the litter industry in recent times have been proposals to ban, tax or impose bounties on non-returnables and other packaging materials.

Litter manufacturers have reacted with dismay and efficiency. Ban-the-can measures were the number one attention-getter during early meetings of the National Industrial Pollution Control Council. Highly incensed, for obvious reasons, were the NIPCC subcouncils on Cans, Glass & Plastics, Containers (Paper), Steel, Beverages and the Ad Hoc Subcommittee on Solid Waste Disposal Systems. Influence within such groups is broadly based. Nearly 50 per cent of all cans used in the country are filled with soft drinks and beer. The beverage market happens to be the container manufacturers' growth area.[5] Ban the can and you kill the "Can People"—American, National, Continental and Heekin. Cans are a major market item for the steel and aluminum industries; by 1976, cans will claim 1.4 billion pounds of aluminum—10 per cent of the national production.[6] The giant bottle manufacturers—Owens-Illinois, Anchor-Hocking Glass, Brockway—have an obvious stake, as do the super markets who smoothly dispense the high-volume throw-aways—A&P, Kroger, Marcor, Super Giant, Lucky Stores. Not to be left out are the soft drink and beer sellers—Pepsico, Coca-Cola, Anheuser-Busch and many others. Add the outdoor advertisers, plastics and forest products industries (who would be hit by a packaging tax) and you have the makings of a respectable political conglomerate.

American Can's President William F. May summed up the crisis before the National Canners Association in 1971: "[Proposals] to risk the destruction of a two-billion dollar segment of the packaging industry to get rid of less than five per cent of litter and hardly make a dent in solid waste —are cropping up every day."[7] *Softdrinks* ("Oldest bottlers' trade journal in the world") offered this editorial call to arms: "Even though the problems would appear to threaten the very existence and foundation of the industry we *shall* overcome."[8] Declarations of desperation preview a determined technological defense.

A brief look at the technological subsidy helps explain why industry prefers to make litter a people problem. Selling a package along with the beverage is good for business. Fifty-seven per cent of the consumer's cost of a can of beer is for the can.[9] By buying containers, consumers contribute $1.5 million annually to growth and sales that would be lost under a mandatory returnables system.[10]

Better yet for business is the cost-free disposal paid for by the consumer through monthly billings for trash haulers and state and municipal taxes. KAB puts the cost of cleaning up litter on public and private property at $1 billion annually,[11] not exactly small change even when compared to the $5 billion or so spent nationally on the collection and disposal of all municipal wastes.[12]

A cost-free disposal system looks better to the beneficiary with each passing year.[13] Disposal sites become more dear, costs ever higher—by 1980 refuse from Chicago will be transported 300 to 400 miles away. The five pounds of garbage discarded daily by each American will become ten within ten years—and non-returnable beverage containers are growing at a rate nearly twice that of other refuse.[14] The 43.8 billion beverage containers made in the United States in 1969, at current trends, will climb to 100 billion by 1980.[15] One or 2 billion of these will end up as litter— enough to encircle the planet several times.[16]

Not only does the throw-away technology solicit contributions from many of the usual sources—the consumer, the taxpayer, the depletable natural resources—it also makes heavy demands on the small businessman. The decade of progress that brought the non-returnable turned the clock back on him. In 1960, there were 8,000 soft drink bottlers in the United States; by 1970, 3,600 remained. The number of breweries dropped from 262 in 1958 to 188 in 1967, a decline of 28.3 per cent.[17] The bottle manufacturers prefer the non-returnables because of their lighter weight, faster loading and delivery times; the big bottlers prefer them because shipping and cleaning empties interferes with high speed assembly lines; big retailers prefer them because they take up less space and require less labor.

The small bottler is the chief victim of these market efficiencies. He has found it increasingly difficult to get returnables from the bottle manufacturers—small orders are rejected, shipments deferred, rebates and discounts offered for the throw-aways. In 1969, Owens-Illinois, the world's largest bottle maker, undertook a "consolidation and standardization" of returnable molds,[18] which was a way of cutting down on returnables. Here's the reaction of Peter Chokola, a little bottler from Wilkes-Barre, Pennsylvania: "The glass bottle manufacturers are presently operating under a planned withdrawal of the returnable bottles from production. At the moment I am fighting to have a returnable bottle made which the glass suppliers told me is no longer a production item. This item covers one-third of my sales and could ruin our company, if I cannot get resupplied. The removal of this item was a unilateral decision without prior notice by the glass manufacturer. I am presently trying to have the bottle made by other glass companies and if they all refuse to make these returnables, I intend to file anti-trust and monopoly charges with the U.S. Department of Justice."[19]

Chokola asked the National Soft Drink Association to take a secret ballot survey of all bottlers on a proposed industry-wide, voluntary ban on non-returnables. Nothing doing; NSDA has worked overtime to bring down the returnable. Chokola took his own poll: thirty-six of forty-five respondents favored a ban but the imperatives of technology wait for no opinion poll from the losers.

The battle of the bottles has been fought in many parts of the country—Oregon and Vermont have enacted deposit measures, as have a handful of municipalities; hearings have been held in the Congress and before dozens of state and local legislative bodies. This story about corporations fighting back and how and why they do it is not unique. It offers a glimpse of the Corporate Country's technological defense—influence, biased research and propaganda.

The special interests began to mobilize in Washington State[20] as early as 1969, in response to a legislative resolution to an interim committee calling for a report and recommendations on the litter problem to the 1971 regular session. Always anxious to get in at the ground floor, the brewers and soft-drink producers, bottlers and can makers, steel and aluminum companies joined in a group calling itself Industry for a Quality Environment to work with the interim committee. These were not sinister operatives but good men, brought together to do good. What evolved was a technological conspiracy, made manifest as the Model Litter Control Law.

The central features of this sorry piece of proposed legislation appeared in a progress report to the interim legislative committee in April 1970. "We have determined from the beginning that half-way measures were not acceptable," announced the industry group, which proceeded to spell out a series of half-way measures, some of them so bad as to be laughable. Among the provisions recommended were proposals for anti-litter labeling mes-

sages on containers, a requirement that vehicles operating
in the state carry litter bags and that commercial firms
catering to the public use state-approved litter barrels. A
modest renovation of the state's criminal fining system for
litter violations was suggested and "a request [was made]
of industry to coordinate its various anti-litter information
and education programs with the [state] Department of
Ecology." A cool response from a legislative committee not
known to be particularly zealous in protecting the environment sent the proposal back to the drawing boards where
new flourishes were added. A band of forty "ecology patrolmen" to issue citations and arrest litterers was prescribed. To meet funding objections and after a great deal
of soul-searching, the group also agreed to the imposition
of an annual litter assessment in the amount of $150 for
every $1 million of gross sales of products thought to be
reasonably related to the litter problem.

The mood of the "model" is unmistakable and will be
extolled before many legislative bodies. Solve the litter
problem with more policemen, more arrests, more trash-
cans and more preachment. Cite the "authoritative" National Academy of Sciences study proving that publicity is
the preferred solution. Deplore the irresponsible few, whoever they are, who decorate the landscape with their garbage. Never forget, "Litter is a People Problem!"

The model is catching on. A December 1970 *Softdrinks*
editorial warmly endorsed it, chastizing those who would
be so low as to use it only as a last resort to ward off
stronger proposals. State legislatures have adopted parts of
it.[21] It was praised by Donald Kendall, Pepsico's president,
before the nation's corporate leadership at a meeting of the
National Industrial Pollution Control Council.[22]

The myth of the model is transparent. The labeling
proposals are the last gasp of every industry hoping to head

off sterner measures, the litter bags a potential new entry in the highway litter index, the criminal sanctions a proven failure as a deterrent, the patrolmen incapable of stemming the flow of garbage. Over the last ten years, according to one industry source,[23] litter fines collected have averaged a ludicrous $100 per state per year. KAB's data on trash receptacles along state highways (around 50,000 at last count)[24] suggest we need a few more.

The single provision in the Model Litter Control Law beyond the band-aid category was the litter assessment or disposal charge, a respectable device for combatting solid wastes.[25] The problem here was that the amount endorsed —$150.00 for each million in gross sales—is a fraction of the cost of cleaning up litter and a tiny fraction of the cost of disposing of packaging waste. Even at that, the litter assessment in the Model Law was to be earmarked for research and development "in the field of litter control, removal and disposal." Part of the fund could be used "for the development of education programs concerning the litter problem." This Litter Trust Fund will hardly rival its counterpart for the highway builders but it's a useful device to make sure that every penny contributed to the "public" comes right back for an assured worthy purpose—industrial research and propaganda.

Washington State subscribers to this fraudulent model included a fair sampling of the litter industry. Among those supporting it financially were Kaiser Aluminum & Chemical Company ($3500), Reynolds Metals Company ($3500), Aluminum Company of America ($3500), Georgia Pacific Corporation ($10,000), Weyerhaeuser Company ($10,-000), Longview Fibre Company ($10,000), American Can Company ($12,000), Continental Can, Incorporated ($12,-000), National Can Corporation, ($3,000), Washington Soft Drink Association ($41,750), Washington Brewers Institute ($3000) and Shasta Beverages ($10,000).[26] While it might appear that these corporate assets went down the drain, they were not invested in the public's interest in litter control; they were invested in a defense of technology, markets and sales.

In Washington State, the litter industry's bluff was called by Initiative 256,* which would have required a deposit of at least five cents on all containers for beer and soft drinks sold for consumption within the state. The idea was to cut down on the numbers of bottles and cans, encourage reuse and commission the citizen in the clean-up effort. It was met by a KAB-inspired propaganda campaign of gargantuan proportions.

The initiative was conceived as an academic project in political science in the spring of 1970 by its sponsor and chief organizer, Dr. Robert Keller of Fairhaven College. It had an auspicious beginning. Petitions began circulating in late April and by July the proposal had garnered a record 188,102 signatures, nearly twice the number necessary to secure a place on the ballot. Ironically, the amateur backers of Initiative 256 called their measure the Keep America Beautiful Act, the ultimate tribute to the industrial front working under the same name. In late July, State Republican Chairman Gummy Johnson advised a gathering of prospective candidates for the legislature that polls disclosed overwhelming support for the anti-litter measure. A poll taken in August for the beverage industry disclosed that 80 per cent of the voters were backing the initiative, a figure that held firm until about three weeks before the

---

*The initiative procedure allows citizens to enact legislative measures directly by vote if enough supporting signatures are gathered to secure a place on the ballot.

election. Professionals and amateurs alike were convinced the issue was a winner. And it was—until the technological defense took hold.

With the people momentarily forgetting that litter is a people problem in Washington State, what was needed was a crash instruction course on how to keep America beautiful. Persuading the public to want what you want calls not for technological innovation but for propaganda.

A strategic move of brilliant iniquity was made in early September when the industry group launched an initiative movement in support of its own model litter law in a bold attempt to turn public sentiment to its advantage. Though the model could not make it on the ballot in time to compete directly with 256, the potential for hoodwinking the voters was irresistible.

Centered in the supermarkets and supported by massive spending through a group called the Washington Committee to Stop Litter, a euphemistic spinoff of the Industry for a Quality Environment, the model law was a surefire winner. Campaign literature averred that the Washington Committee to Stop Litter would take no position on Initiative 256: "Some of the industry members of the Committee, however, are hopeful that the people of Washington will come to recognize the Model Litter Control Act as a better way to attack the litter problem than the deposit-refund proposal of Initiative 256." One syrupy form letter sent to various groups by executives of American Can and Continental Can acknowledged an "extremely awkward situation" brought about by the competing initiatives, and recommended a vote against 256 and support for the Model. A "separate" entity—Citizens Committee Against 256—sprang up to front for the campaign to defeat the deposit initiative. Signatories to the group's paid advertisements were exclusively labor representatives—the Glass Bottle Blowers Association, the Retail Clerks, the

Mineworkers and the Machinists. The money came from big business.

Before long, distinguishing between the pro-Model and anti-256 campaigns was impossible. The Seattle public relations firm promoting the Model handled the publicity for the Citizens Committee Against 256. "Put the Nix on 256" declared campaign literature simultaneously urging support for the Model. Billboards appeared, proclaiming the Model, denouncing 256.

The campaign against 256 was a masterpiece of deception. In the early going the backers of the measure accepted at face value the public utterances of major soft-drink producers and can manufacturers. Industry advertisements were quoted in the statement in support of 256 appearing in the Official Voters Pamphlet, which is distributed to each registered voter in the state. "Pepsi Costs Less in Returnable Bottles" was the message excerpted from a Pepsi billboard. Readers were reminded of Coca-Cola's full page advertisements on Earth Day: "The returnable Coca-Cola bottle is ecologically sound. . . . Because, when a bottle keeps moving it is less likely to find its way into . . . the highways, beaches and parks." Ellison L. Hazard, President of Continental Can, was quoted as saying: "We are convinced that the best answer to solid waste is recycling—finding a way to use the material again."

Considerable embarrassment was created by these references to rhetorical claims made on another day to other audiences for other purposes. For approval of Initiative 256 was something else again: Pepsi would not cost less, it would cost more; returnable coke bottles have nothing to do with making Coca-Cola's world a cleaner place to live in, and requiring deposits was unresponsive to Continental Can's version of "finding a way to use the material again."

The industry publicists soon got nasty. "Deliberate Fraud in Voter's Pamphlet" blared radio and newspaper ads pointing out what was hardly a mystery—that the companies quoted in the statement for 256 actually opposed the measure. News stories were built around disclaimers of the statements in the pamphlet by, among others, Fred W. Dickson, president of Coca-Cola, who sanctimoniously requested the Secretary of State to issue a statement "clarifying" the company's opposition; Ellison Hazard of Continental Can, who protested that his words about recycling had been "used to deceive the voting public and weaken the democratic process," and Donald Kendall of Pepsico, who oozed deep concern "that voters will be misled into believing that Pepsi-Cola is supporting [256]" by being reminded that Pepsi costs less in returnable bottles. (Hazard and Kendall served with distinction as presidential appointees on the National Industrial Pollution Control Council.)

On the merits, understandably, the effort to discredit the backers of 256 was unproductive as the Secretary of State quickly brushed off the suggestion that he could edit or censor materials going into the Official Voter's Pamphlet. Under accepted rules of debate, he pointed out, it was "not unusual" for sponsors to quote their opponents.[27] Nonetheless, the charges were a valuable publicity device and helped portray both sides of the campaign as genuine street brawlers, a position theretofore the sole preserve of the opportunistic promoters of the Model.

Having scored with charges of fraud, the Citizens Committee Against 256 and the Washington Committee to Stop Litter began positively to drive home their points. Most assuredly, it was said, the initiative wouldn't contribute to recycling. Mentioned under this heading were the misfortunes of Pepsi-Cola which, only a few years ago in New York City, experienced the loss of several million returnables in a six-month period. This "proof" of the housewife's laxity in bringing them back is said to be unrelated to the fact that the major food chains often refuse to handle returnables. (Change the issue and you change the tune: in the wake of the ban on cyclamates, the soft drink industry pleaded with the Food and Drug Administration for an extended reprieve on existing stocks of returnables labeled "sugar-free"—as a result of the ban the drink inside would no longer be sugar-free—contending returnables have a life-expectancy of five years.)[28]

The clincher in the anti-256 campaign was flatly inconsistent with the it-won't-work claim. The technology that had put men out of work suddenly would keep them on the job. Predictions of economic gloom were based on a study paid for by the Washington Brewers Institute and conducted by a Seattle consulting firm. Among the four and one-half pages of hair-raising conclusions were the following statistics: 600 jobs lost in the beverage container manufacturing industries, another 1,100 jobs in supporting industries, "lost" wages and salaries in an amount of $12 million, a decline in sales of an estimated $55 million, and a reduction in tax revenues of $1,140,000, all because of a nickel deposit system. To the professional economist this study was nonsense; to an electorate extremely sensitive to depressed conditions—in large part attributable to thousands of Boeing lay-offs—it was a winner.

The employment issue is technology's ace in the hole. Workers displaced by environmental policy shifts must be protected, no less than those threatened by foreign trade intrusions or defense-cutbacks. An easy solution for industry is to resist any policy shift that disrupts existing patterns of production and employment (unless of course the impact on technology brings increased sales and earnings). A proper assessment of the aggregate employment effects of a ban on non-returnables would ask whether "losses" identified in the beverage container manufacturing industry would be spent and taxed elsewhere within the economy, whether consumption of beverages would be adversely affected by a change of containers, whether the abundance of jobs created to handle the returnables would offset predicted losses. A year and a half after the Washington State initiative campaign, a professor of labor and industrial relations at the University of Illinois was to tell a Senate subcommittee that a complete shift to returnables would have a net positive employment effect in the United States of 135,000 jobs.[29]

Elections are not won and lost on economic subtleties. The technological defense's blunt talk of men out of work assured nearly unanimous labor backing. "How Much More Can We Take?" read newspaper ads about unemployment and lost tax revenues superimposed on clippings reporting Boeing lay-offs. "I may lose my job" read stickers appearing on supermarket cash registers. "Initiative 256 a threat to our jobs" was the theme of literature stuffed into the shopping bags of every A&P customer. The scare message drummed home in every conceivable manner was: 1,700 men out of work, $55 million in lost sales and $1,-140,000 in lost tax revenues.

The message for the consumer was equally bleak: "50 per cent higher prices for beer, soft drinks." Initiative 256 "will increase your grocery bill $60.00 annually for an average family of four." "You are already paying the garbageman to haul away your trash . . . why pay your grocer too?" "Deposits and Handling Costs Will Add 48 Cents Per Six-Pack Under Initiative 256." The bilking of the voter mercifully came to a close on election day; the hold on the consumer has a longer run.

This ugly, distorted and false campaign was filled with many of the tricks that marked the 1970 elections. Anti-student sentiment was exploited with ads declaring: "Initiative 256 is a political science project of a Bellingham College Class." "Professor Keller's class project is about to add $80 million to our cost of living." A vice president of Olympia Brewing Company wrote to Attorney General Slade Gorton who supported the measure: "Leaders such as you—and [Governor] Dan Evans—should realize that without business to pay the taxes that provide the funds for the wages of the politicians and the college professors, there wouldn't be any paid government officials or paid college professors. This is very fundamental and should be constantly kept in the back of your mind."[30] "[W]e would like further to state," read another letter from an Olympia representative to the sponsor of 256, "that it has always been our position that the people of this state and nation have, tempered by the public good and welfare, the inherent right of selection, be that in their government or their consumer goods."[31]

So it was that the consumer exercised his inherent right of selection. The measure went down by a narrow margin, 51 to 49 on a percentage basis.

Nobody will ever know how much was spent to beat down Initiative 256 but a fair estimate would be that the discount $6,000 budget of the citizen backers of the measure was matched on a 100-1 basis by industry opposition. Television and radio spots, newspaper ads, billboards, bumper stickers and yard signs were in abundant supply. A plane with a "Nix on 256" streamer appeared over the University of Washington's Husky Stadium on the Saturday before the election. Supermarket patrons were beseiged with leaflets, stickers and warnings driving home the anti-256 message.

The December 1970 issue of *Softdrinks* reported: "Cost

of victory estimated at $2 million by reliable sources. Some $400,000 kicked in by soft-drink parents and plants—remainder from glass and can makers, breweries, retailers and *unions.*" Since Washington law makes it a misdemeanor for a corporation having a majority of out-of-state shareholders to contribute to local initiative campaigns, this is a report of a criminal violation.[32] *Softdrinks* obligingly set the record straight in February 1971: "Expenditures in the Washington (State) battle to defeat Initiative 256 were erroneously reported in this magazine as being in the neighborhood of $2 million. The Citizens Committee in charge of directing the campaign against that initiative has filed a report listing expenditures of $171,487.68. To promote Initiative 40 (the Model Litter Control Law), another group [Washington Committee to Stop Litter] reports spending a total of $127,450. Total spent in the state on the two measures was slightly less than $300,000."

But no report acknowledged illegal contributions by out-of-state corporations which *Softdrinks* attributed to "reliable sources" in December 1970. Nor did any report mention contributions by grocery chains which, according to another item in *Softdrinks,* organized a "segment of the 'trench' battle" by promising price increases of 48 cents per six-pack if the initiative passed.[33] Taking advantage of gaps in the law is one thing, committing crimes is another. Both come easily to the technological defense.

The outpouring from Keep America Beautiful and its followers represents a classic attempt to buy technological peace with a manufactured myth. Look carefully and you will find KAB at work in your neighborhood. KAB has organizations in 38 states, and is looking for more. They are busy fighting litter with cosmetics and fighting laws with commitment. The KAB example has many emulators.

On October 28, 1970, a few days before the Washington State election, Ruder and Finn, a public relations firm, was retained by the Carbonated Beverage Container Manufacturers' Association to "help them find a solution" to the litter problem.[34] The "solution" has been a series of full-page ads by "The Can People"—American, National, Continental, Heekin—announcing the establishment of recycling centers for used cans. "And we hope that eventually every can in every city will be recycled and used to make new cans."[35] This "solution" is contagious. "It's working," reads a Reynolds ad describing the success of its Los Angeles program, where cans were returned by the public for reclamation in response to a bounty offer of one-half cent per can. Alcoa is calling a similar effort "Yes—We Can." The bottle people, too, are promising one-half cent here, one cent there ("This bottle is worth one cent at your Rainier Distributor") to bring them back. "Pepsi-Cola will meet you more than half-way," proclaims the announcement of mobile reclamation centers in a full-page ad run in Washington, D.C. The chorus is uniform—and unbroken.

It is heavy with hypocrisy. Industry can't expect to have its glass collected, sorted and broken, its cans cleaned and crushed by the Cub Scouts and den mothers of America. The return on a project in Salem, Oregon turned out to be less than twenty cents an hour for over a thousand volunteer manhours.[36] The effort, according to one eye witness, involved "long hours of dirty, smelly, dangerous, heavy labor." Owens-Illinois made matters worse by paying $15 a ton for returned glass instead of the advertised $20.[37] There is considerable evidence that some "recycling centers" pay for what is returned, then dump it into the nearest landfill.[38] In a candid moment, Richard Cheney of the Glass Container Manufacturers Institute told the *New York Times* that a high rate of return for a bottle redemption program would be around 5 per cent, which is about the annual rate of increase of bottle production in the United States.[39] Why do these games persist? They are "a great promotional scheme" says the Manager of the Office of Consumer Affairs of one of the Can People.[40] Citizen "recycling" programs provide good copy for the newspapers and good material for the annual report. Everyone is getting into the act because all the others are. It is, in a sense, a vigorous competition in fraud.

In addition to maintaining a steady diet of public relations, the container interests show promise of keeping up their considerable interest in research. Their serious effort will be housed in the National Center for Solid Waste Disposal, quickly renamed the National Center for Resource Recovery, Incorporated.[41] Much of the brainstorming that brought this group into being took place within NIPCC's Ad Hoc Subcommittee on Solid Waste Disposal Systems, chaired by William F. May, chairman of the board of American Can Company. The Center was viewed as a "constructive environmental step as well as a means to forestall alternative and less realistic actions."[42] Its thirty-member board of directors includes executives from U. S. Steel, National Steel, Alcoa, Monsanto, American Can, Continental Can, Reynolds Metals, Owens-Illinois, Anchor-Hocking Glass, International Paper, Mead Packaging, U. S. Plywood-Champion Papers, Marcor, Kroger, Lucky Stores, Super Giant Stores, General Foods, Procter & Gamble, Anheuser-Busch, Adolph Coors, Heublein, Coca-Cola and Pepsico. The little businessman, like bottler Peter Chokola of Wilkes-Barre, Pennsylvania, is not represented on the board.

Chairman of the National Center is Pepsico's Donald Kendall. Kendall is the perfect example of the business executive that influences government. *Business Week* has featured him in a cover story stressing his close relationship with President Nixon[43] (he was a big campaign contributor). As chairman and chief executive officer of Pepsico, chairman of the National Center for Resource Recovery, chairman of NIPCC's beverage sub-council, chairman of the board of the Grocery Manufacturers of America, member of the Business Council, Kendall has a front seat in any governmental moves that might affect his industry. He is proof that today's corporate executive must work full-time to drive his government. "Businessmen have got to be active in defense of the system," he says,[44] and he practices what he preaches.

Kendall has a charge for the Center: "American business has concentrated on the distribution and dissemination of packaging to the virtual exclusion of disposition."[45] He proposes that the Center reverse this trend by launching ambitious inquiries into such areas as reclamation, recycling and reuse of materials; changes in distribution, marketing patterns and procedures; and consumer education. He says the Center "is equipped to go far beyond information assembly and dissemination. We intend to finance trailblazing creative research in the design, operation and evaluation of solid waste management systems." One of the first orders of business was the selection of an ad agency "to prepare a public awareness program for the Center."[46] Abandoning successful strategies, it must be conceded, is not good for business.

The list of genuine research needs in the fields of solid waste and recycling is imposing: packaging that is biodegradable or susceptible to pollution-free incineration, better materials separation techniques, elimination of salvage obstacles (like the inclusion of tin in steel cans), improvements in capturing energy from incinerators. Hard looks should be taken at the transportation rates, depletion allowances and procurement policies that discriminate against recycled materials.

Whether the "trailblazing creative research" of the National Center will fulfill these needs is improbable. The myths of the corporate constitution bar inquiries that threaten prevailing patterns of packaging, distribution, promotion and discard. For example, Reynolds Metals' Director of Environmental Planning, Robert Testin, in obeisance to his industry's indestructible contribution to man's effluent on the planet, calls the search for the degradable container a "technical impossibility," a "search for the 'Holy Grail.' "[47] Taboo for the Center would be research that could be translated into "unwise" political action, like finding a substitute for possibly dangerous (polyvinyl chloride) or unsalvageable (multiple-alloy) containers. More palatable would be purely defensive research, like that of the bottle-makers who favor a study proving their product actually enhances the stability of a landfill[48] or the plastics industry which set out to demonstrate that its product causes no harm to incinerators.[49]

In short, there are countless channels into which limited research and development money can be funneled, and most of them involve no meddling with the basic technologies of the manufacturers who benefit from a cost-free disposal system. Keeping it this way is the function of the technological defense.

Even the National Center will be hard put to better the study that proved instrumental in persuading the federal government to back off on the returnables issue. On September 15, 1971, David Dominick, the Environmental Protection Agency's assistant administrator for categorical programs, predicted in a speech before a Keep America Beautiful gathering that within two years Congress would be forced to enact laws prohibiting or taxing the non-returnables.[50] This slip-of-the-tongue was edited out of printed copies of the speech made available later.[51] Within a couple of weeks EPA Administrator William Ruckleshaus was saying that "official Federal policy" was "that there should be no restrictions on non-returnable bottles and cans because the restrictions do not seem to work."[52] Offered to bolster the conclusion were the findings of a federally aided test in California suggesting that counterfeiters might make bottles to collect a deposit. The threat of counterfeiting could have ended the debate—except for one problem. There was no such study.[53]

Rumors are not so easily quashed. David P. Reynolds, executive vice president of the Reynolds Metals Company, apparently believing what he reads in the newspapers, was quick to cite the non-existent study with approval in his speech accepting the Packaging Man of the Year Award.[54] Said Reynolds: "It is gratifying that a federal statesman like Mr. Ruckleshaus is 'telling it like it is' in this era when so many public officials are tempted, by uninformed public pressure, to impose non-solutions on the litter and solid waste problems."

Whether or not Ruckleshaus continues to tell it like it is, the policy of his agency is clear: study the problem. In September 1970 the position of the Bureau of Solid Waste Management was that definitive recommendations on the returnables issue would be ready in one or two years.[55] One and one-half years later another congressional committee was told that a "wide range of policy actions" relating to solid waste would be ready in a year or so.[56]

In addition to prolonging this study, there is still another role for the National Center for Resource Recovery. It will combine the propaganda and research functions with the all important third element in the technological defense —influence.

The Center claims to be a non-profit, non-lobby organization. Let me offer intuition, as yet unsubstantiated, on another possibility. It will plead for its rightful share of federal research and development money. Through formal advisory committees or informal contracts, it will seek to define the federal research role in the solid waste field (just now getting off the ground), dictate the questions to be asked, influence the selection of contractors, control their findings through the selective release of data, and undermine any "damaging" conclusions that survive this gauntlet—for example, by funding contradictory or related studies, preferably those extending over a long period of time. Any federal impetus threatening established myths that is not captured, diverted, suppressed or repudiated will be directly contested in political forums by the same groups that sponsor the Center. In short, the Center will be hard-pressed to escape the commercial imperatives that insist it perform in the best traditions of the trade association as the technical lobbying arm of special and powerful political interests.

Some observers acknowledge that the 256 initiative campaign in Washington State involved strategic spending by special interests, fraudulent advertising, coercive public relations, wholesale legal violations and conspiratorial deception. Donald Kendall reads it this way: "The American public has made it perfectly evident that it does not want non-returnable beverage containers eliminated, and that it will not accept the higher prices which repressive laws aimed at those containers inevitably would impose on the consumer. In the one instance in which the opposition forces have permitted a direct expression of public sentiment, a proposed state-wide five-cent deposit requirement was defeated by the voters of the State of Washington . . ."[57] That interpretation should be thrown out along with the next Pepsi bottle.

Litter is not the world's most pressing issue, but it is symptomatic of a spiralling solid waste problem. It is symptomatic also of the technological forces that thrive on that spiral. A moving advertisement by Keep America Beautiful depicts an American Indian with a tear running down his cheek and carries this message: "Some people have a deep, abiding respect for the natural beauty that was once this country . . . and some people don't."[58]

2 NO CRACK IN THE CONCRETE

The Highway interest is the public interest*

One Friday afternoon Romaine Terry watched while four men from the county sheriff's office carried things out of his barn and heaped them on the ground—an old sleigh, a wagon, some harnesses and horseshoes.[1] Terry hadn't sold his old brick house and farm in Escutney, Vermont, for he had been born there; the state condemned the property and offered $10,600, but Terry went to court and got the price raised to $13,000.

He never cashed the check. The night the men started to carry his property away, Terry sat down to talk with his brother. When his brother left, Terry went outside and poured kerosene on the junk stacked on the ground, then he soaked the barn and the house. He set them on fire, locked his dogs outside, lay down on his bed and shot himself. Soon the trucks came and Terry's cellar was filled with dirt, then came the concrete, then the traffic. I-90 had arrived.

Each year, 60,000 people like Romaine Terry have to get out of the way of the Interstate System[2]—80 per cent of all black-owned businesses in Nashville,[3] thousands of the poor in Boston, New Haven, Newark, and in scores of other cities. Sometimes the highway swerves to miss the brewery, the mill or the university, but the people move in other parts of town.

---

*The Highway Users Federation, "Moth-Eaten Myths About Highways . . . and How You Can Debunk Them," undated pamphlet.

Insisting that the people move are many of the world's great powers. *Asphalt,* a quarterly publication of the Asphalt Institute, puts it simply: "Roads sustain the existence and promote the growth of our greatest industries—steel, rubber, oil, and of course, automobiles."[4] Ten of the nation's top fifteen corporations are bound inextricably to the automobile—General Motors, Ford, Chrysler, United States Steel, the Standard Oil companies of New Jersey, California and of Indiana, Texaco, Gulf and Mobil.[5] Political allies of this blue ribbon panel include thousands of roadside businesses, motel and restaurant owners, truckers, outdoor advertisers. One of six businesses, nearly one in five jobs in the country has a stake in the highway program.[6] America's surrender to the automobile is unconditional, although the details of the occupation are still being worked out.

The giants making up the highway lobby tread heavily on the laws of the land while conspiring to protect their technologies. An internal General Motors memorandum on air pollution control devices read: "Please note that we are bound by an agreement . . . with the Automobile Manufacturers Association (AMA) to withhold any knowledge about these devices until a joint industry announcement can be made through AMA."[7] A grand jury was to learn also that the auto makers agreed to "participate equally in the public relations benefits that will accrue from a single announcement in the uniform adoption date for any air pollution control device which may be adopted for use."[8] Disclosures such as this prompted the federal government to bring an action against the Automobile Manufacturers Association and its members, charging them with conspiring to frustrate the introduction of pollution control technology. The law suit ended with a piece of paper called a consent decree,[9]* which forbade the defendants from joint research, publicity and politics on matters of emission control. To this day auto manufacturers have not paid a penny nor suffered retaliation for what could be called a conspiracy to commit mass murder.

The highway myth starts with sound premises (the American public wants flexible, safe, inexpensive transportation), it pre-empts debatable ground (the automobile is virtually the only way to fulfill these needs), and comes to rest on a rock-bottomed political proposition: *accommodating the nation to the use of the automobile is in the public interest.* Backed by social and even religious symbolism (the American Road Builders Association has a pledge and an official prayer), the highway lobby's commercial interests are indistinguishable, in their view, from the public welfare. "The 'highway interest' is the 'public interest' " is the arrogant byword of the Highway Users Federation, a key lobby group.

The technological subsidy for the highway interests is unprecedented. Add up the social costs of urban transportation, says Massachusetts Institute of Technology Provost J. Herbert Holloman, and you'll come to maybe $100 billion—10 per cent of the total gross national product.[10] There are thousands of human lives in these costs— some claimed quickly in accidents,[11] others slowly by pollution.[12] There is an astronomical property loss—$2 billion alone each year due to fragile bumpers involved in collisions at under ten miles per hour,[13] $44 million a year for damage to agriculture in California's two major smog

---

*A consent decree is a popular procedure for ending antitrust litigation under which the defendant admits nothing but agrees to refrain from doing what he did not admit to.

areas.[14] Hundreds of millions are exacted by the urban highway for increased rents, moving costs, reduced quantity and quality of commercial services.[15] Billions go to road maintenance, and who knows what for noise pollution, losses of highway-preempted properties from the tax rolls, welfare costs due to lack of mobility.

People who object to paying the subsidy can move. In Los Angeles, doctors are advising at least 10,000 people a year to leave the area, and one-third of the doctors giving the advice are thinking about going with them.[16] Utter helplessness before the technology is conceded in this anti-smog insight from Stanley M. Rokow, medical director of the Tuberculosis and Respiratory Disease Association of Los Angeles County: "Get extra sleep. Avoid stimulating food, drinks and medicines that increase the pulse rate. Do not clean house, shop or cook. Shut the windows and stay indoors, especially if you are young or old."[17]

The list of quotas, allowances, and immunities subsidizing those who insist we shut the windows and stay indoors have been duly chastised in scores of books. But one pinnacle of influence stands out—the federal Highway Trust Fund. Enacted in 1956, the Fund receives and holds revenue derived from taxes on buses, trailers, gasoline, diesel fuel, parts and accessories and other highway-related products. Each consumer makes a contribution at the automobile showroom, the gas pump and the garage to the tune of $138 per year. The money can be spent only for road building and is going to the states in ninety-ten matching funds. The Trust Fund grew from $1 billion in 1957 to $3 billion in 1966 to nearly $5.5 billion by 1970.[18] By 1977, interest alone, paid by the Treasury into the Fund, is expected to reach $525 million,[19] close to five times the figure budgeted by the federal government in fiscal 1971 to combat air pollution.

The Trust Fund is the lynchpin of the highway-auto-oil

technology, and the first "really successful application in our modified capitalist society of a guaranteed annual income."[20] It supplies the capital and the independence for an industrial expansion that has overwhelmed lesser competitors for the federal fisc.

The beneficiaries of the Trust Fund also celebrate a subversion of the state and the principles it purports to serve. Most people in the Republic must reckon with article 1, § 8 of the United States Constitution, which says: "No money shall be drawn from the Treasury, but in consequence of appropriations made by law." The idea is to require competition for the federal dollar, which is the way priorities are supposed to be set. But the Trust Fund doesn't play in this league, for under its "contractual authority" obligations are fixed by the Secretary of Transportation in advance of appropriations, with appropriations committees in the House and Senate reduced to rubber-stamping the bills as they come due. Congress cannot tap this perpetual siphon—"appropriations to liquidate contract authorizations" are a "mere formality."[21]

The argument that "back-door" financing offends the Constitution has been made on the floor of the Congress,[22] but never in court. The Trust Fund rolls on, with its legality assumed by beneficiary and victim alike.

Hand in hand with the trust fund goes the private government that sustains it. Representative John Kluczynski (D-Ill.), long-time chairman of the House Public Works Committee, is the prototype reformers have in mind when they talk of cleaning up the Congress. It was business as usual for Kluczynski in 1968 when he bulldozed through a law specifying not only what highways would be built in the District of Columbia, but also in some cases, the number and width of the lanes.[23]

The Senate version of Kluczynski goes by the name of Jennings Randolph (D-W. Va.), who brought his experience as treasurer of the American Road Builders Association to bear as chairman of the Public Works Committee. One of Randolph's recent capers (unusual only in that it was a losing one) was an attempt to replace Trust Fund money lost by repeal of the excise tax on light trucks with an equivalent amount from excise taxes on liquor, wine and beer.[24] This macabre extension of the "user" concept evidently assumes that enough drinkers drive to justify taxing all drinkers to make it easier for them to drive.

Lending administrative support for the work of the Kluczynskis and Randolphs are people like Francis Turner, who recently stepped down as head of the Federal Highway Administration. Turner joined the Bureau of Public Roads as an engineer straight out of Texas A&M in 1929. A literature search for an assinine quote on highways leads eventually to Turner. He brushes aside the bleeding hearts who say the aged and the handicapped are ill served by our transportation system: they "depend in most cases on their children or friends to personally take them by auto to their destinations. And the same thing occurs with handicapped."[25] He waxes eloquent on land use planning: "I love urban sprawl, and so do most of my friends."[26] In 1970 Turner won the coveted Neil J. Currie biennial award as the individual "who has made the greatest contribution to progress in highway transportation."

Another winner of the same award was California State Public Works Committee Chairman Randolph Collier. Collier may be the only politician in the country who has managed to out-do Kluczynski. Tunnels and roadside parks have been named after him. Sacramento highway lobbyists are known as Randy's Rat Pack.[27] One reporter says of Collier: "Legislative infighters hold him in awe as the 'fastest gavel in the West' when it comes to killing bills opposed by the truckers, auto clubs, oil interests or the Division of Highways."[28]

Having won independence for the technology with the help of the Colliers and the Kluczynskis, the defense digs in. As long ago as 1961, L. W. Prentiss, executive vice president of the American Road Builders Association, wrote ominously of "The Threat to the Highway Trust Fund."[29] Prentiss was worried about a Kennedy Administration suggestion to expand the definition of "construction costs" reimbursable to the states under the Trust Fund to include administrative costs for furnishing housing to the thousands ousted to make way for highways. That the Trust Fund should pay to move its victims was a principle that did not become law until 1968,[30] and then only over the determined opposition of the highway lobby. The lobbyists were there again in 1972 to head off proposals to divert trust fund monies for rapid transit purposes.

Public relations joins political influence to promote and defend the technology. Twenty-five per cent of all advertising in U.S. newspapers comes from auto industry. Typical of the defensive stratagems is a 1971 campaign by the Highway Users Federation, which set about to contradict "the constant bombardment of highway critics." An internal memorandum by the Federation's John Gibbons urged a massive "truth squad" operation for a ten-week period, which would include "hard-hitting, name-calling refutation of the current highway myths; backed up with news releases and supported also by local TV and radio interviews. We'd prepare the talks, coordinate the bookings."[31] The first of six working drafts of talks prepared by the Federation[32] dealt with the "myth" of "paving over America." A sample: "It's astounding how this fabrication has caught the imagination of so many, when any schoolboy can look up the fact that all of our roads and streets occupy less than one per cent of the nation's total land area." Another: "So, if there *is* a highway lobby [the Highway Users Federation isn't saying], it is the American public itself, a most sinister group indeed."

The "truth squads" began their raids in accordance with Gibbons' timetable. In one state the Federation's material—"Moth-Eaten Myths About Highways," "Automobile Pollution and the Great Credibility Gap" and "Let's Talk Sense About Transit" was mailed at state expense to members of the Joint Legislative Transportation Committee.[33] A committee member called them "tired half-truths . . . cheap propaganda for a vested interest."

Public relations tripe gropes for its "scientific" veneer. The myth that people favor highways is supported by public opinion polls proving people are for highways. The Opinion Research Corporation of Princeton, New Jersey was hired by the Highway Users Federation in 1971 to measure public attitudes "in order to provide guidance for highway promotion and public information programs."[34] The poll turned up some good news: 80 per cent of the people have a favorable opinion of the U.S. highway system, and some bad news: 57 per cent of the people favor limiting use of cars in the downtown areas, 42 per cent thought highways affected the environment unfavorably. But the news wasn't bad enough to deter this press release interpretation by D. Grant Mickle, president of the Federation: "This poll, conducted by an unbiased and highly respected leader in the opinion survey field, proves so-called public animosity towards highway transportation to be a fiction. We trust that public officials and legislatures will respond to the preferences of the public in shaping our national transportation policies."[35]

Automobile excesses have achieved new highs in California, so it was appropriate for a few citizens to carry on a debate about the Trust Fund. As long ago as 1923 gas tax money was earmarked for use on state highways and county roads.[36] In 1931 the President pro tem of the State Senate denounced various "schemes to exploit" the gas tax, including one measure to divert gas money for relief of the unemployed.[37] In 1938 Article XXVI of the State Constitution was approved by the voters by about a two-to-one margin. Section one preserves the gas tax "exclusively and directly" for highway purposes, meaning the building, improving and maintaining of roads. Section two says that registration fees may be used both for highway purposes and for the administration and enforcement of laws regulating highway use. As in twenty-eight other states, Californians thus are constitutionally restrained from loosening the purse strings on highway revenues for non-highway purposes. The effect is to place both state and federal gas-taxes (each accounting for approximately 70 per cent of state and local road and federal Trust Fund revenues, respectively)[38] beyond the normal appropriations process. Like freedom of the press and the right to be secure against unreasonable searches, there is something fundamental about the privilege of the highway interests to have their tax payments returned as income subsidies.

During the 1970 elections, Californians, like their neighbors in Washington [Chap. 1], were educated on the politics of technology. It was the same old story—deceitful campaign statements, strategic spending by corporate giants, flagrant violations of campaign reporting laws. The only change was the public relations virtuoso at the helm and the technology defended.

The backbone of the highway program, the fuel tax, was put under scrutiny during the 1970 California legislative session by a half dozen measures aiming to fund balanced transportation.[39] After much backstage maneuvering, Senate Constitutional Amendment 18 was approved by a two-thirds vote of both houses on August 19 and went to the people as Ballot Proposition 18. The idea was to permit a local option for transportation planning by allowing the use of up to 25 per cent of the gas tax for mass transit purposes. The California Highway Commission was directed by the measure to construe a local pro-transit vote as sentiment "to solve . . . transportation problems . . . through public transportation systems, other than state highways." Legislative analyst A. Alan Post estimated that passage of the proposition could result in a maximum diversion of $85 million a year out of an $800 million highway budget.[40]

Support for Proposition 18, if anything, appeared to be stronger than that for anti-litter in Washington. A statewide organization—Californians Against Smog—went to work in favor of the measure. The group was backed by the usual citizen and environmental groups—the League of Women Voters, the Sierra Club, Eco-Action—and survived mainly on the limited funds of the Tuberculosis and Respiratory Diseases Association of California. Proposition 18 got quick and strong backing from the major dailies—the *San Francisco Examiner, The Sacramento Bee* and the *Los Angeles Times.* (The only major newspaper in opposition was the *Oakland Tribune,* whose editor, former Senator William Knowland, was one of two state legislators co-authoring the 1938 restrictions on spending gas taxes.) It claimed impressive support—the League of California Cities, California Medical Association, Governor Ronald Reagan and his opponent Jesse Unruh, Los Angeles Mayor Sam Yorty and most state legislators. State Senator James Mills, the draftsman of the measure, campaigned on its behalf energetically and with sophistication. True to form, Proposition

18 was predicted a winner. An October voter survey by the respected Mervin Field firm hinted at approval by a three to one margin. A week before the election, polls put Proposition 18 in front by better than two to one.[41]

But the technological defense was digging in. At work was a front group called Californians Against the Street and Road Tax Trap, with membership spanning the California State Employees' Association (which is dominated by workers from the Division of Highways), the State Chamber of Commerce, the Farm Bureau, the Teamsters, the Real Estate Association and organizations called the Property Owners' Tax Association of California and the California Taxpayers' Association (with utilities, banks, automotive and oil interests well represented).

The California State Automobile Association (1.1 million members) and the Automobile Club of Southern California (1.4 million members), the two largest affiliates of the American Automobile Association, geared up for the Proposition 18 campaign, as they had for earlier highway fights. Almost indistinguishable from the work of the Auto Clubs was that of the California State Chamber of Commerce, an original supporter of the 1938 constitutional provision. Helping to achieve the homogeneity was Southern Club President Neil Petree, who doubles as president of the Freeway Support Committee, founded by the State Chamber in 1967 as an "educational group." (The Freeway Support Committee took over the work of Californians for Modern Highways, of which the distinguished State Senator Randolph Collier had been president.[42])

A January 1970 Petree speech to the State Chamber on "The Whole Story" of gasoline taxes, given wide distribution during the Proposition 18 campaign, summed up the State Chamber and auto club view. In it, Petree coined a phrase: "There are continued attempts today to indulge in

highway robbery by diverting highway funds." He spoke
with candor. "The purpose of [the California Freeway Support Committee] is quite simple: to encourage the early
completion of California's planned freeway and express-
way system and to prevent the diversion of highway user
funds to non-highway purposes." He demonstrated a sense
of history: "The money from the 1923 California user tax
was to be used for state highways and county roads. It was
not intended that this be the only source of funds for highway improvement, however, and some road expenditures
from other sources continue today . . . as they should."
What is ours is ours, Petree meant, and some of yours is
ours, too.

The tentacles of power slowly squeezed the life out of
Proposition 18. "The buddy system balked us everywhere
we turned," says William Roberts, a coordinator for the
Tuberculosis and Respiratory Diseases Association. "People said they would check with their associates before making a contribution. Their associates were often business
friends in oil companies. I believe the interlocking boards
of directors killed us in trying to get money."[43] Louis Lundborg, chairman of the Bank of America, and John Vaughn,
vice chairman of Crocker-Citizens National Bank, were involved in support of a 1968 mass transit election issue, but
both declined offers to lead the Proposition 18 campaign.[44]
They said they were busy. Each bank has an oil company
executive sitting on its board of directors.

Los Angeles Times staff writer Robert Rosenblatt pointed
out other coincidences:

> Century City, the massive West Side office and real estate
> development of Aluminum Co. of America, (Alcoa),
> donated an office for Proposition 18. But Robert Hat-
> field, Century City president, never issued a public en-

dorsement that had been prepared for him by the campaign staff.

John McComb, Century City's public relations man, says he never encountered any pressure for Century City to soft-peddle its activities.

It's pointed out, however, that two major Century City tenants are oil companies—Humble Oil and Refining Co., and Gulf Oil Corp. Millions of shares of stock in Pittsburgh-based Gulf Oil are controlled by the Mellon family companies, which have three seats on the Gulf board. The family also controls Mellon National Bank, which has made extensive loans to Alcoa, parent of the Century City project. In addition, the Mellons have big blocks of Alcoa stock.[45]

Technological cooperation among oil companies leads to political conspiracy. Rosenblatt explains: "Otto Miller, chairman of Cal Standard, and Fred Hartley, president of Union Oil, took an active personal role in the campaign, according to sources in the oil industry. 'Some of us were reluctant about the bad image we would get by opposing Proposition 18 and we wanted to stay neutral,' one executive says. 'But Miller and Hartley reminded us persuasively of all the joint ventures in exploration where we work with their companies.' "[46] Hartley is the same fellow who won the nation's respect for his comments on his company's contribution to the Santa Barbara oil spill: "I'm amazed at the publicity for the loss of a few birds."[47] And Miller is the same man who was knee-deep in the planning to set up a front-group to kill off another California environmental ballot measure in 1972.[48] The union of politics and big business is born of necessity.

Out in front in the Proposition 18 campaign were the auto clubs. With at least 1,200 of the Southern Club's 4,500 employees making their living from insurance activities,[49] roads and votes were readily mixed. The club's commitment was substantial—the $22,000 in reported contributions didn't begin to tell the story of the value of the pamphlets, leaflets and statements drumming up support.

Of course, the club directors, like the directors of most corporations, didn't ask the members whether they should spend $22,000 to beat down Proposition 18. As Los Angeles City Councilman and club member Marvin Braude says: "The people who run the Auto Club *never* inform the membership about what the club may be up to. The club's membership is *never* informed or consulted about any matter of club policy whatsoever".[50] Inspired by the $22,000 anti-18 contribution, Braude sought election to the board of directors. His request to inspect and copy the membership list was turned down by President Neil Petree.[51] Braude was buried in the election by proxies held by the club, then was put permanently in his place by a change of regulations disqualifying public officials as directors.[52]

The campaign was conducted according to the usual standards of good taste associated with a public relations butchering of a serious issue. Putting legislation directly to the people puts heavy pressures on tacticians to resort to gross oversimplification, misrepresentation and outright fraud—all three if the vote may be close. Explaining your side of the story costs money, and money is the key to success.

Legitimate debate wins few converts; a big lie can win a campaign. In Washington, the slogan was *"Nix on 256"* and the returnable container; in California, it was *"MORE TAXES? NO NO. 18"*. The word was disseminated widely through radio and television commercials, informational booklets and hand bills. Fittingly, the chief means of communication in the battle over highway funding was the motorist's incessant companion—the billboard. Hundreds carried the message *"MORE TAXES? NO NO. 18"*, and the message carried the day.

The billboards couldn't be too specific and say *"MORE TAXES? NO NO. 18 BECAUSE WE BELIEVE THE PUBLIC MUST CONTINUE TO FINANCE ROADS IN ADDITION TO RAPID TRANSIT."* So the message was cut to "MORE TAXES," even though there were to be no more taxes this time. That's the pitch the voter would remember, and it was the voter who posed the threat to the technology and its financial pipeline.

Other subtleties were drowned in the deluge of messages from the Tax Trap Committee: "Don't Divert the Entire Highway Fund" (a "practical impossibility but theoretically possible," said Harry Morrison of the Western Oil and Gas Association),[53] "More Taxes," "Mass Congestion: Not Mass Transit," "A Smog Screen: Not Smog Control." Television ads said roads would deteriorate. Films of cars going through toll booths warned that "the bells will ring" if Californians voted for Proposition 18.[54]

While the big money began the takeover in California, the customary agonizing was heard from the good government sources. Senator Mills called the Tax Trap campaign "a vicious and well-thought-out-lie."[55] Robert Fellmeth, leader of the Nader Study on Power and Land in California, told a press conference: "It is disgusting that they should attempt to defeat [the proposition] with a lie, and it would clearly demonstrate the ineffectiveness of democracy in California should they succeed. Unfortunately, our study suggests that this is not the first time such interests have lied to the public successfully; nor, probably, will it be the last."[56]

Toward the middle of October, the Automobile Club of Southern California was named in two separate suits by members claiming misappropriation of membership fees by club lobbying against the amendment.[57] On October 30 a group of respiratory disease victims filed suit alleging that oil companies sponsoring the anti-18 ads were deceiving the voters with representations that the amendment would raise taxes.[58] Cited as evidence of the fraud was a statement of William Queale, chief architect of the anti-18 campaign, who conceded to a reporter shortly before the election that "additional taxes won't be created automatically by the passage of the amendment."[59]

The citizens were in for a bigger surprise. It was to be a crime, but only a technological crime. A week before the election, in accordance with state law, Arch Brookhauser, Sr., treasurer of the Tax Trap Committee, filed with the Secretary of State a statement of campaign receipts and expenditures. This document should be read fully to appreciate the mockery of campaign reporting in the states today. Brookhauser duly reported that a John Bronson had contributed $25.00 to the Tax Trap Committee and $10 each had come from E. Domingo Hardison and Joseph Gelcher. These three staunch individualists might as well have saved their money, for the big contributors were listed as follows:

San Diego Rock Products	$ 5,000.00
Southern California Automobile Club	10,000.00
Southern California Automobile Club	3,000.00
Interinsurance Bureau	10,000.00
Texaco, Inc.	20,000.00
A. Teichert & Son, Inc.	750.00
California State Automobile Association	10,000.00
Southern California Rock Products Association	2,500.00
California Trucking Association	5,000.00
Newhall Land & Farming	500.00

Standard Oil Company of California	30,000.00
Johnson Tractor Company	100.00
Griffith Company	250.00
R. J. Noble Company	100.00
International Union of Operating Engineers, Los Angeles	1,000.00
Shell Oil Company	30,000.00
M. L. Dubach, Inc.	100.00
Quentin Reynolds	250.00
Asphalt Construction Company, Inc.	100.00
BWB Constructors, Inc.	50.00
Goodyear Tire & Rubber	500.00
Union Oil Company of California	20,000.00
Highway-Heavy Chapter EGCA	1,000.00
Sim J. Harris Company	100.00
Hazard Companies	150.00
Peterson Tractor Company	100.00
Asphalt Service Company	125.00
California State Automobile Association	1,000.00
Vernon Paving Company	100.00
The Irvine Company	300.00
Automobile Club of Southern California	9,000.00
Interinsurance Bureau, San Francisco	2,000.00
Boise Cascade Corporation	1,000.00
E. L. Yeager Construction Company	100.00
Challenge-Cook Brothers	500
International Union of Operating Engineers, San Francisco	2,500.00
Total	$167,175.00

A single entry was posted for expenditures to M. J. Kramer and Associates, the public relations firm handling the campaign: "for advertising and administration expenses— $200,243.48."

The final report was filed after the election on November 25. In the waning moments of the campaign, there were no John Bronsons, E. Domingo Hardisons and Joseph Gelchers contributing less than $25. The full report on receipts read as follows with the "anonymous" benefactors contributing more than half the largesse. (It's a crime under California law for $1,000 and up contributors to neglect to file a report.)

James N. Fulmor	$ 50.00
Firestone Tire	500.00
Anonymous	20,000.00
Sun Oil	2,000.00
California Asphalt	1,000.00
R. E. Hazard, Jr., Inc.	200.00
Douglas Oil	5,000.00
Custom Farm Service	2,000.00
Shell Oil	20,000.00
Anonymous	30,000.00
Phillips Oil	15,000.00
California Portland Cement	500.00
Matich Corporation	100.00
Humble Oil & Refining Company	12,000.00
Granite Rock Company	100.00
Standard Oil of Indiana	5,000.00
Sully Miller Company	15,000.00
Anonymous	25,000.00
Getty Oil Company	5,000.00
Daley Corporation	125.00
Black Top Materials Company	50.00
Marathon Oil	1,000.00
Anonymous	20,000.00
Pacific Motor Trucking Company	1,000.00
California Taxicab Owners Association	335.00
Shepherd Machinery	200.00
California State Employment Association	250.00
T. P. Polich	25.00

Nielson Construction Company	100.00
California Taxicab Owners Association	75.00
Total Contributions over $25	$181,610.00
Plus Total given in Oct. 27 report	167,175.00
Total Contributions over $25	$348,785.00

The disbursements were not detailed. M. J. Kramer & Associates received $131,576.21 "for advertising and administrative expenses." A law firm was paid $1,626.00 "for legal fees." So much for the public's right to know who spends how much for what in a California election campaign.

And so much for the outcome. It was not even close: 54 to 46, by percentage vote.

As Proposition 18 went down, the newspapers offered eulogies. "Money Talks, California Chokes" was the *Los Angeles Times* editorial interpretation. Other headlines told the story:[60] "How Highway Lobby Ran Over Proposition 18," "Oil Companies Battle Prop. 18," "Proposition 18 Foes Can Unmask," "4 Anonymous Gifts Helped Kill Prop. 18," "Big Lie Helped to Kill Proposition 18," " 'Taxes' Tag on Prop. 18 termed 'Lie'," " 'Clean Air' Loses—Court Next." After it was all over, the Sierra Club and the Tuberculosis and Respiratory Diseases Association bravely announced they would try to get the issue back on the ballot.

Some post-election lawyering brought the appearance, but not the substance, of righting the campaign wrongs. Newly elected Secretary of State Edmund G. Brown, Jr., filed suit against the Tax Trap Committee, individuals involved in the campaign and, as it turned out, Standard Oil of California, Mobil Oil and Gulf Oil, charging violations of the campaign reporting laws. It took some time to discover who the "anonymous" patrons were but gradually the story emerged.

Brown was in a position to force disclosure of the names of the contributors through court action; so the offenders, one by one, came out of hiding. Mobil Oil's corporate counsel wrote to the Secretary of State on December 11 with this confession: "Mobil Oil Corporation contributed $30,000 to 'Californians Against Road and Tax Trap.' The contribution was made on October 28 and the funds were transmitted by cashier's check. Mobil did not condition its contribution on anonymity." The letter went on to say that "Mobil is in favor of mass transit," enclosing an ad run in the *New York Times* as proof and requesting that if Brown released the letter, he do so in its entirety, along with the advertisement.

Mobil was to come through again about a year later— another full page ad in the *New York Times* supporting a National Master Transportation Program, and another $45,000 to defeat a New York Transportation bond issue.[61]

Gulf and Standard Oil of California came around shortly. Standard owned up to a $30,000 contribution for the first report, but subsequently went underground, handing over $45,000 in easily negotiated cashier's checks. A query on this point drew the following response from public relations man W. K. Morris: "Since our company made no public statements on this issue, I cannot answer your question regarding the intended nature of our contribution. However, the company does appreciate that contributions on controversial issues, however made, must be considered public property."[62] Especially when forced into the open by a summons and complaint.

These anonymous and illegal investments in corporate security brought success at virtually no cost. Secretary of State Brown won his suit against the trio of oil companies for campaign reporting violations.[63] The maximum penalty? One thousand dollars for each offense.[64] That's like fining an individual with a $20,000 annual income something less than a nickel.[65] Big Oil will stand chastised for its wrongdoing in the campaign. A debit against petty cash will take care of the fines.

The Proposition 18 campaign was but a fleeting example of the relentless squeezing of urban transit options that has been administered by road interests for several decades. Political and economic power, technological stagnation and propaganda have played a part. General Motors was condemned but never effectively restrained for conspiring to foist its buses onto local transit commissions.[66] The whole story of the demise of rail transit and the trackless trolley has not yet been told, but the ingenuity of the executioner is clearly indicated by the famous advertisement of the GMC Truck and Coach Division recommending a purchase of buses as an aid to a fare increase.[67] Buses are promoted on the ground that they "have a shorter amortization period" and are therefore "more adaptable to changes in technology."[68] That is, buses fall apart faster and it is necessary to buy new ones more often. GM's James Roche has said it: "Planned obsolescence in my opinion is another word for progress."[69]

Whatever the contribution of the diesel bus, signs of the death of urban mass transit are everywhere. Between 1950 and 1970, 258 transit companies in the United States collapsed, and they are running a collective annual deficit in the hundreds of millions.

Bringing people movement in the cities back to life will cost money. Some of that started to flow with the Urban Mass Transportation Assistance Act of 1970 which authorizes federal grants and loans for new subway, commuter rail and bus (mostly bus) equipment.[70] But money to buy technology is no guarantee the technology will serve the people. That requires a government of independence, strength and wisdom, however accidental that combination might be.

The Highway Trust Fund is a good reminder of the benefits brought by unrestrained commercial influence on government policies. That monument of fiscal sovereignty is the key to the auto's dominance of the nation, and it continues to crowd heavily on transportation alternatives. What have we learned? After fourteen years' experience with the Highway Trust Fund, Congress, in 1970, enacted an airport trust fund to assist in airport development. It was supported by air carriers and their trade association, equipment manufacturers, pilots, municipal airport operators. It was opposed by a single citizen named Smith who wrote to tell the committee he thought the Highway Trust Fund was a bad precedent.[71]

3 SMELTING THE POPULATION

We found that we could not sell the acid we made and get a profit by it. . . . . I have been able to make sulfuric acid easily and satisfactorily, but my difficulty is to find a use for it. *

Dear Peter. . . . Thanks so much for finding time in your tight schedule to meet with those of us from the copper industry who wished to express our concern over recent actions of EPA representatives. . . . Any assistance you can offer in having EPA acknowledge that it got overzealously involved in Montana's affairs will be appreciated. **

During a break in a hearing on sulfur dioxide in May 1971, a conversation took place at the back of the room between Charles Barber, chairman of the board of American Smelting and Refining Company (ASARCO) and Clarence Gordon, a professor of botany at the University of

---

*Testimony of smelter operator, before the British Royal Commission on Noxious Vapors, 1877, quoted in Semrau, "Sulfur Oxides Control and Metallurgical Technology," *J. Metals,* March 1971, p. 1.
**Letter from John Place, chairman of the board, Anaconda Copper Co., to Peter M. Flanigan, Assistant to the President, Dec. 29, 1971.

Montana. Gordon said to Barber: "I'm not as worried about the sulfur dioxide as I am about the lead and the arsenic. This is turning up in garden vegetables and hair samples taken from the kids in the Helena Valley [Montana]." Barber didn't pay much attention.

Nor, historically, did Barber pay much attention to Smeltertown, a community of 100 or so Chicano families living in tight rows of adobe huts within the shadows of the ASARCO smelter stacks in El Paso, Texas. Some of the men from Smeltertown work at the ASARCO plant, one of the largest metallurgical complexes in the world. Their children play in the dirt streets—there are Rubin Regaldo, Manuel Sanchez, Alberto Garcia and the others. Although the company, over the years, may not have brought prosperity and comfort to Smeltertown, it did provide some jobs, and it surely was doing no harm.

ASARCO's perspective on Smeltertown began to change on February 19, 1972. That was the day company attorneys took the deposition of Dr. Bertram Carnow of the University of Illinois School of Public Health, an authority on lead poisoning who was then advising the city of El Paso. Dr. Carnow testified about serious lead poisoning problems in Smeltertown. He said some children living there ought to be moved and that an extensive testing program should be initiated.

This was a risk deserving attention. Expressing "surprise," the company began its own investigations[1] which confirmed what the city already knew. Children were hospitalized at company expense (the number eventually exceeded 100). ASARCO removed loose dirt from the streets. Roadways were swept and wet down with soil binders to suppress dust; yard soil was carted away. The company pledged to explore with city officials ways of moving the Smeltertown residents out of the reach of the stacks.

ASARCO officials took other steps to combat the lead epidemic on the banks of the Rio Grande—they published ads in the *El Paso Herald-Post* and *Times,* called in their kept experts, forced the city to resort to legal processes to secure data on emissions and reports on lead exposure of company employees, and played down the need for a massive federally sponsored blood sampling program that would reach as many as 60,000 El Paso children.

For two years a small band of dedicated city health officials and lawyers, with the strong support of the mayor, laboriously gathered the evidence that was to prove in court that El Paso was the nation's industrial lead disaster capital. They were fought every inch of the way by the company which agreed to an eleventh hour settlement to avoid the public relations backlash of an adverse judgment. In settling, ASARCO charged city politics prolonged the conflict. "The company has been and will continue to be," said its attorney, "a fine citizen of this community, interested in the welfare of this community in every way."[2]

ASARCO and the other fine citizens of the copper fraternity long ago embraced technology's other tools: research manipulation, political bare knuckles, florid propagandizing. The copper man's equipment, his tactics and testimony have changed very little in the last 100 years.

The industry has a bad case of oligopolitis. The symptoms were spelled out by Hendrik Houthakker, former member of the President's Council of Economic Advisors, in a 1970 speech at Duke University titled "Copper: The Anatomy of a Malfunctioning Market." Pervasive anti-competitive effects among the copper producers include idle capacity, misallocation of resources, suppression of new sources of supply, inflated prices. There is excessive concentration in the mining and refining segments of the industry and unhealthy integration between producers and fabricators. The president of one large and modern tube mill "told us with pride," Houthakker reported, "of his discovery that the firm could make more money by idling most of its facilities." A grand jury has looked at Houthakker's findings, but experience indicates conventional antitrust law enforcement will not soon undo the monopoly power abuses that permeate the industry.

The industry's big four—Anaconda, Phelps Dodge, Kennecott and ASARCO are well known international economic and political powers. Like other subscribers to free enterprise, they are subsidized in many ways. The extractive industries are near the bottom of the taxpaying list.[3] They mine their profits under the bountiful provisions of the General Mining Law of 1872, which essentially hands over the public's mineral rights to anybody who stakes a claim. They get a depletion allowance with the excuse it will encourage them to do more research, then win a direct subsidy for research under the 1972 Mining and Minerals Policy Act.[4] Their legislative spear-carriers, long led by House Interior Chairman Wayne Aspinall, (D-Colo.)* fight off attempts to earmark some of that research money for health and environmental issues just as they have beaten back efforts to interrupt the free ride that began on the public lands in 1872.

The pollution subsidy for copper smelters is old and huge, and a century long corporate winning streak in the courts gives credence to the theory that technological criminality is beyond the law. In 1877 the British Royal

---

*Aspinall's record on environmental matters earned him the enmity of the League of Conservation Voters, which mounted a successful drive to defeat him at the polls in 1972.

Commission on Noxious Vapors heard testimony from smelter owners on how much easier it was to send the sulfur up the stack than to find markets for it,[5] and in the 1970's air pollution officials across the United States were treated to the same story. In 1907 a federal court concluded that smelter emissions in the Salt Lake Valley were a "menace to health,"[6] but the issue was still in doubt sixty-three years later when the copper industry decided to finance an "independent" study at the University of Utah on the health effects of sulfur dioxide pollution from smelters.[7] In 1908 a court in California ordered the owners of the Selby lead smelter to cease creating a public nuisance with "noxious and injurious gases and smoke,"[8] but the public nuisance was still around in 1970 when the loss of dozens of horses and sheep to lead poisoning inspired health authorities to begin monitoring an area of twenty square miles.[9] A 1911 consent decree obligated the smelter at Anaconda, Montana to stop pollution with the "most scientific 'control' processes then practically available,"[10] but in 1971 an Environmental Protection Agency witness so bold as to advise the Montana State Board of Health about what was "practically available" was repudiated on the orders of White House Assistant Peter Flanigan. Flanigan got into the picture at the request of Anaconda Chairman of the Board John Place whose letter is quoted at the beginning of this chapter.

In 1915 the United States Supreme Court laid down a precedent that sets a useful standard for measuring the legal flotsam left in the wake of the copper industry.[11] The defendant operated a smelter in Ducktown, Tennessee, which deposited its sulfur oxides liberally across the landscape of the State of Georgia. That jurisdictional accident helped bring the case to the highest court which ordered the defendant to limit sulfur emissions to twenty tons a day·

during summer months. The decree prompted a technological triumph: development of the lead chamber process
for producing sulfuric acid from smelter stack emissions.[12]
To this day, the Ducktown smelter gets passing grades for
pollution control.

Outside the Ducktown city limits, the copper smelters
didn't make the same progress. The Supreme Court's
recommended tolerance level of twenty tons of sulfur a day
has been upped to sixty tons an hour in some parts of the
country. On a list of the worst single sources of air pollution in the United States, the first half-dozen spots probably would go to copper smelters. The industry's four giants
all have plants contending for top honors.

This industrial extravagance has social costs, which add
up to a technological subsidy. Sulfur dioxide is one of the
most studied pollutants. Commissioner John Middleton of
the Air Pollution Control Office of the Environmental Protection Agency summarizes the data: "Sulfur oxides irritate
the respiratory system, particularly in the young, the old,
and those already crippled with respiratory afflictions.
They attack a wide variety of materials. Metals corrode;
paints disintegrate; fibers weaken and fade; building
materials discolor and deteriorate. Agricultural production
drops as plant growth and yield are suppressed."[13] The
economic toll is huge: "National health costs resulting
from sulfur oxide emissions are conservatively estimated at
over $3.3 billion annually. The effects of sulfur oxides on
materials, property and vegetation cost the Nation an estimated additional $5 billion annually. These total damages
of $8.3 billion amount to about $.20 for each pound of
sulfur now emitted into our atmosphere."[14] Estimates such
as these gave rise to a short-lived Nixon Administration
proposal for a tax on sulfur emissions, to start at a penny
a pound in 1972, increasing a penny a pound each year

until a maximum of ten cents per pound was to be levied in 1982. Applied to one smelter, this sulfur tax would run into millions. ASARCO's Charles Barber and the other copper executives had plenty of help in quickly consigning that idea to the slag heap.

The technology rests secure in the subtleties of its hurts. El Paso is probably the best studied smelter; yet all experts agree it needs more study. Arsenic, lead, cadmium, zinc are ubiquitous contributions from many a smelter, and all agree they need more study. The sulfur dioxide that everybody knows about gets only the condemnation of "more study" when an effort is made to trace the sulfur to the cemetery. Doctors identify a special "risk" population (children, older persons, asthmatics) numbering 8,000 to 9,000 people in the chief "target" area south of one of ASARCO's smelters.[15] But the professional can do no better than offer an estimate of what epidemiologic studies might show: "I tell you this, that there is a reasonable chance that in the susceptible population group . . . there are changes occurring and that indeed these changes may be detectable by death certificates in the age range that I have indicated. . . ." The law looks for corpses, not studies to be, and the money, time and commitment needed to sort out the murder victims from the conventional dead works to the advantage of the technology and its defenders.

Inside the plant, the study has been going on for some time. Here's what a hearing examiner has to say about ASARCO's safety on-the-job in its Omaha plant: "The present safety program of the company, which includes biological testing, in effect uses employees as a test device to determine hazardous conditions."[16] (Ever wonder what the penalty is for creating a hazard "likely to cause death or serious physical harm" to employees? $600.)[17] One worker at the ASARCO plant in El Paso was found to have a lead blood level count of an incredible 700 micrograms per 100 grams of blood.[18] By conventional estimates, this man ought to be dead of acute lead poisoning, but he qualified for work in a smelter.

Affirmative action to suppress information brings greater security. Laying corpses at the company's door is not part of its business. Records of emissions are called trade secrets or privileged communications between attorney and client. Operations are curtailed when the inspectors arrive; business picks up after the sun goes down.

Over the years, collisions between the people and the technology were resolved in favor of the technology. Workers who complained were fired; communities which protested were threatened with a shut-down; citizens who didn't like it could move.

Way back in 1915 the Selby Smelter Commission talked of corporate responsibility: "The policy that 'buys off' trouble, as the most expedient commercial method for abating it, has been responsible for much of the smelter litigation of this country and the intense ill-feeling that unfortunately exists toward smelters in many smelter communities. The principle that right is on the side of the man with the biggest guns is fast becoming an obsolete idea in modern business and is being replaced by equity and open and aboveboard dealings."[19] Today's business practices don't sustain this interpretation by the Selby Smelter Commission.

"Dear Mr. Bessler," read a solicitous note signed by the manager of the ASARCO smelter in East Helena, Montana on August 19, 1968: "During the spring of 1967 and summer of 1968, your property south of the smelter has experienced considerable exposure to SO_2. Under the present state of knowledge, it is not likely that the condition can be improved for a matter of years. Because of this unfortunate situation, it would appear advantageous to all concerned if you were to move out of that location. Possibly you can find another location in the countryside and your house could be moved there. Please let me know if you are interested so that we can negotiate terms of sale." This offer has been made, with minor variations, to many people. They have been advised to remove themselves from the neighborhood, to plant privet hedge instead of the more vulnerable laurel, to shun easily scarred white automobiles or to remove their cars from the driveways at night, where they might be susceptible to smelter fall-out. Beggars at the trough in Tacoma, Washington receive a few hundred dollars a year for property damage, and the company thinks this is outright extravagance. (Montana State University economist Richard Stroup estimates household damages alone during 1968–70 to be about $8 million per year.)[20]

In 1963,[21] an ASARCO letter to a rancher in the vicinity of its East Helena, Montana smelter offered this advice: "I have finally received the results of the soil samples and must report that your soil is highly contaminated with lead. . . . Under some circumstances, it is risky to pasture horses on land, the surface portions of the soil of which contain over 200 parts per million of lead. The risk is great when grass is grown in soil with a content of 1,000 ppm lead. During the times the grass is lush and the animals can graze in the pasture without cropping low, or without picking up some soil, I should say the danger would be minimized. I cannot imagine a very luxuriant growth of vegetation in a pasture which contains such a high concentration of metals. . . . Certainly, in this particular area, it would not be 'up to the stirrups' of an ordinary size horse. My advice, therefore, is that you discourage the use of this pasture for animals, especially horses."

One soil sample from Smeltertown reached 11,000

parts per million, a housedust sample 58,000 ppm. "Might your advice for horses hold true for children?" El Paso City Attorney John Ross asked ASARCO's Kenneth Nelson,[22] the company's top scientific apologist. "It's not really the same thing," said Nelson. "We had tested the horses in the area and had found them to be highly susceptible to blood lead poisoning. Horses as you know graze over large areas of ground, and when they bite the short grass, they eat large quantities of soil." "Are you aware," Ross persisted, "that children also play over a wide area, and could possibly be exposed to the same soil?" "Yes, I am," said Nelson. "But the likelihood of a child eating that much dirt is very small." ASARCO may be an inveterate lead poisoner in the fields of Montana and California and the industrial plants of Nebraska, but it was still a novice in the streets of Smeltertown, Texas.

The advent of "modern" air pollution regimes in the various smelter states in the late 1960's didn't change much. The standards usually covered only sulfur dioxide, not the more sophisticated lead, cadmium or arsenic. For the most part, they created numbers of so many parts per million over certain periods of time that were not to be exceeded. Violations were supposedly punished, sometimes as criminal offenses. By 1970 in El Paso, the law was being complied with, according to the company, "97 per cent of the time."[23] The Tacoma smelter had run up 282 separate violations detectable only when the wind was blowing in the direction of the agency's single recording station. To be sure, Chairman of the Board Charles Barber was not hit with $282,000 in fines nor sentenced to prison for a stretch of 282 years. The only sanctions were thirteen $250 civil penalties against the corporation; ASARCO paid under protest—it was just another technological wrong.

The federal government began to stir in December 1967 with a contract let by the National Air Pollution Control Administration (now the Environmental Protection Agency) to Arthur G. McKee & Company, a San Francisco-based engineering firm, to conduct a systems analysis of the primary copper, lead and zinc smelting industry. The contract called for an assessment of the "technical and economic feasibility" of converting sulfur emissions from smelters to valuable by-products—sulfuric acid, liquid sulfur dioxide, elemental sulfur and ammonium sulfate. Cost estimates were anticipated; future markets were to be assessed. The ostensible purpose of the study was to guide NAPCA in its research efforts. It was no secret that the document also was destined to become a key source for possible enforcement action, since no one, besides NAPCA, had a half-million dollars or so to invest in a study of the industry's indiscretions.

In the early days, the copper companies had the situation well in hand. NAPCA chose McKee as the prime contractor for the smelting industry study because of its close association with the industry. That was understandable—if you want information about the copper industry you do well to consult the people best informed. For some reason, the industry didn't come right out and tell McKee that any firm serving it doesn't do studies for trouble-makers like NAPCA. The probable explanation appears as an acknowledgment in the final version of the McKee Report: "The critical review and suggestions of the Industry Liaison Committee were very helpful." Industry liaison means technology defense.

Under the federal Clean Air Act, NAPCA is authorized to convene "technical advisory committees" composed of "recognized experts in various aspects of air pollution" to assist in the evaluation of research proposals and their progress.[24] Members are supposed to collect $250 a day to work for their government. Among the "recognized experts" on the Primary Nonferrous Smelting Industry Liaison Committee, formed on July 23, 1968, were fourteen company representatives including, of course, spokesmen for the big four—Anaconda, Kennecott, Phelps Dodge and ASARCO. ASARCO's expert was Ken Nelson, a company man with the patience of Job, who with aplomb has been absorbing the barbs of angry housewives for years.

NAPCA's 1969 Second Report on Progress in the Prevention and Control of Air Pollution explains the official purpose of the work of Ken Nelson and his colleagues: "The primary smelter industry liaison committee is established to (a) review the scope of the systems engineering study of the air pollution problems relating to the industry; (b) provide pertinent data inputs from industrial sources as applicable; (c) participate in periodic contract progress reviews; and (d) evaluate a final study report." The liaison committee had quite a bit of evaluating to do.

The minutes disclose that committee members took full advantage of their inside-track opportunities to discuss in depth—and unquestionably to influence—the study that probed so deeply into sensitive questions of feasible control processes and the economics of control. Dispassionate scientific inquiry is not the art of technical lobbyists. At an early meeting, a question arose as to the purposes of the study. The committee "made the point," according to the minutes, "that public opinion will be influenced by the report and that this should be kept in mind when the report is written. Certainly, the report should not present superficial conclusions that control is easy and economical thus endangering the industry." The response reported in the minutes was that "such endangering of the industry is very unlikely; the Liaison Committee was created to help ensure that this does not happen."

The committee worked hard to ensure the report would not endanger the industry. NAPCA was given a new federal version of the hackneyed "we'll move out of town" argument: "If it becomes necessary to stop emissions before economical processes are developed, the smelting industry might be forced out of the country. . . . The study should be made carefully so that it does not present false information that could be used to force the industry into a dangerous situation."[25] NAPCA was given a lesson in priorities: "The industry does not believe that sulfur oxide control is that urgent,"[26] a point reiterated time and again in forum after forum across the United States.

Several times at the October 1968 liaison committee meeting concern was expressed over whether the McKee Report could be used as a "propaganda tool." "No!" was the emphatic response of McKee's project director. It was conceded, however, that "no matter how carefully a document is written it is possible that material taken out of context could be misused." Ironically, the man later charged with misusing the McKee Report by taking information out of context was a spokesman for the federal government.

Committee members suggested techniques for rendering the McKee Report impotent for enforcement purposes. "Is it possible to relate the report to the conservation of a national resource—sulfur from the smelting industry—rather than to control of air pollution?" No, it was untenable for NAPCA to adopt a subterfuge that would deny its role as an air pollution agency. "Is it possible to preface the report with the statement that no part of the report can be copied or used against industry?" No again; presumably it would be difficult for NAPCA to accord information about the smelting industry a classified status akin to that accorded to research into, let us say, biological and chemical warfare.

Nonetheless, industry minions took what appeared to be sufficient steps to undercut the usefulness of the study for enforcement purposes: they would withhold and distort some data and disguise the rest. McKee estimated the emission rate for the Tacoma smelter to be 156 short tons of sulfur a day, a figure contradicting ASARCO's own later admission of 266.4 short tons. The familiar technique of a code was adopted in the report making it impossible to connect a particular smelter with the relevant data. Objections were made at the final meeting on June 11, 1969, that the proposed report "declared that control of SO_2 emissions from smelters was technically feasible without placing sufficient emphasis upon what in many cases are rather dismal economics." The final report published in June 1969 places great emphasis on dismal economics.

Notwithstanding industry's rewrite job, the McKee Report contains useful data. It discloses, for example, that there is ample precedent for controlling all types of sulfur oxide emissions from smelters. The principal barrier for the country's sixteen copper smelters is economic rather than chemical or technical. According to McKee, smelters located in the East recover as usable by-products an estimated 85.5 per cent of their emissions.[27] They do so, says Professor C. B. Meyer, former research director of the American Sulfur Institute, "because they want, or the law forces them, to be good neighbors."[28] Smelters in the West were said to recover an average of only 22.7 per cent of their emissions.[29]

Despite industry's best efforts behind the scenes, the concern expressed in committee a year earlier came to fruition. The threat took the form of a November 1969 document prepared by Terry Stumph of NAPCA's Division of Process Control Engineering, titled "Proposed Emission Standard for Reduced Sulfur from Primary Nonferrous

Smelters." The Report was NAPCA's response to a request for technical assistance from members of the staff of the Montana State Department of Health who were grappling with smelters located there. The Stumph paper cited the three-volume McKee report as "proof of the existence of adequate control technology" and went on to say that control of 90 per cent of the sulfur emissions could be achieved.

To say that industry was displeased with this use of the McKee Report is an understatement. By limiting what is put out, emission controls strike at the heart of the technology. Talk of a 90 per cent emission standard is irreconcilable with prevailing pollution dilution myths—tall stacks, gas heaters to boost the emissions to a higher altitude, curtailment during adverse weather conditions.

It is likely the 90 per cent blasphemy would have been short-lived had it not been for the fortuitous circumstance that Stumph resigned from NAPCA early in 1970 to accept a post in Clark County (Las Vegas), Nevada as pollution control officer. Having saddled NAPCA with liability for the 90 per cent standard, Stumph skipped out to talk about what was going on. He reappeared in March 1970 at hearings before the Puget Sound Board, where the 90 per cent standard was to receive its first stern test.

The occasion for Stumph's testimony was an application by ASARCO for a variance from local regulations to permit the construction of a giant 1,000 to 1,100 foot stack —"one of the tallest in the world" the company proudly noted. The move was designed to head off the rumbling discontent of those beginning to notice that new air pollution regulations didn't do much about sulfur emissions. Invoking a cosmetic action put to shame in the 1915 Ducktown court order, the company's idea was to disperse the sulfur to meet the agency's prescribed ground level concentrations. It was a workable legal strategy that would buy time, protect the technology and earn a possible anti-pollution tax break for rebuilding a stack that was in need of reconstruction. A NAPCA publication exposes the tall stack strategy as a fraud: "Whereas stack heights have increased by a factor of about 4, emission rates have increased by a factor of approximately 6. Thus a good share of the benefits of increased stack height are offset by the release of more contaminants from the stack."[30] Ignored also was a wealth of data indicating ASARCO had no hope of meeting SO_2 standards then in effect, not to mention stiffer standards then being developed.

At the invitation of the local agency, Stumph appeared now as a former NAPCA employee to defend his conclusions about a 90 per cent emission standard. He cited the extraordinary degree of control at Ducktown, and he mentioned the Cominco copper smelter at Trail, British Columbia. (Cominco achieves 99.9 per cent control at its Trail smelter, twelve miles from the U.S. border, a technological achievement credited to legal pressures brought to bear by the U.S. government in the 1920's and 1930's to correct smoke damage to property in Washington State.)[31] Emboldened by developing local opposition to the tall stack and beseiged by requests for help, NAPCA authorized Stumph to speak on its behalf and also dispatched other hearing witnesses whose testimony could not be said to add up to an endorsement of tall stacks.

Notwithstanding the shock of the Stumph appearance, it demonstrated bad taste, even for ASARCO, to call as its key witness Lee Argenbright, the project director of the NAPCA-financed McKee study. Having been paid by NAPCA to study the industry, it made a perverted kind of copper sense for Argenbright to be paid by the industry to rebut NAPCA. Federal conflict of interest laws speak to the point but they are enforced only occasionally.[32] "McKee Report Mis-Used, Company Representative States," read the press release describing Argenbright's testimony. The Stumph document on emission control was condemned for taking extracts from the McKee Report "out of context, with little regard for the derivation or usefulness of the portions extracted." The McKee Report failed to "supply proof of the existence of adequate sulfur-control technology," nor did it "provide a proper basis for setting standards." Argenbright concluded: "The findings of our study are consistent with the proposal of the company to proceed by way of a tall stack, pending development of a workable sulfur recovery process."

Despite this carefully contrived path to success, on March 25, 1970, the Puget Sound Board voted unanimously to deny the tall stack variance, a move that precipitated a crisis within the smelting industry. Though court review of the decision was technically available and ASARCO could go ahead with construction if it wanted to, the tall stack was effectively dead.

Circumstances soon went from bad to worse for the copper smelters. The Stumph Report turned up in Utah and in Arizona which has eight copper smelters and over 50 per cent of the nation's copper smelting capacity. In April 1970 NAPCA's Second Report to the Congress on the costs of clean air estimated that the entire copper smelting industry (16 smelters in all) could achieve 98.9 per cent control with a modest capital investment of between $33.8 and $81 million.[33] Hearings were held on a proposed 90 per cent emission standard by the Arizona State Board of Health on April 17 and by the Montana State Board of Health on May 21. Both states were to adopt the 90 per cent standard. Similar proposals were aired before the Puget Sound Board on June 10 where representatives of

ASARCO bitterly attacked the Stumph report and criticized its author as one whose thinking was "superficial and unrealistic."[34] That the issue now claimed priority was demonstrated by the ashen appearance of ASARCO's Chairman of the Board Charles Barber who vowed that the technology was unavailable and pleaded with the board: "Why then would NAPCA send an attractive young man out to appear before you with a proposed emission standard for control of sulfur from non-ferrous smelters, calling for removal of 90 per cent of the sulfur in the gases? Frankly, I do not know the answer to that question."[35] Barber declared: "I do not minimize for one minute the problem of control of sulfur dioxide emissions from non-ferrous smelters. It has been the number one, bar none, challenge to which the considerable energies and talents of our research and engineering staff have been devoted over the last two years. The same can be said for other companies in the non-ferrous smelting industry, particularly the other copper companies."[36] The board, which knew something about the smelter that Barber didn't, went ahead and adopted the 90 per cent standard effective mid-August 1970.

The "considerable energies and talents" of the smelting industry of which Barber spoke were already at work in Washington, D.C. It took about a year to complete the job. On June 29 J. Allen Overton, executive vice president of the American Mining Congress, wrote to NAPCA's John Middleton to tell him to get rid of the 90 per cent standard: "Dear Dr. Middleton," came the word from Overton, "Several member companies of the American Mining Congress, producers of nonferrous metals in the western states, have reported to us their concern about a NAPCA document entitled 'Proposed Emission Standard for Reduced Sulfur from Primary Non-Ferrous Smelters.' The paper was originally prepared by Terry L. Stumph, a former NAPCA employee, and submitted to the State of Montana Department of Health. This paper subsequently was received at least by the States of Utah and Arizona and by the Puget Sound Air Pollution Control Agency." Our concerned member companies don't like the 90 per cent standard, was the thrust of Overton's message, because it "does not include data on cost effectiveness or on the enormous economic impact on the copper, lead and zinc industries if the proposed emission standards are adopted and enforced by air pollution control agencies." Not only was the 90 per cent standard economically indefensible, Overton continued, it was legally flawed: "In the Act there is no authorization for the Secretary to set industry emission standards. Proposing such standards and permitting strong endorsement of them by NAPCA representatives at public hearings held by air pollution control boards in Arizona, Montana, Utah and Washington is considered far beyond the simple rendering of technical service provided for in the Act." He had a solution: "Because of these and other grave objections we are compelled, on behalf of our affected member companies to request prompt withdrawal of the proposed emission standards contained in the Stumph report from the air pollution control agencies which have received it and a full review of the entire problem with industry representatives and other government departments and agencies. We further request that the authorities who conducted the public hearings be notified that the proposed standards have been withdrawn and that the problem is under review." This invitation to surrender unconditionally eventually was accepted by the Environmental Protection Agency (NAPCA's successor) although the negotiations were of sufficient duration to provide insight into the corporate interpretation of the Clean Air Act.

The attack on the 90 per cent standard was intense, bitter and carefully orchestrated, with ASARCO's Charles Barber in the middle of the picture. The pitch that the 90 per cent standard was an illegal attempt to set federal emission standards was backed in a memorandum of law submitted to NAPCA on ASARCO's behalf by Covington & Burling, Barber's old law firm and Washington, D.C.'s well-known counsel for the mighty.[37] The politics were helped along by a Barber letter to Senator Henry Jackson (D-Wash.) complaining that the 90 per cent standard was a NAPCA-inspired attempt to foist a solution that was neither "technically nor economically feasible."[38] James Owens, director of the Department of Commerce's Office of Basic Materials, was brought into the picture with a letter from Barber warning that copper production essential to the national security was jeopardized by application of the 90 per cent standard to the Tacoma smelter.[39] David Swan, Kennecott vice president and chairman of the Environmental Matters Committee of the American Mining Congress, appeared on the scene to coordinate the effort to kill the 90 per cent standard.

A key figure in the struggle was Hendrik Houthakker, who in July 1970 put in a call to NAPCA's Edward Tuerk, special assistant for program operations, to explain that industry was threatening to close up shop if the 90 per cent control requirement was affirmed.[40] A July 20 Tuerk memorandum explained: "Mr. Houthakker is looking for some compromise solution whereby each smelter would make a public statement as to what they would do in the next two years in order to achieve what they consider to be technically feasible. He talked about a control level of about 75 per cent as a compromise figure. I explained to him that our position of 90 per cent was based on what, in fact, had been achieved by smelters and that, as I understood the issue, the concern of the industry was with the cost of achieving this level of control and its effect on their price and competitive situation." Tuerk promised a background paper for Houthakker defending the 90 per cent standard and spelling out what the cost of achieving control would be. William Megonnell, NAPCA's assistant commissioner for standards and compliance, was assigned responsibility for pulling the data together.

An August 18 Megonnell memorandum to Tuerk contained this summary conclusion of NAPCA's position: "Mr. Stumph's analysis regarding technological control of sulfurous emissions from nonferrous smelters is substantiated by the authoritative and comprehensive McKee Report. It appears that control costs for copper smelters will be nominal, about 4 per cent of product price at most [based on a price of 60 cents per pound], and a sound investment in protecting health and welfare in accordance with the purposes of the Clean Air Act." Around this time NAPCA re-issued the Stumph report on the 90 per cent standard as an official agency document.[41] It was to be one of the last acts of defiance of an agency that was about to meet its master.

Elsewhere during the summer of 1970, as NAPCA was preparing the documents that nobody would read, industry was hard at work to undo the damage. A useful entree was the Mining and Non-Ferrous Metals Sub-Council of the National Industrial Pollution Control Council which was already in business in the Department of Commerce to give top executives a direct pipeline to the administration on pollution control issues. Of all the accomplishments of NIPCC, the Mining Sub-Council is probably the best example of a government-sponsored conspiracy to defeat antipollution laws. The sub-council chairman is Frank Milliken, Kennecott's chairman of the board and includes the chief executives of ASARCO, Lone Star Cement Corporation, Utah Construction & Mining Company, Alcoa, American Metal Climax [see Chap. 7], Hecla Mining Company, and International Minerals & Chemical Company. Anyone else interested in killing the 90 per cent standard was welcome at the meetings.

The first sub-council get-together was held in Washington, D.C., on July 6, 1970. There as participants were David Swan of Kennecott and an ASARCO man. The highlight of the session was a blistering communique from Kennecott's Frank Milliken.[42] "In Government's development of criteria and the subsequent setting of standards," said Milliken, "it seems to me, the testimony and data presented by industry have not received due consideration by government. . . . And in the *present* critical stage of action—the planning and implementation of [environmental] quality control measures—government *must* grant us a fair and honest forum. . . . Imposition of uniform but unnecessarily severe ambient air standards across the country can place an undue economic burden on industry. But when *emission* standards place restrictions on industry that are even *more* repressive than the ambient air standards—and are even less necessary—the resulting economic impact on industry is serious enough so that it might lead to the shutting down of smelters."

Inspired by Milliken's remarks, the Mining Sub-Council dictated a series of "recommendations" into the summary minutes: "We are seriously dissatisfied with the role NAPCA has played in the standard-setting process at the state and regional level." NAPCA's use of an "unofficial paper" (soon to become official) was singled out for criticism; submission of the Stumph Report "as part of NAPCA testimony at state hearings has lent an entirely unjustified but authoritative significance to it. We believe that the use of this paper as the basis for establishing standards for sulfur dioxide should be discontinued, and that the states who have received it should be informed that it does not reflect the official position of NAPCA."

By September, the technological defense moved to call up the scientific platoon. The Mining Sub-Council's minutes reported that "[a]n industry-financed independent study is being made at the University of Utah on health effects of atmospheric SO_2 pollution from smelters." Not only was industry going to study the problem, it was going to look for a solution: "The Smelter Control Research Association is being organized to demonstrate on a pilot plant scale the technical and economical feasibility of at least one method of SO_2 removal from smelter stack emissions."

These projects with all the appearances of the best of motives offer a lesson in anti-pollution research and development. The concern of the industrial lobbyist is pronounced if a research effort takes on applied overtones, and becomes acute when somebody (invariably the federal government) talks about funding a project as dangerous to established commercial patterns as a pilot plant to control pollution. Industries have two basic strategies when it comes to scientific and engineering studies that could adversely affect the current technology, and the choice may not always be theirs. The first is to allow the government to pay for the study, relying upon capturing the grant, influencing the research team, controlling data input or even outright censoring to avoid damaging results. Taking over a single major research project assures twenty legal victories.

The smelting industry had gone the government research route with the McKee Report and the NAPCA criteria document on sulfur oxides, and despite the protective device of the advisory committee, twice had come up smarting. It was time to take the second route which is to pay for the study yourself and decide whether to release the findings and, if so, in what form. This tack offers protection against "damaging and arbitrary" findings but it costs money, and sometimes public officials and the people tend to discount the reliability of industry-purchased science. Sometimes they don't.

The copper makers preferred to do it themselves and to do it together. The purpose of a joint research effort through the Smelter Control Research Association is highly suspect because, as Kennecott's Milliken explained in July 1970, "[e]nvironmental quality control measures [at smelters] have to be integrated into individual processes and have to be tailored to a variety of factors peculiar to each operation and each locale in which we operate."[43] The types of concentrates and metallurgical processes, in particular, make the problems different. Sulfur dioxide, moreover, leads the list of all pollutants under attack from a variety of directions. None of the big four were without funds for research, all were engaged in sulfur dioxide research individually (ASARCO, with Phelps Dodge, had a pilot plant under construction, as did Anaconda.) One is left with the impression that the Smelter Control Research Association was formed to prove that it was *not* technically and economically feasible to remove sulfur dioxide from smelter stack emissions. There certainly would be no confusion among Association members about the viability of the 90 per cent emission standard, for the man who led the attack against it as the chairman of the Environmental Matters Committee of the American Mining Congress, Kennecott's David Swan, was to serve as the president of the new Smelter Control Research Association. Fungibility of views is one of the strengths of the smelting industry.

The March 8, 1971 meeting of NIPCC's Mining Sub-Council marked the high-water mark of the industry's formal assault against the 90 per cent standard. Interestingly, NIPCC's Executive Secretary Walter Hamilton defended his group's closed door deliberations on the ground that a small get-together encourages candid exchanges.[44] That this notion was designed chiefly to still congressional inquisitors is suggested by the fact that those in attendance at the March meeting numbered a chummy fifty-nine. Chief executives of the big four were there along with their counterparts from the other copper companies. From the government came Hendrik Houthakker, NAPCA's John Middleton and James Owens of the Department of Commerce.

Deserving special mention was Barry Grossman who appeared near the bottom of the list of those in attendance as a representative of the Justice Department. The reason for his attendance was concern about the antitrust laws. Grossman has spoken for the Department on the special dangers of joint research ventures on environmental problems. His former boss Richard McClaren, when head of the Justice Department's Antitrust Division, put it this way in a speech to the American Bar Association: "It is for this reason—i.e., to avoid the risk that the group may be slowed down to the pace of the slowest—that we urge that members of an industry present their views to government agencies on feasibility and timing on an individual, rather than on a joint, basis."[45] Words mean little. Industry members routinely present joint views on feasibility and timing to government agencies, and the copper makers are very good at it. All in all, March 8, 1971 was the finest hour for the newly born Smelter Control Research Association.

ASARCO's Ken Nelson who turned up in the Commerce Department on March 8, has attended many hearings in his time. He has taken the trouble to spell out his views on the public hearings mandated by the Clean Air Act, which contrast sharply with the hearings to which industry is accustomed: "A parade of witnesses begins.

Housewives, garden club members, physicians (most of whom know little or nothing about the subject), and anti-establishment students. All will demand tighter particulate standards—fewer micrograms per cubic meter, tighter SO_2 standards—lower fractions of a part per million, than the standards proposed by a competent technical advisory committee. . . . One or more industry experts, or scientists retained by industry, will describe the technological difficulties. They will express a willingness to cooperate in every feasible way. The audience will respond with jeers and hisses. . . . So it goes. The Board will invariably discard the standards originally proposed and adopt tougher ones. . . . Judgments that should have been made on scientific, technical and economic grounds have been made on the basis of politics and emotion."[46]

On March 8, 1971, in a conference room of the Department of Commerce, there were no jeers and no hisses.[47] It was supposed to be science, technology and economics. But the copper man's technology and his politics and emotion are inseparable.

Industry served up a carefully coordinated performance aiming, once and for all, to kill the 90 per cent emission standard. One by one, the distinguished chief executives recited a tale of impending economic disaster precipitated by environmental regulations. Kennecott's David Swan presented data from an "independent study" by Fluor Utah, an engineering consulting firm, setting forth cost estimates for industry-wide pollution control which were ten times those of EPA.[48] (Simon Fluor, president of Fluor Utah, is a member of NIPCC.) The data was good enough to get results.

Part of the March 8 industry package was an alternative to the 90 per cent standard. "We have had considerable experience at our El Paso and Tacoma smelters with the so-called closed-loop emission control system," was the way it was put by ASARCO's Charles Barber. The "closed-loop" calls for curtailing production if the weather makes dispersion difficult. ASARCO's skilled practitioners of the closed-loop in three years ran up hundreds of violations at its various smelters. The closed-loop is a cosmetic strategy for keeping smelting technology intact, a reason for putting men out of work, an excuse for avoiding emission controls, another pitch for a tall stack. It is a lawyer's paradise of uncertainties in meteorological prediction, instrument calibration, reading of ambient data and sorting out of sulfur dioxide sources. The closed-loop was good enough for EPA.

It didn't take long for the March 8 message to sink in. On April 7, EPA's proposed guidelines for the states' air pollution implementation plans set forth firm federal sponsorship of the 90 per cent emission standard. In an appendix containing examples of emission limitations in various jurisdictions was a formula for emission control of copper, lead and zinc smelters, accompanied by an explanatory note: "This rule, in effect, requires removal of about 90 per cent of the input-sulfur to the smelter."[49]

On August 14 the final version of the same formula had a different explanation: "These emission limitations are equivalent to removal of about 90 per cent of the input-sulfur to the smelter for most copper smelters and somewhat higher for most lead and zinc smelters. Technology capable of achieving such emission limitations may not be applicable to all existing smelters. In such cases, less restrictive control can be coupled with restricted operations to achieve air quality standards."[50] The "closed-loop" espoused by the American Mining Congress, was well on its way to becoming law.

This villainy from EPA had predictable results: a rekindling of the spirit of opposition within industry, expressions of betrayal from state officials and a minor revolt within the staff of the Environmental Protection Agency.

Within weeks of the publication of EPA's final guidelines the companies were rushing to state forums, citing federal support for new initiatives to repudiate the 90 per cent standard.[51] "The True Position of the Federal Government is Now Available" read the communication from an ASARCO attorney to one state board then considering an appeal. " 'National Priorities' Have Been Reassessed"[52] was the advocate's happy interpretation.

State officials, already embarrassed by EPA's failure to adopt an hourly national ambient air standard for sulfur oxides despite widespread sentiment for it, were left further out on a limb by the turn-around on the smelter standards. Typical of the reaction was a letter from Norman E. Schell, director of Arizona's Division of Air Pollution Control, to Dave Calkins,[53] director of EPA's San Francisco office, saying he was "somewhat amazed" at the language changes. "As your agency is well aware," wrote Schell, "it has been a most difficult road in getting to a point where Arizona has arrived whereby all of the smelters save one have presented plans utilizing available technology to reduce their sulfur emissions in accordance with the formula which EPA has validated. These commitments were made under oath at public hearing. . . . We are now developing control strategies under the implementation plan and feel that technology is applicable as has previously been testified to by federal staff people in public hearings. . . . If there are any smelters in this state which your agency believes the 90 per cent control would not apply to," wrote Schell, "please advise which ones these are and the explicit reasons why this standard would not be applicable."

Early in September 1971, the political screws were

turned again. Terry Stumph, now back in EPA's San Francisco office, was invited by Nevada officials to testify on emission standards for smelters. Had Stumph testified, he undoubtedly would have reiterated that it's economically and technically feasible to control 90 per cent of the sulfur emissions. But Terry Stumph didn't testify although he did get as far as Reno with statement in hand. The official explanation was that the testimony wasn't cleared by headquarters. EPA was making good on the demand of the American Mining Congress that a muzzle be imposed on federal spokesmen supporting the 90 per cent standard.

This strategy of prior restraint became *ex post facto* censorship on the next occasion an EPA staff man spoke about copper smelters. The offender was George William Walsh,[54] assistant to the director of APCO's Standards Development and Implementation Division, who testified in December 1971 in Montana that EPA's ambient air quality standards "tend to represent minimum goals to be achieved" and that emission limitations generally "are required to minimize administrative and regulatory problems and to insure necessary enhancement of air quality." Walsh offered cost estimates of achieving 90 per cent control at about three cents per pound of copper and said that this "could be passed on without significant effects on sales revenues."

The testimony prompted John Place, Anaconda's chief executive, to fire off a letter to EPA Administrator William Ruckelshaus. He demanded a meeting "to learn from you directly whether or not the views expressed by this EPA employee do in fact reflect those you hold and endorse."[55] Recipients of this missive, for some reason, included the chief executives of Kennecott, Phelps Dodge and ASARCO along with Commerce Secretary Maurice Stans (soon to become chief fund raiser for the President's re-election campaign) and Peter Flanigan of the White House staff. Place also wrote to Flanigan with a special plea for assistance (quoted at the outset of this chapter). The meeting was held, not with Ruckelshaus, but with Flanigan, and the return on influence was soon forthcoming.

A draft "correcting" the Walsh statement was sent to John Green, Walsh's boss, by EPA's Donald Mosiman. "Sorry" scribbled Mosiman on the message to Green, as he sorrowfully spelled out the decision: Walsh's cost figures "should be considered as expressions of his point of view derived from review of information available to him." EPA, after the flip-flop, "does not have a position on the costs to the industry of pollution abatement and the impact of these costs on product price and industry profit."[56] Copies went to John Whitaker and Peter Flanigan at the White House, leaving no doubt about who was pulling the strings. The decision was formally executed in a letter from Regional Administrator Green to the Chairman of the Montana State Board of Health on January 6, 1972, disavowing agency responsibility for Walsh's figures and affirming unequivocally that emission limitations were *not* a requirement for implementation plan approval. The Clean Air Amendments of 1970 say quite clearly that emission limitations *are* a requirement for implementation plan approval.[57]

Out of such administrative intrigue will be shaped the smelting industry's technology of the future. EPA's waffling brought good news to the industry immediately: in Montana the governor refused to approve a state implementation plan calling for 90 per cent control; in Arizona the State Board of Health proved eager to flee from commitments once thought ironclad. In the next few years, EPA will have to face down the White House and fight off indus-

try to make up for the ground lost.* Getting rid of the
standards is easier than getting rid of the technology.

Sound judgments should be made, says ASARCO's
Ken Nelson, "on scientific, technical and economic
grounds." But sound judgment suffered a dizzying reversal
from the day in 1970 when the American Mining Congress
charged EPA's predecessor with an illegal attempt to set
emission standards to another day in 1972 when EPA con-
fesses a willingness to flout the Clean Air amendments by
approving state plans without emission limitations. In August 1970 control costs for the industry were said to be
"nominal" and "a sound investment in protecting health
and welfare in accordance with the purposes of the Clean
Air Act,"[58] but a year and a half later EPA "does not have
a position on the costs to the industry of pollution abatement."[59] An agency statement puts cost figures at something less than 2.5 cents per pound of copper in August
1970, but a witness who mentions three cents per pound in
December 1971 is repudiated.**

This is not science and law; this is mush. And the copper industry is vigorously stirring the pot. It is time to
recognize that the great changes in the industrial organizations that rule modern technologies have brought changes
also in the political decision-making that affects these technologies. The studies, hearings and consultation proffered

---

*EPA's Approval and Promulgation of Implementation Plans contains
both good and bad news in the pursuit of stringent emission limitations
for copper smelters. See 37 Fed. Reg. 15080 (July 27, 1972).
**A recent contribution to the cost-study debate puts costs per pound
of refined copper at 0.1 cents in 1972, 2.5 cents in 1976, with a possible
high estimate of 5 cents in 1976. Council on Environmental Quality,
U. S. Department of Commerce and U. S. Environmental Protection
Agency (joint publication), "The Economic Impact of Pollution Control: A Summary of Recent Studies," June 1972, p. 34.

the people can become a well-staged charade, vulnerable to the snap of the fingers of a Peter Flanigan. A capable agency staff can be undercut unmercifully. Concentrated economic power brings with it a concentrated political power that relentlessly bends the law and the science to the needs of the corporation's economic efficiency.

The remedy is to reform the state and build up its resistance to the industrial planning process. There is some good news in the lead poisoning tragedy of El Paso. A few people who cared managed to piece together the evidence that was beyond compromise. A measure of success was realized not by appealing to the corporation but by appealing to a law that was not entirely written by the corporation.

4 COUNTRY LIVING

*Boise Cascade does more than develop rec-
reation communities. We stay around to see
what develops.* *

*The developer has announced a decision to
accelerate its withdrawal from the recreation communities business, and has discontinued retail land sales at several of its
projects in California. It may discontinue
such sales at any or all of its remaining
projects in the future.* **

Joe Curia says you don't need excitement to sell a piece
of Boise Cascade's multi-million dollar Ocean Pines development on the coast of Maryland.[1] Mr. and Mrs. Ross Horworth of Dover, Delaware, might not have looked like
prime prospects when they showed up on a rainy January
morning driving a car eight or nine years old. But Joe
toured them and sold them. He sold them a lot that was six
feet under water. For $18,000, $10,000 down. Salesman
Joe Curia creates his own selling excitement: "I just told
them how beautiful Ocean Pines was *going* to be. I told
them there was nothing like it along the entire Eastern

---

*Boise Cascade Recreation Communities Group, Advertisement for
"The Hideout," *New York Times*, Sept. 17, 1971, p. 22.
**Excerpt from federal registration statements of Boise Cascade Home
and Land Corp., October 1972.

Seaboard from Maine to Florida." Sales Director Bill Gibbs was ecstatic as he approved the contract: "Boy, oh boy, oh boy."

There was a time during 1972 when neither Joe Curia nor anybody else was doing any selling at Ocean Pines. Boise Cascade Recreation Communities was sitting out a ninety-day suspension order of the Maryland Real Estate Commission.[2] The reason: some of their salesmen didn't have state licenses. Officials of Boise expressed "shock and dismay" at the ruling. They said the violations resulted from "administrative oversights"[3] and legal niceties, "not instances of intentional deceit, failure to fulfill contractual obligations or selling of a product that has proved less than satisfactory to purchasers."

Boise ought to know. Intentional deceit, contractual violations, product dissatisfaction plagued its land development ventures. Outlawed in Maryland, sued in California, investigated in Hawaii, Boise watched in astonishment as its lunge for the real estate pot of gold threatened to pull the company under. From a high of $74.50 a few years ago, Boise's stock had fallen to $13.00 in June 1972. The company's rise was another case of technological preservation, its fall a prescription for a cure.[4]

Boise Cascade is a relative newcomer to both the real estate field and the ranks of corporate giants. Once a small company locked into the lumber business in the late 1950's, Boise rode the merger movement into pulp and paper, plywood, packaging, building materials, office supplies and the distribution of these products all the way to the retail level. It has moved into engineering and construction services—factory built houses, on-site houses, mobile homes and urban development.

By 1969 Boise's sales exceeded $1 billion, and the company ranked 55th on *Fortune*'s list of the 500 largest American corporations.[5] It was making plywood in the Philippines, trailers in Holland, France and England, containers in Austria and paper products in Guatamala and Costa Rica. It had run up the second highest annual sales among United States pulp and paper companies. In thirteen years the company had grown thirty-fold, consummated thirty-three mergers and compiled a phenomenal annual growth rate of 33 per cent. In recognition of his achievements and status, Boise's top executive, Robert Hansberger, was selected in 1970 to serve on the President's National Industrial Pollution Control Council.

The values shared by the company leadership and communicated to the 50,000 or so corporate employees are traditional. Chiefly, Boise is committed to making money. The aim is not "growth for growth's sake," says Hansberger. "It is, instead, but a means to the goal of increased earnings per share."[6] "One hundred thousand acres of pure profit" is the description of Boise timber holdings appearing in the company magazine, the *Boise Cascadian.*

In addition to making a profit, the company is committed to fighting pollution. In June 1970 Hansberger issued a seven-point statement pledging that Boise would achieve "reduction and prevention of air and water pollution to the full limits of existing technology" and "compliance in letter and spirit with all applicable regulations designed to protect the environment." That there might be a conflict between complying with the "letter and spirit" of the law and increasing earnings per share wasn't given much thought at the time.

A careful company historian might have noted the stress. Boise boasts the "singular distinction," according to the Council on Economic Priorities,[7] of having opened the only brand new kraft mill pulping operation in the United

States—it began production at De Ridder, Louisiana, late in 1969—without benefit of an odor control system. As of 1970, none of the company's nine pulp mills at six locations provided adequate pollution control and five were under state order to do so. Recent years have brought continuing conflict as the company's effluent claims a share of the most popular of all technological subsidies. The "full limits of technology" pollution control policy was to meet its sternest test as Boise went to work on the land.

With its eye on the trends, a few years ago Boise moved into the "leisure-living" business—the market for recreational communities. By 1969 its sales of recreational products including resort land, amounted to $209 million— about 12 per cent of the company's sales.[8] Boise had twenty-six projects underway in twelve states in 1969— double the total of one year earlier. It planned and promoted developments at Ocean Pines in Maryland, Woodridge in Connecticut and Incline Village on the shores of Lake Tahoe, California. At its twelve projects in California alone, Boise had, by 1970, staked out 63,000 acres (about 100 square miles).[9] The properties included many lakes (most man-made), fourteen golf courses, a ski resort, swimming pools, tennis courts, equestrian facilities. Building cities was the name of the business.

It's a big business. The lot sales industry is one of the largest and fastest growing businesses in the country, with rumored annual sales of $6 billion. There is money to be made.

"The total price of lots in one of these promotions can reach $50 million, and they can be sold out in a year or two," says Nevada County, California, District Attorney Harold Berliner. "Representative promotional developers have stated that of this sum, one-third is spent for the land, engineering, streets, water supply, sewers, if required, country clubs, lakes, etc. Another third is spent on advertising and sales. . . . The last third is profit."[10]

Traditionally one of the last domains of the small entrepreneur, real estate development is succumbing to the necessities of technology: high capital investment, extensive planning, minute division of labor. "Front-end cash requirements for new towns can be stiff," says *Business Week*, "even for large corporations."[11] Meeting the requirements are familiar names—ITT, Republic Steel, Weyerhaeuser, Standard Oil of California plus land development specialists like the Horizon Corporation, GAC Properties, Cavanaugh Communities and the General Development Corporation. These giants can bring innovation and improvement to the housing market. They can bring also a sophistication, not in quality, but in political subversion, marketing technique and professional machination.

Like the other big companies who have entered land development, Boise discovered that the rules of the old real estate tin-shack huckster are remarkably similar to the dictates of modern business. The huckster stuck to one iron principle: buy low and sell high. For the modern corporation, the words are different but the result is the same. The corporate analyst sees two principal variables: the cost of preparing the homesites and the returns from sales. By manipulating each of these, he ends up buying low (putting not one extra penny into the sites before they're sold) and selling high (devising sales pitches that will loose hordes on the sales office). Lots are sold for investment but there is no secondary market; they are sold for recreation but it is too expensive to live there; they are sold for retirement but the land is uninhabitable. The crucial target—the end of time as far as the company is concerned—is the sale. After that, it's on to another tract.

This philosophy can lead to some discouraging before-

and-after comparisons: a promise of paved streets brings dirt roads; a promise of access to a lake brings a title dispute; a promise of a deposit for an electric line extension brings nothing; a promise of a dam and a lake may bring a dam and a lake—by 1980.[12] Boise's golf course at Lake-of-the Pines, designed for profit, not golf, would bring Jack Nicklaus to his knees; one group of golfers needed seven hours to tour eighteen holes, losing six to twelve balls apiece.[13] Another Boise development in California, described by one critic as "hardly the flagship of the fleet," offers water to any lucky lot owner who can find it at the bottom of a deep and expensive well.[14]

But business has risks as even large corporations understand. There is always the chance that this delicate financial equation may be upset by a government agency or an angry consumer. Who can tell when the Main Streeters are going to overhear one of the pre-sale promises or be suspicious about the project from the start? To make sure that these non-business uncertainties don't interfere with the business calculations, corporations like Boise divert some of their manpower from selling the lots to buying the government, or at least to influencing it to listen to reason. The pattern is endemic to the technological defense.

Land-use planning today invites political influence. Major development decisions are now being made by backwoods boards that are hopelessly ill-equipped. Not long ago most major real estate development took place in the urban centers, where governments were forced to acquire a semblance of competence. But when developers moved to the country they found the going easier. The smooth real estate hustlers come by Lear jet to a political system more accustomed to wandering livestock, isolated junkyards and real estate men with tested reputations.

The local planning commission or county commissioners ruling on a recreational development usually will be making the most important decision of their public lives. They must, after all, decide whether a city is to be built, and, if so, to what specifications. Decisions must be made about sewers or septic tanks, water pipes or wells, a million-dollar bond or a promise, utilities above ground, underground, or maybe in the future. So, too, with storm drainage, roads, fire, police, school services, building restrictions, public access to amenities and disclosure requirements for lot buyers. State and federal laws intrude occasionally, but the big decisions are local responsibilities.

The legal system for land-use planning, born in a different age, presents few barriers to the smooth-talking lawyer with his multi-colored charts and stable of experts. The process begins—and often ends—with a forty-minute slide show before the planning commission, typically comprising a real estate salesman, a bank clerk, and perhaps a former president of the local League of Women Voters. The law usually says that a zoning change will be granted or a planned unit development approved, where compatible with "the public interest" or if "in consonance with the purposes of this ordinance" or some such phrase. The question boils down to whether the planning commission or the county commissioners think the developer ought to go ahead. Typically, everything is informal, with no disclosure of documents the applicant wants to suppress, no cross-examination of witnesses and no notice about what evidence will be offered. Twenty years hence, when lot-owner Smith sues lot-owner Brown for polluting his well water with a septic tank, all will be conducted according to formal procedures. Not so where the decision is whether to allow 5,000 septic tanks to pollute 5,000 wells.

This process calls for no firm plan—it calls for a forty-minute slide show. It invites promises of economic benefits. It requires making friends with the commissioners, buttering up the local editor, joshing with the Chamber of Commerce. This is what Boise did best. You keep the options open: if the planners demand sewers, you promise sewers; if they're worried about what the dams will do to the fish, you promise to protect the fish; if the marina looks a little too big, you promise to make it smaller; if somebody has heard of eutrophication, you say that it can't happen in your company's lakes.

A slide show Boise presented to the planning commission of Kitsap County, Washington, is exemplary.[15] At issue was the propriety of going ahead with a recreational development to provide homes for 20,000 people.

The show took forty minutes. There were shots of the area in its natural state, many of them taken from a helicopter, contrasted with multi-colored plans for its development. There was a picture of morning frost on the edge of ponds and one of the beautiful Olympics [In other shows substitute Poconos, White Mountains, Rockies, etc.] looming in the background. There would be the golf course with a club house, a teen center, and a dance bandstand. "There would be a boathouse located at this point that would have a lounge, boat service area, and clean, well-lighted, heated restrooms. . . . This shows a number of parks and open spaces that we tried to design in the project." There would be a big dam and some lakes. "We believe that we would be able to develop all of the potable water from wells." There would be a "private fire department." "We propose that the road system be private." Any questions from the Commission? There were a few, and then this exchange between Boise's Bob Johnson and Ray Richards, a planning commission member:

Richards: What projects of this nature, this size, have you undertaken, you and the company, and where are they located?

Johnson: Me as an individual?

Richards: As a company then, as a representative of the company.

Johnson: Well, at the present time this is going to be the number one nicest thing that we intend to do.

Richards: We should be complimented.

Johnson: And one I can think of—of course, I am from down California way and one that I am thinking of is Incline Village. Another one is Lake-of-the-Pines. I know that we have some back in around the Chicago area.

Richards: What about the size?

Johnson: Nothing of this size. I would say Incline Village.

Now Bob Johnson didn't quite tell it like it was. Boise had several projects as large as this one; some were disasters. But Bob Johnson probably didn't know or care about these other projects. His job was to sell this one. Bob Johnson was only doing his job.

Some fibs are never told. They just happen. Boise Project Manager Dave Carey promised to protect the marine environment—"We will suspend work during extremely rainy periods when there may be excessive silt"[16]—then left town. The man who must fulfill the promise neither made it nor heard of it. The "Declaration of Protective Covenants" that Boise prescribes for each lot sale makes another promise: "Neither Declarant (Boise) nor the Association shall be liable for damages by erosion, washing or other action of the water of any lake or stream."[17] It was only a case of the project manager and the lawyer not agreeing on promises. Both were doing their jobs.

Working with a law that is so amenable to change, other

skills enter into the decision of whether Boise's needs mesh with the local communities' wants. Influence within the government becomes a commodity in demand no less than a long term, low interest rate. A pattern was detectable as Boise went to work in California:

> One local D.A. was hired by B-C [Boise Cascade] to handle a water problem in an adjoining county; a county planning director was hired off the public payroll by B-C midway through a development project; the mayor of a North Coast city is also B-C public relations man for the area and two of the five-man city council work for B-C and a third depends upon it for his business; in another area, the B-C task force patronized the hotel and restaurant of one of the county supervisors, who also received free advertising in the company newspaper; in another county, the head of a project which was purchased by B-C saw fit to take out a $40,000 life insurance policy from an obscure mid-Western company, through its local agent, one of the county supervisors, while another supervisor was awarded a sizable campaign contribution and yet another was graced by the project's purchase of three automobiles from his local dealership. . . .[18]

This partnership between business and government means that planning for "governmental" relations becomes an ever more dominant corporate objective. Boise has developed computer-based profiles of legislators in states where the company is active.[19] W. L. Mills, Boise's director of governmental affairs, admits to devoting twenty-five per cent of his time to helping candidates who seek elective office: "If I can help get good people elected to office, I don't have to baby-sit them. But I can get in to see them if I have to. In any case, they will make the best decisions without any arm-twisting. In the long run, Boise

Cascade will benefit most from this policy."[20] In another era Mills could have come out and said what is good for Boise is good for the United States.

A near miss from California lends further testimony to the company's technique.[21] Boise dammed a stream flowing through its Lake Wildwood development to make a 320-acre pond and persuaded county officials to abandon a road fishermen had used to gain access. Spoiling this move for marketable exclusivity was the local prosecutor, who discovered a 1917 law saying that anyone who dammed a stream must allow the public continued access for fishing. Boise lobbyists set out to tailor the law to the needs of the market. Eugene Chappie, who represented the subdivision area in the state legislature, was persuaded to tack onto an unrelated bill a provision exempting non-profit corporations from the fishing-access law. This was fine because the company had set up a non-profit corporation to operate Lake Wildwood. Chappie approached the chairman of the Assembly Rules Committee, Robert Lagomarsino, and talked him into accepting "technical amendments" to a bill then pending on the assembly floor. As amended, the Boise-inspired measure passed in the last minute rush of business. Upon discovering he had been taken, Lagomarsino went to the extraordinary ends of requesting Governor Reagan to veto the measure, which he did. Boise says these manipulations in its name were "completely unauthorized."

Boise follows the conventional practice of writing laws for state legislators. The company man in the Hawaii State Senate, for example, is John T. Ushijima, who managed in 1968 to push through the Senate a bill drafted by O'Melveny and Myers, Boise-hired blue ribbon lawyers from Los Angeles.[22] It would allow developers like Boise to operate virtually as a city through a development district, floating bonds, financing improvements, assessing lot owners.[23] People could vote according to how much land they owned, and the developer would own the biggest chunk. At an opportune moment, with sales well advanced, the district could dissolve itself, leaving the public holding the bag. Some still insist there are significant differences between governments and corporate governments.

Boise and the other giant developers usually don't have much trouble prescribing political independence for their second home communities. The legal device is the home-owner's association which is given the power to impose assessments creating liens upon the members' properties. All lot owners must be members. It is the association that is supposed to maintain the roads, hire the security force, take care of the golf course and fish hatcheries and keep the undesirables out. The association is controlled by the developer. It gives him authority over land use decisions within a development, allows him to mulct lot owners into paying for frilly improvements that will help future sales, and provides an argument for persuading local officials that they won't be stuck with his maintenance and service promises. "Can you mention a single case in which a homeowner's association has provided the services on the scale envisaged?" Boise was asked at hearings on its Nettleton (Kitsap County) project. No answer.

With the preliminaries out of the way, the game of beat-the-clock begins: trying to unload the acres before the plaster falls off the sales office walls, before the customers ask about those promised sewers and before the commissioners think again about what's going on in their town. Like other developers, Boise used a crack sales team, drilled them in the best hard-sell tactics, and rewarded its aces. Commissions ran as high as 20 per cent, though 12 to 14 per cent was more common. *Developments,* the corporation's sales magazine, reported on a training film for salesmen made with the cooperation of the late Vince Lombardi, coach of the Green Bay Packers and the Washington Redskins. His dicta for success: "Control the Ball. Mental Toughness Is Essential. Fatigue Makes Cowards of Us All." Read the sales manager's message to headquarters announcing that the Lake Wildwood lots had been sold out, "Mission accomplished. Wildwood is dead. Where do you want us next?"

Corporate programming for sales is not foolproof, but it can prove to be a low capital resuscitator of dubious projects. Joseph Timan, chairman of the board of the Horizon Corporation, which sells better than Boise, can't quite bring himself to concede a corporate role in creating demand: Horizon's twenty-seven consecutive record quarters "were not accidental, were not due solely to skillful marketing, but actually due to our ability to creatively meet a strong and sustaining market for land, new communities, and a new life-style for America."[24] But then Timan can't say Horizon leaves the market to chance: "The intangible hunger to own land is pervasive, and we must not exploit this desire but simply direct it properly, and responsibly, so that the customer gets the most for his money, and society also benefits."[25] And Mr. Timan admits to planning sales strategies: A major factor "contributing to the development of our housing market has been the refinement of our own selling techniques, and the creation of a separate, specially trained sales force which sells only housing."[26]

The sales psychology relies on two basic urges: the urge to live in the beautiful wilds and the urge to get rich. The realities of things being what they are, few put much stock in the first pitch. The people who intend to live on their bit of precious land are often dissuaded when they actually see

136162   EMORY & HENRY LIBRARY

it. But the speculator persists where the homeowner is discouraged. With the stock market acting sickly and inflation devouring the dollar, even a weed-covered parcel in a desert may look like a good investment.

While Boise formally rejected the speculative sell in 1970, its early Lake-of-the-Pines ads stressed that "the first investor makes the most." And, of course, Boise is the first investor. Boise's ads for Circle XX Ranch were designed to make even the most cautious householder feel he was throwing his chances away: "YOU CAN'T BUY A BAD PIECE OF REAL ESTATE IN CALIFORNIA. . . . The State Board of Equalization states: California property increases in value $1,000 every single second (In the time it took you to read the facts on this page, California Real Estate has appreciated in value by $1,000)." Under the circumstances, the company's promises about lakes, parks, green belts and beaches were not the syrupy song of a builder of cities luring future residents. They were, instead, a speculator's come-on to the next eager speculator. Since the buyer has no intention of living on his property, this is just another reason for withholding the investment that would make it livable.

All that's missing from these pictures of a rosier tomorrow is someone to buy the house from the speculator who bought it from Boise. Joseph Timan—whose Horizon Corporation lures buyers with ads screaming "You can make money here even if you can't spell ALBUQUERQUE" or "You can invest in land no matter how modest your income"[27]—turns around and tells a group of financial analysts, "[A]s yet, a secondary market has not been created for the sale of these properties." There is a lot of slack to take up before today's buyers can sell.

New Mexico, it is said, has subdivision roads that, strung out together, would go all the way to Mongolia;

there are enough lots to house 8 million people, not bad for an area with an expected state-wide population by the year 2000 of 1,336,000. Nevada County, California, has enough lots to last 400 years. Boise spokesmen admit the building rate at Boise developments may be only 1 or 2 per cent a year,[28] and Boise has the experience to prove it: Lake-of-the-Pines has 1,944 lots, 1,300 acres—and 100 houses.[29] Ranch Calaveras has 3,600 parcels, 5,200 acres— and nine houses. Diamond XX Ranch, with 190 lots on 4,000 acres, has a single structure—the former sales office converted into living quarters. Bar XX Ranch, with 230 parcels on 5,000 acres, has one house—owned by a former Boise executive. You can get rich, all right, if you don't mind waiting a century or so.

Exploitive development and fraudulent sales, one might suppose, can be good for business. That's sometimes true. But somewhere along the way Boise came unmoored, lost the caution which has made other companies cover their flanks, started reaching for slices too big to be decorously devoured. The accumulation of hurts was gradual but telling. The company merged with trouble back in 1967 when it took over United States Land, Incorporated, which was the predecessor of Boise's land development division, now known as Boise Cascade Recreation Communities. U.S. Land had problems, and some of them carried over to Boise. There was, for example, that unfortunate incident during the summer of 1967, when a U.S. Land subsidiary, along with Robert Onorato, was indicted by the Nevada County, California, grand jury for misleading advertising in connection with land sales. It seems that Onorato, who after the merger became a Boise vice president, ran a newspaper ad declaring, "There are no assessment bonds [and] . . . all improvements will be installed and paid for," although a $950,000 water district was to be paid for by assessing lot buyers at a rate of $32 to $40 a year for some twenty-five years. The case ended with a plea of no contest. Onorato got a two-year suspended sentence.

One misstep by a single executive does not a course of criminal conduct make. But after a while, the accumulation of anecdotes conveys the flavor of the operation. Disgruntled officials, disappointed lot owners and investigative sleuths ganged up on Boise.

Read the reports as they trickle in. New Hampshire's planning director: "If we hadn't stepped in they would have been dumping that refuse from the 5,200-acre development into the lakes." Director of the Torrington, Connecticut Health District: "I am endeavoring to get the real estate commissioner to lift their license to sell, as the sewerage problem solution is very dim and far in the future if at all. They, however, continue the big sales and TV push." (Boise's federal registration for the Woodridge Lake-Ravenswood Estates project in Connecticut was later suspended by the Office of Interstate Land Sales Registration.) The California attorney general's office: "This firm [Boise Cascade] has developed a number of subdivisions in California of a highly speculative nature which have received the attention of local authorities because of misrepresentations and lot-owner dissatisfactions." Deputy administrator of OILSR: "Boise Cascade in recent months has experienced several problems with regard to subdivisions located in various parts of the country. Most frequently the problems involve the company's failure to follow through on promised investments, sales abuses, or failure to properly register new tracts of land with this office prior to selling."

Ignoring officials who still have some bite can hurt. On October 12, 1971, California (largely due to the efforts of a persistent deputy attorney general, Neil Gendel) brought a major action against the Boise land sales subsidiaries and sought to enjoin fraudulent sales tactics at several pro- jects.[30] The state won a temporary restraining order, only to return to court charging continuing misrepresentations by salesmen.[31] Private suits were soon to follow.

Boise met this novel challenge by resorting to an an- cient technology—deceit. Misrepresentations about the case were liberally distributed to critical groups—the press, the company's lot owners, and the shareholders. Minimiz- ing the business risk was the aim.

One Boise press release reported the trial court as holding "void"[32] several of the state's claims, but forgot to emphasize that a sweeping injunction had been entered. That ruse brought a few helpful headlines—"Boise-Cas- cade Suit Tossed Out of Court"—but didn't bring relief from the company's legal difficulties.

The dread of thousands of buyers coming unstuck from their commitments called for aggressive action. Boise's 30,- 000 or so lot owners in California were blessed with a message of concern that "the adverse publicity being gene- rated may have a harmful effect on the value of the property you have purchased. . . . We will do everything we can to prevent that from happening," the company said, "but your help is needed." Enclosed for inspiration was a copy of a *San Francisco Chronicle* column by financial editor Sidney P. Allen, reciting the company line about "Who's Hurt by Class Actions." (Some of Allen's other work has found its way into Boise's sales kits.)

President Robert Hansberger himself wrote to the shareholders[33] to quiet their concern with a list of decep- tions, including a claim that the company did not oppose a court restraint "since our policies clearly prohibit unlaw- ful and improper practices." (Boise's non-opposition is re- corded in over 10 pages of formal objections.) Hansberger told the shareholders that "less than one-half of 1 per cent" of Boise's 30,000 property owners had joined as plaintiffs, but he forgot to tell them that named plaintiffs are hardly indicative of the number of complaining lot owners, and he didn't tell them how many complaints Boise had received. (The California attorney general has over 500 complaints, and he says, "It is reported that hundreds or even thousands of lot purchasers have complained to private attorneys, Boise, other district attorneys, and the Department of Real Estate.")[34] Hansberger told the shareholders that the company had a firm policy of refunding payments and rescinding sales "when legitimate complaints are presented," but he didn't tell them about the numerous practices repudiating that policy. And he didn't enclose reprints of an internal Boise memorandum written by Alice Hennessey to Torri Smaus with a copy to John Fery, a vice president and director of the parent corporation:

> "Torri, please work with George [McCown, a Boise vice president and general manager of the Boise Recreation Group subsidiaries], the attorneys, and whoever else is necessary in having an appropriate draft of a Hansberger response prepared for Mayor Reading of Oakland. This one appears to be a little delicate and I have decided not to acknowledge it in *the usual, non-committal fashion* [emphasis added]."[35]

And Hansberger didn't send the shareholders a copy of another internal company memorandum depicting intolerable conditions at the Ranch Calaveras project: "The real question that has to be answered is [whether] Boise . . . is going to budget appropriate funds to complete their legal obligations and some moral responsibilities to the Ranch Calaveras property owners, which are long overdue, by completing the construction of roads, utilities and amenities with the same vigor with which the 3600 M/L lots were sold, or are we going to continue the firefighting as it arises to temporarily satisfy the governmental agencies and property owners."[36]

By the end of 1971, the *Wall Street Journal* was reporting "Boise Cascade, One Time Wonder Company, Loses Wonder, Investors and Profitability."[37] Much of Boise's distress stemmed from its land development fiascos: costs were up; sales down. The sheep who sit on land use boards or other agencies and the suckers who buy the land were displaying considerable resistance to foolproof corporate planning. One project was abandoned in the face of an attack by those disenchanted with the idea of 1,300 new septic tanks draining into the lake;[38] development costs at another soared to more than 50 per cent of the project's market value;[39] still another project got a go ahead to develop with septic tanks, then was forced to come up with $6 million for a sewer system.[40] A class action on behalf of members of the homeowners association at yet another project ended with a court order compelling Boise to come through with promised improvements. Fraud made a dramatic appearance in May 1972 when a California jury hit Boise with a $500,000 verdict for punitive damages arising out of misrepresentation on sales at the Klamath River Ranches project in Northern California.[41] (The court later set the verdict aside as being excessive.)

When the shareholders desert, the corporate ship is approaching the shoals. In June 1972 the shareholders of one of Boise's merger victims joined the bandwagon by filing suit against the company and its accountant, Arthur Anderson, charging a long list of fraudulent activities.[42] The plaintiffs were not pleased that the value of a Boise share they got for their previous property on November 3,

1969, had plunged from $74.50 to $13.00 by June 1972. They pointed out that Boise had lost $40 million on its land operations. They charged phony accounting, suppression of fact, seat-of-the-pants investment, and something else: "The practices and business methods followed by Boise in the development and marketing of its recreational properties were improper, fraudulent, and false, as a consequence of which Boise was, at the time of the merger, and remains exposed to substantial civil liability with the possibility of recision of [the] land sales." It was "foreseeable," plaintiffs charged, that fraudulent practices "would materially impair Boise's business and its ability to market its recreational properties to the public."

Boise was determined to botch it to the end. On the morning of August 30, 1972, John Borgwardt, Boise's associate general counsel, walked into the Washington offices of John R. McDowell, deputy administrator of the Federal Office of Interstate Land Sales Registration, and presented a balance sheet for Boise Cascade Home and Land Corporation showing a deficit of $57,330,000. Borgwardt told McDowell that a deficit of this magnitude, "plus or minus a few million," was known to the company "for approximately a month before August 30." McDowell pointed out that the law required, in the event of material changes in information, amended federal filings on registered subdivisions within fifteen days. A memo on the meeting explains:

> Mr. Borgwardt acknowledged that he was thoroughly familiar with this aspect of the regulations but that he personally—Mr. Borgwardt's primary responsibility being [Boise] legal work—had not become aware of the situation until August 16 or thereabouts. He did not pose this as an excuse for not having filed amendments but admitted that they should have been filed. However, he was of

the opinion that the parent company would be able to provide sufficient capital to put them in the black before 15 days expired, thereby causing the problem to evaporate—that being the reason why he had not filed an amendment.

What this meant was that Boise clearly deserved suspended sales for fraudulent non-disclosure on all of its forty or so subdivisions filed with OILSR. Peace was purchased only by the senior corporation immediately kicking $100 million into the real estate subsidiary to offset the losses.

Sales continue at the Boise projects. But they do so against the background of a stunning announcement by Robert Hansberger* that Boise was considering a $200 million charge against income (one of the largest corporate write-downs of recent years), mostly in anticipation of a withdrawal from the recreational land business.[43] The lot buyer today is told that Boise is getting out of the business. The haunting refrain of the company advertisement of the year before is heard: "Boise Cascade does more than develop recreation communities. We stay around to see what develops."**

It would be comforting to conclude that Boise's downfall proves the old morals: haste makes waste; crime doesn't pay, and he who reaches too greedily for the goods may get his fingers smashed. But fraud has precedent in the land sales business, indeed is sometimes an indicium of success;

---

*Hansberger recently stepped down as Boise's chief executive.
**Late in 1972 six lawsuits against Boise were resolved in a $58.5 million settlement. The company agreed to return $24 million to buyers who wanted cash, to spend $21.5 million on administration and maintenance of the properties and to invest $13 million more to complete certain portions of the projects.

so it, alone, does not distinguish Boise. The good news in Boise's case is that the law was kept immune from the corporate risk-reduction planning process. There were commissioners, administrators, lawyers, journalists and citizens who could not be planned away. Perhaps Boise's experience is unusual because the business is not yet dominated by monopolies, the wrongs not entirely obscured by mysterious technologies while governmental decision-making authority is still widely dispersed and immune from a knock-out blow. But Boise's case is not unusual in demonstrating the need for a bright line between the corporations and the country to keep their policies distinguishable.

5 DDT: DEFENDING THE THRONE

The industry recognizes that continuing safety education is necessary. Accidents do not result from use of pesticides; only from misuse!*

This material is sold without warranty as to hazards or results.**

Louis A. McLean, who used to work for the Velsicol Chemical Corporation, was the choice of the National Agricultural Chemicals Association to lead the defense of DDT. As the attorney for the Industry Task Force for DDT during the 1968-69 hearings before the Wisconsin Department of Natural Resources, McLean could set the tone and map the tactics that would deflate the critics of DDT. From industry's point of view, McLean's credentials were impeccable—and he understood the problem. He had the proper attitude toward the opponents of pesticides:

> Long ago it became apparent that the pesticide controversy was led by two types of critics—purposeful and compulsive. The purposeful include those who use the controversy to sell natural foods at unnatural prices, to give color to their books, writings, and statements, to gain notoriety, or in any way to profit from the controversy. The compulsive were described by Sigmund Freud

---

*James R. Mills, Director of Public Relations, National Agricultural Chemicals Association, in *Canner/Packer*, March 1971.
**Label on container of Ortho Rose Dust, California Spray Chemical Corp.

in *Totem and Taboo* as neurotics, driven by primitive, sub-conscious fears to the point that they see more reality in what they imagine than in fact. If you read medical journals . . . , you will learn that the same purposeful and compulsive types, the anti-pesticide people, in almost every instance hold numerous beliefs in nutritional quackery and medical quackery and that they oppose public health programs. The compulsive see simplicity as purity, feel rejected by mankind and man-endeavors such as science, medicine, and business. They are not able to adjust to the assaults on ego we all experience: failure to achieve the ultimate socially or in business, and especially the ego-shattering fact that we all grow older. Thus while they seek youth and purity in the simple and primitive, they suffer increasing fear of loss of health and physical powers. While presenting a holier-than-thou attitude, they are actually preoccupied with the subject of sexual potency to such an extent that sex is never a subject of jest.

The anti-pesticide leader, as distinguished from the fair-minded person who is merely misinformed about pesticides, can almost always be identified by the numerous variant views he holds about regular foods, chlorination and flouridation of water, vaccination, public health programs, animal experimentations, food additives, medicine, science, and the business community, or by his insistence that insecticides should be mistermed "biocides."[1]

In August 1962, Louis A. McLean, Velsicol's secretary and general counsel, wrote to Houghton Mifflin suggesting the company might wish to reconsider publishing Rachel Carson's *Silent Spring*. He argued that some attacks on the chemical industry were designed to reduce our food supply to "east-curtain parity."[2]

In the intervening years—important ones for DDT—

McLean had no second thoughts. "The New Hate Literature" was the title he chose for a 1971 book review appearing in *Agrichemical Age.*[3] McLean wrote:

> Like those two classic examples of hate literature, "Das Kapital" and "Mein Kampf," these two paperbacks [*Eco Tactics: The Sierra Club Handbook for Environmental Activists* and the *Environmental Handbook*] provide easy answers to anyone who wishes to blame someone else for the world's problems. In fact, there is more than a bit of Marx in each of them.
>
> This is not to suggest that most of the numerous co-authors are Commies. One or two may be; but most are too nihilistic and too undisciplined to be trusted with a card.
>
> The Commies, however, must be delighted with the activists' teachings.

Introduced editorially as "one of the most effective and frequent defenders of agrichemicals," McLean's views were warmly endorsed by *Agrichemical Age,* and the fraternity was exhorted to take the truth to the people: "Our readers communicate with the public in many ways. We think they need all the coaching we can pass along from reliable authorities, and from sound thinkers like Louis A. McLean."[4]

Sound thinkers like Louis A. McLean have celebrated a renaissance during the chemical conflicts of recent years. They wait in ambush for scientific truths that threaten the product. They loyally serve the pesticides state, perpetuating its myths, protecting its wares. Despite rumors to the contrary, the technological defense is one of the best.

Pesticides for farm use were first manufactured in 1902.[5] But the industry didn't take off until the close of hostilities in World War II when it reaped returns from government research on DDT and various nerve gas compounds. The four chemical giants—Du Pont, Union Carbide, Monsanto and Dow—account for more than 50 per cent of sales although pesticides are a small part of their diversified output.[6] Pesticide manufacturers number at least fifty while more than 2,500 other companies, many of them small businesses, formulate the chemicals into brand name products and market them to farmers, public health agencies, foresters and homeowners. The value of the products sold rose from $440 million in 1964 to $12 billion in 1969. Enough pesticides are produced annually to provide each person in the country with five pounds.

Pesticides are strongly driven by the imperatives of technology of which John Kenneth Galbraith and others have written. Bringing a new chemical from the laboratory to the farm involves time (five years), capital ($4.5 million), patience (one compound out of 5,000 tested emerges as a marketable product) and specialized manpower.[7] Pesticide manufacturing is low in labor intensity and wages, with agricultural chemical workers last on the list of all chemical sub-groups and below the manufacturing norm.[8] It is high in profits, pollution and power consumption (chemical and aluminum production alone account for about 28 per cent of the total industrial use of electric power in the United States).[9]

The pollution subsidy is extorted by commercial necessities and protected by legal realities: It's technologically simpler and good for business to develop broad spectrum poisons with a wide market appeal. Somebody else has to worry about agricultural losses from pest resurgence (because of destruction of predators of the target species) and secondary pest outbreaks (due to elimination of the enemies of a heretofore innocuous species), not to mention losses to fish, wildlife and human beings. A pesticide's secretive origins and subtle effects add up to legal im-

munity: Tracking down the consequences is an interdisci-
plinary extravaganza, and uncertainty in proving a product's bad effects works to the advantage of those who sell
the good effects.

No corporation puts $4-5 million down on a 5,000-1
shot without taking a few steps to shorten the odds. A
valuable odds-shortener for the chemical pesticides industry was the United States Department of Agriculture's Pesticides Regulation Division, whose derelictions were principally responsible for its transfer to the Environmental
Protection Agency in 1970. PRD's sorry history of administrative malfunctioning meant security for the corporate investment in chemical pesticides.[10]

The idea of near total control pursued by large corporations is within reach of pesticide manufacturers. The gift
was a government choice. It all began with the Insecticide
Act of 1910 which required labels on Paris greens, lead
arsenate and other primitive poisons.[11] (As of 1971, lead
arsenate was still being labeled and sold and still poisoning
people). The year 1947 marked the arrival of the federal
Insecticide, Fungicide & Rodenticide Act (FIFRA),[12] which
was good law twenty-five years and a technical revolution
later. Under FIFRA economic poisons were to be registered prior to sale. Instructions for use were made mandatory. Warning statements on the label were prescribed to
prevent injury to man, other animals, insects or plants.
Virtually the sole instrument of legal control was the label.
The man responsible for reading the label was the user.
Protecting the manufacturer from the next-to-nothing
sanction of a change in label was a prolix procedure of
advisory committees, hearings, reports and appeals.

With this legal slap-on-the-back, the industry, its academic hangers-on and government promoters proceeded to refine and perpetuate one of the most powerful technological myths of modern times: *careful use* became the all-encompassing answer to health and environmental objections to chemical pesticides. Responsibility was passed along to the homeowner, the commercial sprayer, the aerial applicator. Labeling exhortations became the credo of the chemical makers, a principle of free enterprise, nourished by propaganda, perpetuated by politics and invoked to flay the deviant who suggested that something other than preachment was a proper regulatory response. The technology that exacted its costs near or far, today or tomorrow, through direct or subtle attacks was in the clear.

To this day, the careful use policy is the dominant theme of pesticides regulation. It is everywhere—in pamphlets, handbooks, warning signs to field workers, speeches and sales literature. "Wise usage" is a message drummed home by the National Agricultural Chemicals Association. ". . . Stop . . . Read the Label," says NACA's Director of Public Relations James R. Mills. "The industry recognizes that continuing safety education is necessary. Accidents do not result from use of pesticides; only from misuse!" Mills told believers at the 1970 annual meeting of the National Canners Association.[13]

Manufacturers, regulators, extension agents, applicators alike subscribe to exhortation as the key to regulation. The United States Department of Agriculture dispenses millions of reminders a year to "read the label and follow the instructions." An annual meeting of the National Aerial Applicators Association was told that pilots should "avoid spraying workers or animals in the fields they treat."[14] Workers are advised to wear rubber suits and felt masks. People are advised to stay one step ahead of a cloud of

TEPP, the deadliest organophosphate compound presently in use (a single drop can be lethal).

> Mild poisoning in people and severe symptoms and death in cattle have resulted from exposure to static clouds of TEPP dust. When TEPP dust is applied in very still, hot weather, note should be taken of the position and movement of the dust cloud. If, even at a point distant from the area of application, the TEPP dust cloud tends to settle over homes or pastures in more than usual concentration, the people should be urged to remove themselves and their cattle to an uncontaminated area until the cloud has dissipated.[15]

Sprinting is a job requirement for workers at the Giegy Chemical Company plant at McIntosh, Alabama:

> "The plant has an interesting safety device. There are windsocks on tops of buildings. In case of major leaks of dangerous fumes, the men are instructed to glance at the wind and run up-wind, or cross-wind. There is no time to hold a wet finger in the air."[16]

Sometimes there's no place to run:

> "There's no place in the Shell plant [in Denver] to get away from trouble. Some years back several men quit their jobs in the Acedrin manufacturing unit and bumped back into the labor gang to get away from the stuff. Some employees think this is why the company eliminated the labor gang—to close one of the escape routes for the men."[17]

Getting out of the way of the chemical pesticides industry and its technology is a principle so widely accepted on faith that its perpetuation no longer depends on collaboration, if it ever did. Careful use began as a good idea and grew

into a group-think apologia independent of explicit conspiracy.

The result was technology run amok. While the user
read the label and followed the instructions (sometimes),
United States pesticides policy sank to the depths of an
international scandal. Relying on a label to protect against
misuse called for a product that was controllable, an accurate label, a user who understood it and was inclined to
obey what was understood. This defense proved as porous
as the thinking that placed reliance upon it. The chemical
mobility and broad spectrum effect of many pesticides and
the job pressures, contract deadlines and inexperience of
the applicators combined to put the lie to the labeling
lobby. The labels themselves were notoriously bad: clinical
lessons in lilliputian print, contradictory instructions and
chemical double-talk were available to anyone who
browsed in his local hardware store.

With the assistance of the myth of careful use and laws
that insisted upon it, the chemical pesticides manufacturers
moved against other risks—conscientious regulation, consumer knowledge and scientific truth. The technology
sought refuge and security in political persuasion, the sales
pitch and data control.

The "controlled use" dogma has significant meaning in
the regulatory process. Screening for safety or effectiveness
is relegated to the back seat, since the "bite" of the law is
to be found in the words on the label. At the point of
registration, commercial momentum is powerful: the
chemical candidate is one survivor among thousands; process development and pilot plant studies have pushed the
investment into the millions; time is of the essence, for
patent rights remain unexploited during registration. The

result is a very shaky governmental finger in a very large industrial dike.

Is it any wonder the corporation might be tempted to overwhelm the registration hurdle standing in the way of the return on investment? It is here that industrial and state activities, policies and personnel can be wedded. The technology is secure if a dispirited and understaffed government is run over, conned or bought off. It is secure if independent tests are rarely conducted or outside comment irregularly solicited. And it is secure if data submitted is proprietary and on that ground withheld from public scrutiny.

The Pesticides Regulation Division shows the scars of industrial influence:[18] products were approved for uses without satisfying safety procedures, and they were approved for uses practically certain to result in the illegal adulteration of food. Labels surviving the registration process failed to inform users of possible hazards or to give accurate directions. Actions to cancel registered products were long-delayed and bungled; PRD, during its years in the Department of Agriculture, never did secure a single registration cancellation in a contested case. Following uncontested cancellations, hazardous products lingered in marketing channels for years, awaiting unfortunate buyers. Despite repeated violations, no case in thirteen years was referred to the Department of Justice for criminal prosecution. Enforcement of the central legislation for the regulation of chemical pesticides disappeared in a sea of administrative indifference and lawlessness. Sending the law to the bottom, to be sure, gives the technology a certain buoyancy.

Influence shaded into conflict of interest. A House subcommittee explained how Shell's popular DDVP strip made it to market:

Registration of Shell's DDVP strip was originally approved in 1963 after John S. Leary, Jr., then PRD's Chief Staff Officer for Pharmacology, overruled an objection raised by a subordinate. In November, 1966 Mr. Leary gave notice that he was leaving PRD to accept employment with Shell Chemical Co. In December 1966, before leaving PRD, Mr. Leary recommended that PRD ignore a Public Health Service report opposing continued sale of DDVP strips. In 1968, as a Shell employee, Mr. Leary participated in a meeting at which Shell opposed the addition of a warning notice to the label of its DDVP strip.[19]

In a 1971 speech to the California Weed Conference, Dow Chemical's Julius Johnson explained the industrial need to be close to the action:

I would stongly advocate that we worry less about conflict of interest and see to it that government, industry and university personnel communicate more effectively. Industry has been excluded from these councils for too long and as a consequence both university and government are making mistakes that are hurting the country. Industry has pulled its share of boners which helped to give pesticides a bad name but a congregation will be strong, meaningful and exciting if us sinners come to church along with all you good people.[20]

But the large corporation cannot be satisfied by going to church. It must be elected to the board of deacons, hire the minister, write the sermon. Keeping a big corporation in suspense is a *non sequitur*.

While a figurative pat on the back has been known to get a chemical registered, it takes a good deal more to get one unregistered. The label serves industrial certainty coming and going. Since it is the key to control, the sanction is to take somebody's label away, which means you have to write another and have it approved. Protecting the manufacturer from this label change under FIFRA was one of the most devious procedures ever devised by imaginative lawyers:[21] years could be eaten up by advisory committee deliberations, administrative rulings, public hearings, more rulings, appeals. The special form of corporate due process found in the 1947 FIFRA underwent some changes in 1972, but the pesticide cancellation proceeding will be remembered nostalgically by administrative lawyers.

A legion of case studies on milking the process that is called regulation comes from the files of the Shell Chemical Company, a subsidiary of Shell Oil. It took five years, over strong resistance, for public officials to compel Shell to inform Azodrin users that the pesticide was highly toxic to bird life.[22] Shell hired Mitchell Zavon to lobby for approval of its DDVP Pest Strip, a major market item, while he was simultaneously serving as a consultant to the Pesticides Regulation Division.[23] Zavon originally was appointed by PRD to advise on problems relating to Dieldrin, another major Shell product.[24] John Leary, a key PRD official instrumental in the approval of the DDVP Pest Strip, later resigned to join Shell, as previously described.[25] Shell's K. R. Fitzsimmons threatened suit against *Environment* magazine if it went ahead with publication of an article raising safety questions about the Pest Strip. He promised a full disclosure of safety data and didn't produce although Shell brought in Zavon and others to meet with representatives of the magazine.[26] On another occasion Fitzsimmons promised that Shell would go on selling Aldrin (a big market item) if it was banned,[27] only to explain he meant a cancellation does not forbid continued sales. The activities of Dr. Roy T. Hansberry, an official of one of Shell's affiliates, were singled out by a House Subcommittee, and the

Justice Department was requested to investigate the possible conflict of interest involved in his service on a task force looking at pesticide registration criteria applied by PRD.[28] (No criminal charges were filed.)

Isolated abuses? Occasional aberrations? Or a systematic attempt to rule the state on issues of safety and environmental quality? The technology is defended by the means available.

Information control serves along with political control. Greatly expanded sales and marketing staffs and fewer production workers are marks of the chemical industry[29] no less than they are for the recreational lot sellers. Unlike the detergent manufacturer who strives for control of sales and growth through massive television advertising, the seller of pesticides usually baits his hook in more selective waters. He offers, instead, a technical service, a specialized know-how, and the buyer looks not for a product but for a solution to a complex problem.

"The salesman is the key to the system," explains Robert Van Den Bosch, professor of entomology at the University of California, Berkeley, "for he serves as diagnostician, therapist, and pill dispenser. And what is particularly disturbing is that he need not demonstrate technical competence to perform in this multiple capacity."[30] It is the salesman, pushed by competition, pulled by the lure of incentives, who dictates "careful use" down on the farm. The professional independent, giving reliable advice, is an unwelcome interloper in this field of commercial sovereignty.

The salesman's conflict of interest has been nowhere better explained than in a 1966 speech to the California Agricultural Teachers Association by George Poppic, president of Corestox, Incorporated and at that time a

member of NACA's Board of Directors.[31] Poppic pointed
out the conflict:

> "Bug chaser," "Field Tramper," "Insect Distributor,"
> "Manure Salesman," these are all good-humored nick-
> names for a position of great responsibility. These peo-
> ple offer more advice and direct more decisions as to
> farm practices than do the university or the farm advisors
> or the county commissioners. The "why" of it is very
> simple. They are basically "salesmen" but have the dual
> responsibility of paying their way for their employers as
> well as to serve farmers with responsible technical knowl-
> edge. They are in contact with growers five days per
> week. . . .

He expressed disdain for a trained adviser to help the deci-
sion-maker in the field:

> The position of this individual might be considered as a
> "nurse" among "doctors," or a "brother" among
> "priests"—a position of dedication to service of the farm
> community yet perhaps short on the highly technical as-
> pects of the industry being serviced. In my opinion, and
> in the opinion of others, it is not necessary to have a
> Bachelor of Science degree to sell agricultural chemicals
> or to make recommendations for their use.

"A thorough study of entomology is not necessary," Poppic continued, although it wouldn't hurt to know a little bit.

He seconded the need for a soft sell, which can hardly
be described as compatible with principles of minimal use:

> What do manufacturers and suppliers of pesticides and
> fertilizers desire in farmer contact salesmen? Needed are
> young men who are agriculturally oriented, of pleasing
> personality, of clean, neat appearance, and of such integ-

rity that their services in any direction will be unquestioned.

The finesse required of a salesman must also be considered:

> In order for the student to use this knowledge for industry he must sell himself as well as his company's products and services. Here, two points must be emphasized: salesmanship and psychology. The industry is not interested in the normal high school or retail salesmanship course offered in Junior Colleges. It is seeking to create a relatively sophisticated presentation of a somewhat technical nature to a very intelligent person (a farmer) who is about to spend a large sum of money, usually at the purchaser's place of business. This situation is common and continuous and in no way resembles selling thread or shoes or a suit. The psychology of human nature must be studied so the student may develop an avenue of approach to his very limited number of customers that will eventually lead to sales and to mutual respect and trust.

Well documented are the returns from this exercise of "mutual respect and trust": gross overuse, destruction of beneficial insects, resistance in target species, a grower hooked on a chemical diet. Overall, as much as 50 per cent of the pesticides used are believed to be wasted or wholly counter-productive.[32] That's good news for the seller, bad news for everybody else.

While propaganda to advance the technology is usually a one-company venture, propaganda in defense of it can be more broadly based. Expectations are not disappointed by the activities of the National Agricultural Chemical Association. NACA propagandizes profusely through television and radio spots and canned editorials for thousands of daily and weekly newspapers.[33] Public relations men for the trade claim major victories in recent years: (1) providing material for "The Senseless War on Science," appearing in the March 1971 issue of *Fortune;* (2) guiding a January 1971 *Life* article toward "the beginning of a balanced view of the pesticide controversy"; (3) helping the managing editor of *Better Homes and Gardens* come up with a "balanced" editorial for the June 1971 issue; (4) feeding syndicated columnist Walter Trohan of the *Chicago Tribune* a "highly favorable column" on the pesticide controversy; (5) providing information for a pesticide article appearing in *Senior Scholastic* magazine which is circulated among high school students; (6) funneling information to the Newspaper Enterprise Association which earned a "highly favorable syndicated editorial reaching some 150 newspapers throughout the country." There's nothing wrong with getting a point of view across, but a point of view, like a pesticide, can be dangerously oversold by heavy investments, cunningly spent.

Research and development is the lifeline of the chemical industry; "test tube competition" is said to be a vital competitive force, the key to productivity gains. Predictably, the same forces serving growth and innovation serve also to stifle and suppress. If there is a way to manipulate research, the pesticide makers have found it. Secrecy, defensive spending, exploiting "right-thinking" advocates are a few of the favorites.

Classifying knowledge assures it will never be used against the corporation either commercially or by the regulators, consumers and workers whose interests might collide with efficient production. So employees are denied information about safety data on commonly used chemicals, obliged to handle chemicals identified only by code numbers, instructed to falsify safety reports, ordered to curtail production and visible pollutants if television cameramen are in the neighborhood, denied information about their own physical examinations and laboratory tests.[34]

The Monsanto Company's Security Manual illustrates the iron curtain that descends on plant operations under the guise of trade secrets. The company advises employees in doubt to suppress: "To reasonably err in favor of denoting information, a document or a project as Company Confidential can do no harm to Security and in most cases causes little or no legal or administrative inconvenience."[35] Employee "orientation" and "retraining" emphasize news management: ". . . premature and fragmented disclosure of releasable information in advance of the Public Relations Department's handling could negate an opportunity to exploit favorable news or minimize the impact of bad news." Security is a continuing thing: "The Personnel & Administrative Services Department will develop and coordinate throughout the company the conduct of indoctrination and refresher courses for all employees on the importance of company security." A pollution control, safety or health official who wants to peek at secrets is asked to sign a secrecy agreement: "Should he refuse, his authority or board should be contacted to resolve the issue. If an impasse is reached, the Law Department should be notified promptly." So it is that the state rules the corporation—on terms the corporation strives to write.

Defensive research also has come to the fore in recent years. "The biggest thing that has happened to us very lately is that we have had to spend, I would guess," says a spokesman for Hercules, Incorporated, "about 50 or 60 per cent of our research money in defense of our current products, to try to keep them registered and satisfy all the questions that are being asked about these."[36] An industry-wide survey discloses that during 1970, 23 per cent of research and development expenditures went for "Regulatory Maintenance of Existing Products."[37] It is too bad that the technology is caught without the answers while markets are booming, but it is also unfortunate that defensive research is research for the lawyer, the publicist or the hand-picked consultant working within the phony frame of reference toward the more-study-to-buy-time alibi.

When a study in the late 1960's disclosed that 2,4,5-T, a widely used herbicide, caused fetal defects in test animals,[38] Dow Chemical's defense came through, pointing out that the samples used in the tests contained a contaminant not found in current commercial grades. A repeat experiment with "pure" 2,4,5-T was conducted with the same depressing results. But nearly four years elapsed between the first suggestion of birth defects and initial governmental restrictions, during which time 20,000 tons of 2,4,5-T were dropped over Vietnam. The defense then turned to the science advisory committee system and, after that, to the courts, playing out the legal strings while running up the sales.

The FMC Corporation and Chemagro used workers as guinea pigs to head off an emergency order by the California agriculture commissioner that would have required a thirty-day interval between the application of certain compounds to farm fields and worker re-entry.[39] Earlier experience with a seven-day re-entry rule resulted in poisoned workers, so the manufacturers set up an "industrial hygiene study" to contradict this data. "Volunteers" from picking crews, including women, children and people with physical defects, were enlisted. Picking was begun seven days after application and, sure enough, the results were the same: poisoned workers. But they weren't poisoned badly enough to persuade the manufacturers to discontinue the tests before completion of the scheduled regimen.

Reliable professional advocates are another ingredient of an industrial policy reluctant to leave science to chance. One of the pesticide industry's gladiators is Mitchell Zavon whose scientific skills as a consultant for Shell Chemical Company were brought out in a 1969 House Report. One study of food samples collected under his direction and sent to Shell laboratories for analysis found that the use of Shell's DDVP strips in restaurants for one- and two-hour periods left no residues in exposed food. Others disagreed although measuring residues and reporting results wouldn't appear to invite scientific conflict. It was Zavon who wrote to the Public Health Service as a "health officer" —he then was an assistant health commissioner for the City of Cincinnati—to ask that pesticide vaporizers like Shell's Pest Strip "be re-reviewed."[40] His letter—"the only instance known to the subcommittee in which a health officer wrote PHS to endorse use of DDVP pest strips"—did not mention his relationship with Shell Chemical Company.[41] It was Zavon who "pooh-poohed"[42] a study funded by the Department of Health, Education and Welfare, raising serious questions about adverse health effects on workers at Shell's plant in Denver. And it was Zavon who is credited with the insight that "labels are primarily designed to protect the manufacturer from legal action."[43]

One of NACA's most reliable experts is Donald Spencer who probably knows what is going on in every pesticides research laboratory in the country. The December 1969 issue of *NACA News and Pesticide Review* honored Spencer for "vision and dedicated effort" in contributing to the "great, positive story" of chemical pesticides. Industry's

faith in Spencer is aptly placed. He told one audience that
during his five-year stay in the Pesticides Regulation Division he did not know of a single chemical accepted for
registration without the support of the conservation agencies of the United States;[44] but a House subcommittee told
another that hundreds of registrations were approved by
PRD over the objections of the Public Health Service.[45]
Spencer is a one-man scientific repudiator of pesticides
critics, and his publications are given wide circulation by
NACA.

All of the industry's skills in home-made science, public
relations invective and political might were on display during the ten-year struggle over uses of DDT. That the
chemical makers' proudest contribution, one that had
saved millions, could also be a worldwide pollutant, perhaps without parallel, was a proposition unacceptable to
the pesticides state. From the beginning, when Louis
McLean of Velsicol sought to head off the publication of
Silent Spring, the conflict was submerged in propaganda
that was bitter, vitriolic and prolonged. Critics were bug
lovers, pure food nuts and worse. Efforts to discredit them
regularly strayed from the merits. "You understand of
course that Dr. Wurster is generally regarded as the most
extreme member of the scientific community on this left
side but your readers don't know and understand this,"
NACA President Parke Brinkley wrote confidentially to an
editor of *Reader's Digest* which had published an article by
anti-DDT researcher and spokesman Dr. Charles
Wurster.[46]

The elimination of DDT, it was said, was an attack on
all pesticides that would bring famine and plague on a
worldwide-scale. No responsible and few irresponsible critics urge immediate world-wide bans, but the technological

defense feasted upon the strawman: a pesticide ban would produce deaths and suffering greater than those of World War II, said a ubiquitous pro-DDT spokesman;[47] forbid the use of pesticides and the total output of crops and cattle would be cut by 30 per cent, echoed the U.S. Department of Agriculture.[48] The message was backed by a "virulent form of pesticide 'McCarthyism' first directed at Rachel Carson":

> Dr. Max Sobelman of the Montrose Chemical Corporation of California charges DDT critics with being anticapitalistic; Louis McLean of Velsicol Chemical Corporation suggested they are "preoccupied with the subject of sexual potency." Dr. Wayland Hayes, Professor of Biochemistry, Vanderbilt University, suggests that they are aiding the machinations of foreign agents; Dr. White-Stevens, Professor of Biology, Rutgers University, charges that they may be responsible for the death of millions [by] malaria, and *Barrons* has accused them of plotting world famine—despite the fact that banning DDT in the U.S. will have no legal effect on overseas shipments and that DDT critics make an exception for use of DDT to control epidemics.[49]

Four government committees studying DDT between 1963 and 1969 recommended that it be phased out. While the scientific evidence was accumulating, NACA was responding with science of its own, highlighted by such gems as Donald Spencer's "The Peregrine Falcon Populations," questioning the widely shared hypothesis that chlorinated hydrocarbon pesticide residues have contributed to the species' decline; his "Chlorinated Hydrocarbons and Runoff," explaining why the mobility of these pesticides is highly overrated; and his answer to a self-evident question, "Fruit Pesticides Are Affecting Wildlife: Fact or Fiction?"

The legal system protecting DDT worked precisely as

designed. It took several Court of Appeals decisions in suits initiated by outsiders to get the government unstuck. The first, in May 1970, ordered Secretary of Health, Education and Welfare Robert Finch to start thinking about whether DDT causes cancer and, if so, whether that might have some bearing on the tolerances allowed in raw agricultural commodities.[50] The second, decided on the same day, ordered Secretary of Agriculture Clifford Hardin to explain why he didn't move against DDT as an "imminent hazard," and as such, take it off the market.[51] The third decision, in January 1971, ordered EPA Administrator William Ruckelshaus to issue cancellation notices with respect to all uses of DDT and invited him also to explain why he didn't take the stronger step of ordering DDT off the market.[52]

With the formalities out of the way, the suffering called a cancellation proceeding got under way: Montrose opted for an advisory committee report; some formulators preferred a public hearing. Months passed; a committee was appointed; the hearings got under way. The report was filed; many months later the hearing was concluded. Finally, in June 1972 EPA announced a ban on virtually all domestic DDT usage. The technology was on the way out, but it was a strategic retreat, hardly a rout brought on by a respectable rule of law.

In September 1972, as this is being written, two monuments to the chemical pesticides industry linger like residues after a spraying operation. One is DDT, for the ban would not be effective until December 31, 1972. The other is the Federal Insecticide, Fungicide and Rodenticide Act (FIFRA) which contributed so much to extending the life of DDT.

The endurance of both are good examples of the technological defense and the remedies to combat it. Looking back over the ten-year struggle a key move was the transfer of the Pesticides Regulation Division from the Department of Agriculture to the Environmental Protection Agency, a new agency not yet indentured to the industry it regulates. With a bright line between the corporation and the state, unvarnished science was able to surmount the technological defense.

Whether FIFRA will be rewritten with the distinction between the corporation and the state in mind is in doubt. The years 1971 and 1972 brought to the Congress proposals to look at the technology as well as the user—strict pre-clearance requirements, disclosure of registration data, severe use limitations, streamlining of cancellation procedures. But the "reform" legislation that passed the House in November 1971 was a credit to the labeling lobby and a measure that in some respects was worse than the 1947 FIFRA. The crowning insult was a provision that called for public compensation for a manufacturer who suffers losses as a result of a registration cancellation. This covering of private risk with public monies holds uncompensable the victim's hurt but rewards the bandit who turns in his shotgun. It is a parody of the confusion between the corporation and the state.

Prospects for strong legislation were not enhanced when the Nixon Administration's position became quite clear as a result of a memo authored by Howard Cohen, director of EPA's Office of Congressional Affairs, and distributed to the regional administrators in January 1972:

> Once EPA has developed its positions, John Whitaker [White House assistant] must be consulted with in order for EPA to ascertain the degree, if any, of flexibility which this Agency will have in dealing with the Senate Committee. The result of these conversations will hopefully be a solid EPA/White House position on the [House] bill.
> . . . .

Any further public hearings on the bill ought to be avoided, since they would put EPA on the spot in trying to defend the House bill or attacking the House bill as being too weak. Under no circumstances should EPA attack the Pesticide Bill as being too weak. This would cause serious problems for the President in farm states. . . .

The important point to remember is that the White House can live with [the House bill]. If EPA can improve upon the House version then we ought to do so, but not at the risk of jeopardizing the bill on the Senate side or in the Conference.

EPA should attempt to get a pesticide bill out of the Senate as soon as possible. The President is in an election year and he needs some legislative victories. While the environmentalists will strongly object to the lack of further hearings, they will not, for the most part, be voting for the President. . . .

When this indiscretion became a matter of public record, Howard Cohen was suddenly no longer working for EPA. But he found another job as a member of the White House staff.

It is bad enough that the White House chastens EPA to go easy during an election year. It is worse if the price of going easy is to give the technology the free rein it abused so thoroughly for most of this century.*

---

*The price was paid in large part when the Federal Environmental Pesticide Control Act was enacted into law in October 1972 with a strong indemnity provision calling for government payments to businesses suffering losses as a result of pesticide registration suspensions or cancellations. *See* Pub. Law 92–516, Oct. 21, 1972.

6 THE WASHDAY MIRACLE

*I can't believe that any industry, any member of our industry, would knowingly produce a product they felt could be a real hazard to the public.**

*The manufacturers of laundry detergents would find themselves forced to change the composition of their product—to use some unproven or perhaps unsafe materials— simply to maintain their competitive position on the market place.***

No less a power than the detergents industry was paying close attention as the debits mounted against the phosphates in its products during 1969 and 1970. These included a report of the International Joint Commission (Canadian-American) on Lake Erie pollution, restrictions imposed by the Canadian government, a House subcommittee report recommending elimination of phosphates from detergents by 1972, tough talk fom the Federal Water Quality Administration, a contract announced by Secretary

---

*Edward K. Hertel, vice president, FMC Corp., in Hearings on Environmental Pesticide Control Act, before the Senate Subcommittee on Agricultural Research and General Legislation, 92d Cong., 2d Sess. 1972, p. 258.
**Edgar H. Lotspuch, vice president, Procter & Gamble Co., statement of April 26, 1971, before the Federal Trade Commission.

of the Interior Walter Hickel for the development of a phosphate-free laundry product. In September 1970, FWQA released test findings on specific detergents "to clear up any confusion as to phosphate content . . . and to serve as a general standard for the housewife shopping in the super market." Names were named and the percentage of phosphates in the products disclosed in the newspapers and on television. There were Biz, Tide, Axion, Drive and the rest, looking bad in an unaccustomed public role.

In the months following the technology was in full retreat as citizens took steps to protect their water resources from phosphate-based detergents: Suffolk County, New York; Dade County, Florida; the states of New York and Indiana; the cities of Akron, Detroit, Chicago—one almost felt sorry for the detergent industry.

No sooner did the tears begin to flow than the law and the science began to change. "EPA Explains Position on Publication of Detergent Lists" was the quiet announcement in the summer of 1971. The list of the damned published in September 1970 was said to be no longer "a reliable basis for comparison of products on today's market." "The rate of introduction of new products and reformulation of old products has become so rapid," the explanation went, "that it is essentially impossible to prepare a list which doesn't become obsolete almost as soon as it is published." This, "coupled with the fact that some manufacturers now apparently market products of differing composition for different geographical areas, has led us to decide to refrain from publishing any further lists at this time."

Where the list went, the policy was soon to go. In mid-September 1971 came a press conference extravaganza featuring Surgeon General Jesse Steinfeld, Food and Drug Administration Commissioner Charles Edwards, the Environmental Protection Agency's William Ruckelshaus and Russell Train of the Council on Environmental Quality. The increasing use of "highly caustic substitutes" was labeled a "cause for serious concern;" phosphates were back in favor. Their statement went so far as to urge states and localities "to reconsider laws and policies which unduly restrict the use of phosphates in detergents."[1] The Surgeon General equivocated not at all: "My advice to the housewife at this time would be to use the phosphate detergent."[2] His words were soon immortalized in full-page ads paid for by the Lever Brothers Company: "My advice to the housewife is to use phosphate detergents."[3]

That phosphates in detergents could rise from utter disrepute to government preferred in just about a year brought signs of skepticism. Congressional hearings were held; angry editorials written. A publication as staid as *Business Week* went so far as to detect "tattletale gray in detergent regulation."[4] The magazine editorialized: "This sort of floundering not only suggests that the federal regulators are using fragmentary, inconclusive evidence to make their decisions. It raises the ugly suspicion that political pull as well as scientific research is involved. Government regulators owe the public some explanation." The explanation is that the government has difficulty regulating the technologies of the larger corporations.

A vigorous defense of phosphorus was preordained. The size of the sales and the size of the sellers made it so. Each year Americans buy an estimated 6.6 billion pounds of soap and detergents valued at $1.7 billion.[5] Each of us goes through an average of thirty-two pounds per year, twenty-seven pounds of it synthetic detergents.[6] Sharing about two-thirds of the detergent market (and 85 per cent of the market for heavy-duty products) are the big three—

Procter & Gamble, Colgate-Palmolive and Lever Brothers.

Essays on corporate power tend to come around to Procter & Gamble whose undisputed sovereignty of the-soap and detergent market (about 45 per cent) is but one feather in a very well decorated cap.[7] P & G is the nation's largest advertiser spending more than $250 million a year on media and promotion. Its annual sales are close to $3 billion, with profits in excess of $200 million. At the top, P & G's board of directors includes six Harvard Business School alumni and graduates of other prestigious institutions. The board has included a former Secretary of Defense, a former ambassador to West Germany and two members of the Business Council, an advisory group with considerable influence. Bryce Harlow, the company's Washington lobbyist, served for two years as personal counselor to President Nixon. Howard J. Morgens, the company's president, was chairman of the National Industrial Pollution Control Council's Detergents Sub-Council and had in hand in writing the two NIPCC publications on the industry's pollution problems. P & G is much admired as a money maker and "impenetrable," according to the *New York Times* and just about everybody else. (Following a leaked story about the removal of enzymes from Tide, discussion of product changes was forbidden by company order). Watching P & G and its allies respond to technological crisis is to observe a private government in action.

Like other large corporations, detergent makers strive for total control of their economic and legal environment. Public relations and politics are invaluable servants of this commercial certainty, and both were to be invoked while phosphates were briefly at bay.

The industry publicizes and politicizes with the best. Theories on the imperatives of technology rest upon the advertising techniques of detergent manufacturers. In all, the big three spent over $452 million in advertising during 1969, a sum in the neighborhood of 225 times the amount budgeted by the federal government for research into water pollution blamed on detergents.[8] Procter & Gamble and Colgate-Palmolive were ranked first and third, respectively, among the leading network television advertisers based on 1969 expenditures.[9] Leading the 1969 list in amount spent on television promotion, $7,249,000 and in percentage phosphate content, 73.9, was Procter & Gamble's Biz.[10]

That the purpose of advertising is to achieve maximum consumption and control over demand is no secret. Colgate-Palmolive's 1969 Annual Report sums up the philosophy: "With the advent of television in the late 1940's, Colgate-Palmolive was one of the first to visualize the tremendous effect this new medium would have on the packaged consumer goods market. The Company immediately embraced television and through the years has continued to be among the leading and most sophisticated exponents of this prime selling force. . . . Comprehensive testing and evaluation before and after the production of commercials insures imaginative and persuasive selling messages that motivate consumers to try our products."[11] The Association of National Advertisers—a trade group made up of the 500 top advertisers—calls it *"Stimulating Desire. . . .* Few, very few of us, even in our own best interests act without a nudge. The nudge . . . can come through dictation as in a controlled economy; or it can occur through the suggestions imparted through advertising." Advertising, insists the association, "has made voluntary that which, in the past and even today in the evolving countries of Africa and Asia, could be done only by dictation and compulsion."[12]

Imaginative nudging pushes of sales of detergents far

beyond expectations—and need. In parts of the country served by soft water the consumer each year is buying and throwing away twenty-seven pounds too much; overuse in any event is rampant: ten times what is needed for best results, says the project engineer credited with the development of Tide.[13] Manufacturers insist excessive consumption is not a problem, and if it is, consumers are to blame. This myth, like that of the pesticide salesman, writes off responsibility for waste, misuse and damage.

Political clout joins advertising skill to reduce business risks. The law has always been a personal erector set for detergent makers, who are notorious technological recidivists. They work in the erratically regulated worlds of advertising, packaging and labeling, and traffic in products of many formulations. They bargain with a collection of agencies—the Environmental Protection Agency, the Food & Drug Administration, the Federal Trade Commission, local consumer protection and health authorities. Perpetually in litigation, they are perpetually "losers," although not much happens to them when they break the rules.

In March 1971, Colgate-Palmolive and Lever Brothers consented to judgments enjoining them from selling detergents in violation of a New York State labeling law.[14] The penalty: $2000 for costs. During the same month the FTC sought consent orders against the big three and eight of their advertisers restraining them from falsely claiming enzyme detergents can remove all types of clothing stains.[15] In the summer of 1971 Colgate-Palmolive was compelled to recall 86,000 cases of Crystal Clear, a dishwashing detergent being test-marketed in milk-type cartons, which the FDA said were unsafe and especially attractive to children.[16] Later in the year, the FTC charged Procter & Gamble with fraud by using promotional games that neglected to award all prizes promised and failed to disclose the odds. (Optimistic participants in the "Join the Jet Set" sweepstakes had about one chance in 30 million of cashing in on the grand prize).[17] By the year's end, P & G was answering a water pollution suit for spilling caustic soda into Long Beach Harbor.[18] The new year opened on a familiar note with a consent judgment proposed to restrain Colgate-Palmolive from antitrust violations in connection with the sale of mineral supplements like iron dextran,[19] and with another charge that the company knowingly marketed a laundry product without cautionary labeling despite the completion of laboratory tests demonstrating that it was an eye irritant.[20]

Skills in law-breaking and opinion-making were to serve the manufacturers well as they came under increasing fire for the phosphates in their products. Despite the multi-disciplined disguise shared by most technologies, phosphates in detergents have been seen for what they are. They are justified as "builders," which soften hard water by tying up minerals such as calcium and iron that otherwise might interfere wth cleaning action. Phosphorus also makes clean water dirty.[21] It fertilizes the growth of plants and leads to accelerated eutrophication typified by excessive algae and oxygen depletion. Too much algae means the water stinks, fish die, green mats of slime clog the beaches, and people get upset. While algae need many elements for growth (fifteen to twenty, says the Soap & Detergent Association), phosphorus is, in many waters, often the one in short supply, making it the "critical" nutrient. Phosphorus is also the one nutrient most easily controlled. Municipal sewage is an important man-made source and detergents are responsible, on the average, for at least 50 per cent of the phosphorus in sewage.[22] Phosphorus is a people problem, but three manufacturers of detergents are a bigger problem than the rest of the people put together.

Reciting the dogma about the contribution of phosphates to eutrophication outlines the technology's defensive perimeters: minimize the role of phosphorus while stressing that of other elements (e.g., carbon or nitrogen) as the cause of eutrophication, play down the pollution, play up the loss of cleaning power that would attend the elimination of phosphates, and prove substitutes to be unacceptable. Developing a myth that requires no change in technology is all important. The detergent makers' principal myth is that phosphorus in sewage should be handled in the treatment plant, not in the laundry product. This is a commendable aim, no less than cleaning up hundreds of millions of beer cans. But it will cost billions; it will take years, and the public will pay for it.

So commanding is the myth that E. Scott Patterson, while president of the Soap & Detergent Association, viewed the subsidy his industry seeks as an everlasting favor to the public. Drawing on "social dynamics theory," Patterson envisaged "counterintuitive behavior" in the move to restrict the phosphate content of detergents. "Less use of detergents, lowered phosphates, instantly degradable surfactants may in fact delay a recognition of the need for full-scale sewage treatment, with a consequent decline in water quality," he opined. "I am sure no politician would buy . . . any suggestion that a detergent *ban* could make lake pollution *worse*. But maybe some day a computer model of the feedback-loop dynamics will command more respect than the judgment of a local mayor or councilman."[23]

Research is the cheap answer to an expensive problem. The technological defense draws on old stand-bys: commandeering governmental inquiries, dragging out uncertainties indefinitely, exploring politically useful hypotheses.

As long ago as 1967, Secretary of the Interior Stewart Udall sought to touch off a search for a non-polluting detergent: "We enlist the aid of the soap and detergent industry in this work, asking that you intensify your program to research and develop substitutes for phosphates in detergents." At a July 1967 meeting with industry people, Assistant Secretary Frank DiLuzio conceded that "nutrient pollution is complex." But he insisted, "We . . . have sufficient knowledge *now* of the . . . eutrophication problem to know that action must begin immediately to limit phosphates added to our waters."[24] By January 1968 the Soap & Detergent Association was formally—and hypocritically—committed to seeking a substitute for phosphates in detergents.[25]

Out of the mid-1967 meetings between industry and Interior Department officials came a press release announcing a "Joint Task Force to Investigate Eutrophication." Made up of industry and agency representatives, the Joint Task Force was "to make recommendations on a cooperative program to research the problem of controlling eutrophication (overfertilization) of lakes, including the role of phosphates and any possible replacements."[26] Members of this group charged with redesigning the industry's technology came from, among others, Allied Chemical, Colgate-Palmolive, Hooker Chemical, Lever Brothers, Monsanto, FMC Corporation, and inevitably, Procter & Gamble.

Copies of the minutes of the Joint Task Force are available, not in federal offices, but in the offices of the Soap & Detergent Association,[27] which gives a hint about who was making policy on this dry and dusty run. A May 1968 editorial in *Industrial Water Engineering* was more explicit about the work of the Joint Task Force: "The plain fact . . . is that FWPCA [the federal Water Pollution Control Administration, now EPA] needs industry help. And it is to industry's advantage to give it. Consider, for example, how the Soap and Detergent Industry helped turn an ill-conceived plan for phosphate substitution into a progressive program for studying eutrophication. More of this type of cooperative action is needed."

Cooperative it was. At the opening meeting, putting first things first, the Joint Task Force selected Charles Bueltman of the SDA as chairman and Mary P. Kilcoyne of the SDA as recording secretary. Later, T. E. Brenner, research director of the SDA, became the executive director of the JTF,[28] and he was housed with desk space in Washington along with the necessary back-up services.[29] No one gave a moment's thought to the recommendation of the Justice Department, made back in the 1950's,[30] that the antitrust laws require the disqualification of trade association officials from industry advisory committees.

It was decided at the first meeting that industry and the government would speak with a single voice; it soon became clear who would write the script. The minutes report: "[i]nquiries directed to the Task Force or concerned with its activities should be referred to either Mr. Bueltman, as Chairman, or Dr. [Leon] Weinberger [of the Federal Water Pollution Control Administration], as Vice Chairman, in order that they can coordinate replies, thus avoiding any possibility of government and industry appearing in the press to be divided."[31] (As of mid-1971, Dr. Weinberger, no longer working for the public, was still "coordinating" his replies with industry when he showed up before the Federal Trade Commission to oppose a warning label for phosphates in detergents)[32] "In order to do the job right," one JTF member explained, "an effort of this type has to demand maximum participation by industry at a point where decisions are being made and where they can influence it [sic] in a proper way."

As this technological conspiracy got under way, the members were self congratulatory but cautious. The detergent makers were selected for participation on the Joint Task Force, said a spokesman for FWPCA, "because of the excellent experience government has had with the detergent industry in the past." In discussion with other groups, the detergent industry is "cited as a model," for it was "essentially taking the lead in the problem." A government spokesman "hoped that an attitude of coming up with answers and not one of banning products could be transmitted to other groups, such as the agricultural people." But there were dangers: "Concern was expressed by the SDA representatives that the soap industry was taking a calculated risk as an industry by taking the lead. It was hoped that such a step would not be looked upon as acceptance of responsibility for the whole problem. Eutrophication is a problem of mankind and not of the detergent industry." To this day, eutrophication remains a problem of mankind.

The first JTF meeting could not pass without a baring of the federal laboratories to industrial eyes. Task Force members were given a full summary of federal research and development activity and a 200-page literature review.[33] The chairman and vice chairman of the JTF later agreed upon a letter to Secretary Udall "suggesting that the Secretary request [the] Water Resources Scientific Information Center to develop a procedure by which its information retrieval services can be made available to industry members of the JTF."[34]

It is by such incremental methods that influence takes hold. The issue is not access. It is special access. Getting information unavailable to others and free services besides are reasons enough for staying close to the government. More important, where political judgments are determined by technological advances, the tables are turned by putting the brakes on the technology and traveling that leisurely route to political success. Knowing where every penny of federal money is being spent, who is doing the research, what methodological or institutional restraints are governing it—these are the talismen of future policy directions.

Directing governmental research away from applied solutions, if it can be done, is twice blessed—chances of intervention are minimized and the field is abandoned to researchers proceeding at a "proper" pace toward "sound" solutions, as defined by industry and its economic constraints. It is thus no surprise—indeed it was inevitable—that JTF gradually moved to develop a standard eutrophication ability test method to measure the potential for algal bloom (that is, how much phosphorus algae requires in host waters to support its growth). A Lever Brothers spokesman stumbled on the premise: "The lack of a test method at this time was not holding up the replacement of phosphates in detergents." All the more reason to press ahead on refining the means for measuring the problem. Even then, care was essential:[35] "Dr. Weaver [of Monsanto] recommended that the Task Force not proceed with a eutrophication index, if its primary purpose would be to serve as a mechanism to remove phosphates from detergents. Basically, the test methods should enable the [Joint] Task Force to have an understanding of every component of eutrophication. Dr. Stephan [of Interior] said such a test would become a tool in learning the causes and effects of eutrophication and not put a finger on phosphates."

With obvious chagrin, Congressman Henry Reuss (D-Wisc.) opened hearings in December 1969 to inquire into

the role of phospate-based detergents in the eutrophication of the nation's waters. "The principal result of the
Joint Industry-Government Task Force seems to be an
agreement to develop a 'Provisional Algal Assay Procedure' for field testing about two years hence. The mountain
has labored and brought forth a mouse,"[36] said Reuss. He
was optimistic. The standard procedure for measuring the
problem, reports the SDA, "is expected to be completed in
1972,"[37] not 1971.

The Joint Task Force was so demonstrably unproductive that the SDA's Bueltman had to draw on his imagination when he sent a progress report to the new Secretary
of the Interior, Walter Hickel, in June 1969: "Perhaps the
accomplishment of greatest long-range significance has
been the establishment of a common meeting ground in an
area where divergent and often controversial views have
been frequently expressed."[38] As for the benefits hatched
in this common meeting ground, Bueltman could think of
two: a Eutrophication Information Center at the University
of Wisconsin and a nutrient removal study at Pennsylvania
State University, both jointly funded by SDA and the federal government.

An information center is a useful exercise and one unlikely to embarrass the technology. As for the Penn State
study, the Joint Task Force minutes disclose "some discussion" regarding its "significance."[39] Dr. Weinberger of the
Interior Department "noted that while the project was one
which the [federal government] would be pleased to support independently of the SDA, he had some questions as
to whether it was the kind of project which should be identified as a [Joint] Task Force inspired project. Dr. Weinberger pointed out that the exact same procedure will be
evaluated through other [federally supported] groups. He
said that in all likelihood the City of Detroit with its own

independent groups will be doing this work and their report would probably be issued before the report of the Pennsylvania State Project." As it turned out, the Penn State project was worthy of JTF association: in 1971 John Nesbitt, chief academic recipient of the funding, joined Dr. Weinberger and the big detergent makers to oppose the FTC's labeling proposals.

By the meeting of August 12, 1969, industrial subversion of the Joint Task Force was complete. New members had arrived—from the Department of Agriculture, the Tennessee Valley Authority, the Manufacturing Chemists Association and the National Plant Food Institute. None of the original four Department of the Interior appointees showed up (some undoubtedly had left with a change of administration). Bueltman, Kilcoyne and Brenner of the Soap & Detergent Association were still there. The minutes showed a diminished fury in the attack against eutrophication: "Caution was expressed regarding the possible implication that the JTF was going to pass judgment on whether or not there are adequate programs and attack being made on the problem of eutrophication in the Great Lakes. It was agreed that such action would fall beyond the objectives of JTF." So much for the commitment, made two years earlier, to inquire into the role of phosphates and any possible replacements.

The meeting had more important business. It was time to discuss "The Greeks Had a Word for It," a proposed fourteen-and-one-half minute motion picture, in color, live action and animation "on what eutrophication is, what is being done about it by government and industry, and what can realistically be expected in the foreseeable future in alleviating this problem." Sponsors, distribution, costs, scheduling were the important topics of the day.

The JTF's most memorable contribution was yet to

come. At the Reuss subcommittee hearings in December 1969, a new variant on the "all deliberate speed" theme was heard: "with all the deliberate speed, perhaps never." Delivering this bleak communique was Charles Bueltman of SDA, chairman of the JTF: "Although, as I shall discuss in greater detail, the industry is intensively searching for replacement materials *should they be needed,* there is at this time no suitable phosphate replacement available for detergents [emphasis added]."[40]

The industry testimony was clear enough to persuade even the feds that they had been had. The February 1970 meeting brought the charge that industry was not following through in "good faith" with its commitment to get rid of phosphates. FWPCA retaliated by resigning from the task force it created. Company control over the phosphorus issue missed scarcely a step as it soon took up residence in the Department of Commerce's National Industrial Pollution Control Council.

The Joint Task Force typifies the technological conspiracy. Brought together with a ringing declaration by the Secretary of the Interior that water pollution could be combatted by eliminating phosphorus from detergents, the Soap & Detergent Association commandeered the ship and set sail 180 degrees away from its members' products. The pirates did not even reach the prescribed destination, however remote that was. A break-through against eutrophication is hard to find in a fourteen and one-half minute movie, an informational service, a duplicative nutrient removal study and a measuring procedure to be field tested some time in 1972.

Throughout 1970 and 1971 the publicity and politics grew in response to the scope of the threat. Just as the manufacturer spends to promote the positive virtues of his products, he invests to allay fears about side effects that could cut into sales. The FMC Corporation, a leading producer of phosphates, fits the stereotype perfectly by churning out commercial myths in its "scientific" reprints, carrying such titles as "Lack of Correlation between Phosphorus and Algae Growth," and "The Eutrophication Problem: A Review and Critical Analysis (The Non-Role of Detergent Phosphates in Eutrophication)."

The Soap & Detergent Association is a skilled practitioner of the transplant technique: feed the line to a source who repeats the message in the appropriate forum, whether it be a newspaper column, a story in *Good Housekeeping* or a semi-technical publication. Next, make reprints and disseminate widely the views of this "independent, free-thinking" authority. "The attached reprint from *Good Housekeeping* magazine, entitled 'The Detergent Dilemma' is one of the most comprehensive, up-to-date discussions of the subject we have seen; and we believe it would be an excellent reference for your files," says the Soap & Detergent Association. (It also tells the story the "right" way). Accept *Good Housekeeping's* invitation to write for additional information on water pollution and phosphate detergents, and the return mail brings a comprehensive bibliography, padded with such authoritative writings as the NIPCC publications on detergents, Lever Brothers' "Detergents and the Environment," SDA's "Enzymes in Laundry Products," and a booklet of SDA's Cleanliness Bureau, "The Facts About Today's Detergents." The propaganda bootstrap is not foolproof but the odds of being hurt by regulation are shortened by strategic, heavy investments. The gullible, forgetful, uninformed or just plain ignorant—most of us fit in one or all of these categories—can be nudged in the direction of the prevailing mythology.

The nudging can be helped along by deception.[41] In January 1971 the Cooperative Extension Service of the New York State College of Human Ecology at Cornell University, published Informational Bulletin No. 12 by Mary E. Purchase, titled "Phosphates and Detergents in Water Pollution." Dr. Purchase, a home economist, has attracted support over the years from Soap & Detergent Association members, and her views hew closely to the industry line. Eager to spread the word, SDA got permission from the director of the Cooperative Extension to reprint without charge 40,000 copies of Bulletin No. 12. The bulletin clearly says: "Single copies free to New York State Residents; additional copies 10 cents each," but nobody expects the SDA to labor under the same financial disadvantages as, let us say, an interested high school biology class. SDA distributed copies of the Purchase article bearing the extension service monogram and a new "March 1971" date. But there was no notice that the text was re-written. Mary Purchase wrote that "[s]ome no-phosphate detergents are presently on the market," but the SDA preferred that there be "few no-phosphate detergents presently on the market." Mary Purchase wrote that phosphates were considered "pollutants," but the SDA preferred that they be considered "a contributing factor to cultural eutrophication." Mary Purchase wrote that "phosphates added to waste water may contribute to cultural eutrophication," but SDA wanted an amendment so that "[p]hosphates and carbon added to waste water may contribute to cultural eutrophication."

Dr. Purchase insists these and other changes were made with her consent and under circumstances "not unusual" for extension publications. But the SDA's reproductions of the Bulletin and changes made in it were not consented to by the college's publication committee,[42] which is the customary procedure. And it smacks of fraud, albeit a popular one, to pass off the work of a trade group as a government document. But it is a wrong in defense of technology, and that often turns out to be no wrong at all.

The federal government also contributes to industry's programming of the public. Write to the Environmental Protection Agency for information on detergents, and included in the return package will be a NIPCC sub-council publication on detergents, authored in part by Procter & Gamble's Howard J. Morgens. Why the Department of Commerce must pay for the printing of Morgens on detergents and the Environmental Protection Agency pay for its distribution appears questionable, until it is understood that today's trade propaganda is a strong candidate for tomorrow's governmental policy.

The top executives of the leading producers, convened as NIPCC's Detergent's Sub-Council, were thinking substance as well as form. Secretary of Commerce Maurice Stans told a press conference in July 1970 that the sub-council had met three or four times and that he had attended most of the meetings.[43] The minutes the law requires when businessmen convene to advise the government[44] are available for only one meeting before then, suggesting that either Stans' memory is poor or the law undependable. It is nonetheless easy to believe the report that the industry was making "a detailed case against hasty action" behind closed doors.[45]

Out of such public-spirited gatherings come cynical initiatives. In November 1970 the Soap & Detergent Association announced a "voluntary" labeling program, ostensibly to clear up confusion occasioned by the spate of detergent-content lists.[46] Coincidentally, the Nader Report on water pollution points out, "By writing its own labels, . . . the industry also got a chance to 'correct' the form in which the information had been presented on most lists, the percentage of phosphate as the compound sodium tripolyphosphate (STPP). The percentage of elemental phosphorus in any given product is roughly four times lower than the percentage STPP; Tide labeled '12.6 per cent phosphorus' sounds a lot more innocuous than Tide with 50 per cent phosphate.' "[47] By writing its own labels industry also got a chance to leave out a few details and improve upon a label that was wending its way through the Federal Trade Commission.

Heading off meaningful regulation with cosmetic concessions is an old and reliable tactic: industry takes a bow; the government has an excuse for doing nothing; the people are appeased. Given SDA's sudden commitment to labeling, one might suspect there would be no objection from its member companies when the FTC proposal broke into print early in 1971. All it required was a listing on detergent containers of all ingredients by common name, with percentages, and a warning statement:

> "Warning: Each Recommended Use Level of this Product Contains _____ Grams of Phosphorus, Which Contributes to Water Pollution. Do Not Use in Excess. In Soft Water Areas, Use of Phosphates is Unnecessary."

This was no ban, tax or mandated reduction in the phosphorus content of detergents. This was providing the consumer with information—albeit limited—about the consequences of the normal use of products whose virtues are extolled incessantly through massive advertising campaigns. But it was a question that might embarrass the technology, and the industry preferred it not be asked or if asked, not answered.

Shortly before the hearings opened before the FTC,

the detergent industry's lawyers and lobbyists assembled in the Washington law offices of Pierson, Ball & Dow for a strategy session on how best to head off the phosphate restrictions the FTC and various states and cities were considering.[48] Procter & Gamble's Bryce Harlow had been busy touching bases with presidential aides John Whitaker, Charles Colson and Peter Flanigan. Industry's idea was to get legislation giving EPA open-ended control over detergent content, pre-empting other authorities. EPA's William Ruckelshaus would set phosphate limits of 35 per cent, which was agreeable to the industry. The promised government delivery, however, must await passage of the law and EPA's implementation of it.

The strategy is consistent with a trend in defense of technology. Growing sophistication in technologies leads to the centralization of political authority on grounds of incompetence at the grass-roots, and this centralization is welcomed by industry. One win at the federal level and the heat is off. Concentrating political responsibility and then overwhelming it with monopolized know-how and old-fashioned muscle helps the corporation run the country.

The exercise before the Federal Trade Commission was likely to be mooted by flanking movements elsewhere, but the industrial planning process takes few chances even with the inconsequential. Lever Brothers emerged from the backrooms long enough to run up to the federal court in Portland, Maine (home of the company), where it was joined by Proctor & Gamble, SDA and Colgate-Palmolive as intervenors in an effort to restrain the FTC from conducting further proceedings on the proposed rule. Tossed out of court, they went back to the agency where Procter & Gamble took over to dominate the data before the commission. Calls by the company were put through to virtually every expert in the country whose testimony could help.

The *modus operandi* was to solicit scientific statements favorable to P & G's position from witnesses who could accept no fees (like public officials), although where consulting arrangements were feasible, professionals were paid for their comments. (Several neglected to inform the commission that they were hired to tell the truth). The "good" statements got national renown when they were widely distributed by P & G. Indeed, some new science came into being by this short-order method, including the famous—and questionable—estimate of Dr. Daniel Okun that 85 per cent of the population has no eutrophication problem.[49]

The commissioners also got a chance to hear the old myths. Cornell University's Mary Purchase, a member of the Procter & Gamble team, explained why a little knowledge for consumers is a dangerous thing: "Neither consumers in general nor some of their professional protectors know what each component in a detergent is nor why it is there. The proposed ingredient listing, if adopted, would only cause confusion. False rumors will spring up, arising from ignorance. Consequences of these false statements may be worse than the consequences of omitting the labeling which is proposed."[50]

Another P & G team-member, Dr. Jack A. Borchardt of the University of Michigan, told about burdens of proof in technological conflicts. "For the past two decades, I have been intimately associated with the problem of phosphate enrichment of natural aquatic systems," he said. "In good conscience, I must oppose any form of labeling, restriction or active attack on phosphate-bearing materials until the facts of the situation are abundantly clear. . . . A truly concerned individual or group should press for more research to define the issues before demanding action. . . . And yet, action at this time and not research, is being demanded. This is a destructive approach to correction of a

serious problem. If total logic does not prevail in the face
of such [uninformed] pressure, only more chaos can result." Industry's 5.5 billion pound annual contribution of
phosphorus to the environment, according to this "total
logic," does not qualify as "action" and does not offend Dr.
Borchardt's first principles of research. P & G's rise to the
top in the detergent industry was founded on no such doc-
trine of restraint.

Making the good and bad of the technology indispens-
able is central to the defense. The record before the FTC
is cluttered with ghastly predictions about how the adoption of a warning rule would lend a competitive advantage
to technologies with a greater tendency to kill, maim and
pollute. Procter & Gamble's President Howard J. Morgens
told the Commission that "industry would have to replace
the phosphates with other materials before those other
materials have been proved to be safe for people and the
environment."[51] The observations of Edgar H. Lotspuch,
P & G's vice president in charge of advertising, bordered
on blackmail: "The manufacturers of laundry detergents
would find themselves forced to change the composition of
their product—to use some unproven or perhaps unsafe
materials—simply to maintain their competitive position
on the marketplace."[52] A detergent maker, said Lotspuch,
would be faced with the alternative of "either discontinuing
his advertising altogether or moving precipitously to the
use of untested substitute materials to replace phosphates."[53]

Hinting that it might move "precipitously" to "some
unproven or perhaps unsafe materials" simply "to maintain [its] competitive position on the marketplace" is a
crude concession coming from the industry's finest. But the
fate worse than phosphates argument is common enough:
ban DDT and we'll bring on a nerve gas substitute, cut

down on particulates and we'll increase nitrogen oxides, reduce jet noise and we'll risk a crash. Contrived need and safe substitutes pretty well explode the indispensability of phosphate-detergents. Soap is one forgotten cleanser in good supply,[54] albeit one whose sales bring lower profit margins.

Procter & Gamble practices what it preaches by moving to replace phosphates in detergents sold in Canada with nitrilotriacetic acid, NTA.[55] What is good enough for Canadians is not quite good enough for Americans: The industry has refrained from using NTA as a replacement compound at government request pending the completion of safety studies that have been proceeding for a number of years.[56] Subjecting P & G to the "more study" policy it so often inflicts upon millions of consumers was not accomplished without a *quid pro quo.* The government decided to trade phosphates for NTA, one for one with no draft choices involved.

So it was that the nation was treated to the September 1971 press conference where administration spokesmen made merry with the myths of the detergent industry: substitutes are unacceptable, phosphates are safe, upgrading sewers is the only way to take care of the technology. On September 22 Russel Train of the Council on Environmental Quality wrote to the FTC to protest against the "misleading" warning proposal, pointing out it would be "very difficult" to draft an accurate one. As for a statement of ingredients, it was enough that the manufacturers voluntarily were including one on their packaging.

The administration's reversal would effectively undercut the FTC which initiated its labeling proposals only after receiving commitments of strong support from the staffs of EPA and the Council on Environmental Quality. An FTC staff memo in mid-1972 acknowledged the controversy created a "dilemma" for the Commission, since the agency "will be considered by some as wrong regardless of its decision."[57] By this time, the staff was recommending dropping both the warning proposal and the requirement that the percentage of each ingredient be disclosed, leaving only an ingredients listing not much different from the Soap & Detergent Association's idea a year and a half earlier. The differences that remained were worked out in secret meetings between the FTC staff, SDA and the three big manufacturers.[58]

Above the cries of political deal occasioned by the turnaround on phosphates were heard the measured tones of Howard J. Morgens of Procter & Gamble: "We are encouraged that the federal government has at last given a clear direction to the country for dealing with the complex question of phosphates in relation to detergents, the environment, and public health."[59] It was the federal government, it must be understood, which had given the clear direction.

7 ALUMINUM'S ALLOYS

It is cheaper to pay claims than it is to control fluorides. *

Manipulative techniques in defense of technology are limitless. Harvey Aluminum Company has refined an ancient one: the lie. The liar can patch up a balky technology faster than an engineer.

Back in the 1960's a judgment was entered against Harvey Aluminum (now Martin Marietta) for fluoride pollution from its plant at The Dalles, Oregon. Shortly after the court brought in the bad news, the company came up with test data proving fluoride emissions had dropped spectacularly from 1,300 pounds a day to around 640 pounds. Lawyers rushed the glad tidings to the Court of Appeals in San Francisco in an unsuccessful attempt to get the lower court's decision upset. Unraveling the mysteries of this technological marvel took some imagination.

Joe Schulein, a teacher of chemical engineering at Oregon State University for 17 years, was convinced Harvey was still putting out at least 1,300 pounds of fluorides per day, despite the lawyers' claims. He decided to investigate by studying the power charts for the two-hour test period on November 11, 1964. The charts record the conversion of alternating power into direct current for use in the production of aluminum. Schulein asked Harvey's Fred Blatt for the charts.

---

*Manager of a Reynolds Metals aluminum plant quoted in *Reynolds Metals* v. *Lampert*, 324 F.2d 465 (9th Cir. 1963).

[Blatt] said, "We don't have any power charts." I said, "Of course you have power charts." He said, "We don't keep any power charts, no such thing." He looked me right in the eye. And I said, "Fred, I know you have power charts." He said, "Do you think I would lie to you?" And I said, "Yes." But I didn't get a chance to see any power charts.[1]

Schulein eventually did get the charts. They made interesting reading. The voltage and current showed decreases during the time of the test—"way, way down for a considerable time." The reason the voltage and current was way, way down was that Harvey shut it down, then took the tests. Turning off the power turns off the fluorides. It was done intentionally. Harvey Aluminum doesn't pay claims or control fluorides willingly.

Technological stability is not new to the aluminum industry. The metal was first made in this country in 1888 by the Pittsburgh Reduction Company soon to become the Aluminum Company of America.[2] For nearly fifty years Alcoa was the nation's sole producer of virgin aluminum ingot, building an integrated empire extending from bauxite ore deposits to the rolling mills and other fabricating plants. Playing monopoly called for the usual fencing with the Justice Department. A 1912 consent decree forbade Alcoa from engaging in predatory practices. New litigation was begun in 1937, culminating in a famous 1945 decision by Judge Learned Hand condemning Alcoa as a monopolist of the aluminum ingot market.[3] During World War II the government contracted for more than thirty aluminum reduction and fabricating plants, virtually all built and operated by Alcoa. Reynolds and Kaiser charged at the time that Alcoa purposely built mammoth plants at out-of-the-way sites to make peacetime operation by competitors impossible.[4] But competitors got their chance after the war when the disposal of government properties greatly strengthened Reynolds and gave Kaiser a substantial start. Alcoa was rewarded with a 1947 court decision refusing to break up the company despite its monopoly.[5] The big three have learned to live together, working through international consortiums, joint ventures and sometimes plain old conspiracies.

The aluminum industry's marriage to the state is long standing. A blizzard of subsidies comes as guaranteed loans, depletion allowances, tax-free bond financing. A state-guaranteed market called the government stockpile justifies in the name of national defense the storing of $750 million worth of aluminum at depots throughout the United States.[6]

The supreme ransom is delivered by transmission line. A tax on electricity proposed by Senator Warren Magnuson (D-Wash.) in 1972 brought a suggestion from sources friendly to aluminum that each user in the country pay $1.20 a year, to be stepped up to $240 for the biggest users. This 200:1 graduated tax rate is just only in the eyes of an industry whose plants consume several million times the electricity of the average householder. In 1940 the 4-1/2 billion kilowatt hours going to aluminum amounted to 2.5 per cent of the electricity generated in the country; in 1950 industry's share was 3.4 per cent; in 1960, 4.3 per cent. By 1980 aluminum may consume as much as 5 per cent of the total electricity generated in the United States.[7]

Aluminum's power is built upon rate structures riddled with inequities. In fiscal 1970 the Bonneville Power Administration, a Department of the Interior bureau which sells the energy from the federal dams in the Pacific Northwest, sold about 40 per cent of its electricity—just over 22 billion kilowatt hours—to aluminum plants accounting for perhaps one-third of the nation's ingot capacity. The basic rate was $18.60 per kilowatt year, one of the lowest rates in the nation. This steal takes place under cover of economics: dams built without reflecting costs to the environment, absurdly low interest rates on the dams, discounts for interruptible power supplied on a firm basis,* more discounts for power used next door to a dam. The John Day Dam on the Columbia River is the largest in the free world, and nestled next to it, soaking up the energy, is Martin Marietta's giant aluminum plant with pot lines nearly two-thirds of a mile in length. Researchers are beginning to think about such trivia as the effect of higher electricity rates on the homeowner's use of his waffle iron, but the Bonneville Power Administration is firmly committed to stable rates for the aluminum industry until at least 1980.

Inflicting damage and not paying for it is another popular technological subsidy. The economic wisdom of this policy is summed up in the memorable remark of the manager of the Reynolds Metals plant in Troutdale, Oregon: "It is cheaper to pay claims than it is to control fluorides."[8] Judging from the number and variety of suits against the aluminum industry, it's still cheaper to pay claims than to control fluorides. Cheaper yet is to do neither.

One of the most notable cases in this regard was the 17-year fight of Paul and Verla Martin to protect their 1,500 acre cattle ranch east of the Reynolds plant in Troutdale.

---

*The interruptible power category, no longer available from BPA, gave lower rates to customers who bought subject to prior demands of buyers assured of "firm" power.

Martin caught the attention of the company lawyers when he erected a billboard on his property denouncing Reynolds for killing his dairy cattle. He was sued for that, and his own damage suit against Reynolds was met by a phalanx of top attorneys from the likes of Harvey, Alcoa, Georgia Pacific, Weyerhaeuser, and the Association of Oregon Industries.[9] Years later Paul Martin died. His widow sold out to Reynolds.[10] The technology got its breathing room. While some succeed by confronting a legal system that puts a premium on high-priced lawyers, understanding experts and long waits, many do not. The questions are only how big the industrial subsidy will be and for how long will it run.

No industry grows and fluorishes without planning for the entities of the state whose policies make a difference. The aluminum industry honed its skills as a state planner throughout the fifties and sixties, winning one favor after another. Political influence and behind-the-scene deals were in order, though in retrospect they seem to lack the life-and-death fervor of latter day collisions over the technology. Three examples of plant siting controversies convey the spirit of the occasion.

Oregon and Washington learned the hard way about aluminum influence in the 1960's as they sought to outgrovel each other for the favors of Intalco Aluminum (jointly owned by American Metal Climax and the Howmet Corporation) which eventually settled on a site near Bellingham, Washington. Intalco got the expected gifts from the Bonneville Power Administration—$4.3 million for transmission lines and a substation, a long-term contract for power to be provided without significant interruption at the cut rate for interruptible power.[11] Help came from the Whatcom County Public Utility District which agreed to build a $500,000 water line; the Port of Bellingham found $200,000 for a deep water dock; and the Great Northern Railroad, future beneficiary of freight shipments, volunteered about $50,000 worth of needed trackage in addition to supplying the land for the site. But the "irreducible" advantages of the Washington site were said to be a tax give-away, now appropriately named the "Intalco tax law," a bit of fiscal engineering that cost the taxpayers $25 million in two years but by 1969 had done nothing to lure new industry into the state.[12] "Oregon's constitution prohibits such tax favors," wrote one commentator.[13] "That situation drew cries of 'socialism' from bitter Oregonians, but it didn't deter Intalco."

Harvey Aluminum was another pace-setter in the plant siting game. The company came into being, flourished and matured with the support of the state and its wartime needs. During 1952 the government was anxious to get new producers into the industry to help with expansion during the Korean War.[14] As part of the deal, Harvey got a rapid tax write-off (85 per cent of a $65,240,000 investment over a five-year period) assured by a certificate of necessity from the Defense Production Authority. The General Services Administration came through with a commitment to buy up to 270,000 tons of the early aluminum output "and, if necessary, make advance payments on this output to help the firm finance construction."[15] The Bonneville Power Administration was to provide front door transmission line service.

Preliminary construction began in May 1953 but ran into a principle: the Eisenhower Administration was insisting that only crucial military items like titanium should qualify for federal handouts. This brought the threat of a suit for breach of contract from Harvey. As a result, a sweet deal became still sweeter in the form of a federal guarantee on Harvey's borrowing to finance the plant, said to be a "new concession" granted by the General Services Administration as "part of the price of the out-of-court settlement."[16] Government spokesmen were subdued but not contrite: "We are simply making good on commitments more than two years old. If the proposal came in today, we wouldn't touch it."[17] An Associated Press story noted: "Officials today insisted nothing has been sacrificed except an administration principle . . . The Federal guarantee of any additional bank borrowing required by [Harvey] does not establish a precedent for other companies seeking to enter the aluminum field."[18] Nor, the country was promised sixteen years later, would precedents be established by federal guarantees on borrowing by a company threatening to depart from the aerospace field.

A third example of industrial siting by heavy politics comes courtesy of the Northwest Aluminum Company which was interested in locating a plant on Guemes Island off the coast of Washington State in the late 1960's. In the Pacific Northwest the key to land use for the electroprocess industries is the Bonneville Power Administration. Northwest Aluminum went to Bonneville and got a long-range power commitment—"without the knowledge or consent of the affected states," an irate Governor Dan Evans was to say later.[19] The states weren't consulted because they didn't count.

With the Bonneville contract secure, all that remained was the familiar pattern of pressuring local planning authorities until they saw things industry's way. A show called a public hearing proceeded on schedule, while the serious work between Bonnneville, Northwest Aluminum and the county commissioners was conducted behind closed doors. A zoning change emerging from this "governmental" process predictably hewed closely to options held by the company.[20]

That would have ended the matter were it not for feisty

Seattle lawyer, John Ehrlichman, representing property owners on Guemes Island. Ehrlichman argued that behind-the-scene deals in "executive sessions" made a mockery of the planning process. He took his case to the state supreme court, winning a judgment upsetting the decision of the county commissioners as offensive to due process.[21] (Judging from the work going on behind the scenes in the NIPCC, Ehrlichman left his monument to open government in Seattle when he traveled to the White House to be a key advisor to President Nixon.) Northwest has since sold out to American Metal Climax which is planning to develop another site at Warrenton, Oregon. The first order of business was the quiet consummation of an agreement with BPA consenting to the assignment of the power contract to the new owner.

The aluminum industry's long-accustomed role as the government's step-father made it well prepared for the crises that would come with the awakened interest in environmental issues. The industry locked up the state and the state of the art and has not come close to letting them go.

There is not a business executive in the country who would deny that tight control over operations is the key to economic success. Uncertainties eliminated from production, distribution and marketing are assurances of profitability. Risks to the technology must be banished also. When they take the form of the public regulation of allowable effluent, the best industrial security is to write the rules for the public. The technological defense swarms on the state at every opportunity.

The Aluminum Association has gone to the trouble of preparing recommended air quality standards for fluorides.[22] The numbers are obscure to the non-professional, but are said to be inadequate to protect some types of vegetation and dairy cattle.[23] They clearly afford no margin for error. They are warmly recommended in three scientific brochures distributed by the Aluminum Association.[24] They are now the law in several states.

Oregon and Washington offer a representative example of deference to this industrial expertise. Early in 1970 the staffs of the two states' agencies charged with air quality control looked around for a handle on the problem of fluoride emissions and grabbed hold of the Aluminum Association's recommendations which were just about the only recorded wisdom on the subject. The question became how best to defend this industrial insight.

Washington's Jerry Hildebrandt and Oregon's Fred Skirvin came up with the idea to invite the association's experts to attend public hearings in both states as guests of the agencies. On January 7, 1970, Hildebrandt wrote to Skirvin: "Our Board has now set a hearing on the aluminum plant and fluoride regulations for February 25th . . . at the Olympia airport. The hearing is scheduled to begin at 1:30 p.m. to allow time for Professor [W. J.] Suttie [author of one of the Aluminum Association's scientific brochures] and Mr. [Leonard] Weinstein [an industry consultant] to fly in that morning if they can. . . . Thanks for your assistance in requesting Messieurs Suttie and Weinstein. Please let me know as soon as you hear of a firm schedule so that arrangements can be made to provide the gentlemen with local transportation if they are unable to attend our hearing." A copy of the letter went to Don Winson whose Pittsburgh law firm represents the Aluminum Association. On January 20, Winson wrote to Suttie, Weinstein and Delbert McCune [author of another association brochure] spelling out these comfortable arrangements: "The air pollution staffs of Oregon and Washington have asked the Aluminum Ass'n to arrange for you to be present at the public hearings in those two states on the proposed primary aluminum industry air pollution regulations to testify in support of the fluoride positions of those proposed regulations." The hearing "has been scheduled for 1:30 p.m. [on February 25] to permit you and any others from the East to travel in the morning. . . . Pete Hildebrandt of the Washington staff has offered to provide transportation for you from the Seattle-Tacoma Airport to the hearing in Olympia as well as transportation to Portland after the conclusion of the Washington hearing. . . . I suggest that Joe Byrne be the coordinator in the Northwest with regard to your appearances since I will not be able to attend the hearings." Copies of Winson's letter went to, among others, Harvey's Joe Byrne, J. C. Dale of the Aluminum Association and Alcoa's L. V. Cralley, all three of whom sit at the right hand of the throne as conspirators on EPA's Primary Aluminum Industry Liaison Committee about which more will be said.

In addition to getting the Aluminum Association's views in person, the state staffers also got them in writing. They sought to plumb the opinion of recognized authorities and soon discovered the aluminum industry owns the science like it owns the pot lines. Although head-counting is unscientific, it tells much about balance among those who look into the less publicized industrial pollutants. Thirteen names appeared on the original list of experts whose opinions were solicited by the state staffers. Of these, three (Weinstein, Suttie and McCune) were brought in courtesy of the Aluminum Association to defend the regulations; others testified for Harvey during its legal difficulties; another was Harvey's Joe Byrne; still another, Washington State University's Donald Adams, has been Intalco's defender for years and a recipient of its research funds. A single spokesman, A. C. Hill, a biologist at the University of Utah and choice of the growers as arbitrator in the Harvey litigation, could be said to represent those anxious to avoid fluorides. Hill wrote that "your proposed standards are not adequate to protect vegetation from extensive injury from gaseous fluorides."[25] He recommended ambient standards less than half the levels thought tolerable by the aluminum interests and, by extension, the state governments regulating them.

Of the thirteen experts, the only one not tainted by some kind of bias was Dr. Walter Heck of the Division of Economics Effects Research, National Air Pollution Control Administration, who sent a strong letter to NAPCA's San Francisco office:[26] "I was somewhat surprised at the recommended standards because they represent the values applying to The Dalles situation. . . . There is adequate information in the literature to suggest that these levels are barely marginal and give no latitude for error. I believe the states of Washington and Oregon would be doing a disservice to the aluminum industry, the farmers and the general public by adopting these standards." The disservice Heck protested is well on its way to being written into law by many states with a fluoride problem.

It is not spectacular corruption that helped the aluminum industry write the state standards for fluorides. Conscientious administrators, trying to do their best, were simply denied options. The premises of the law succumbed to the planning prowess of the Aluminum Association—the data, the experts, the weight of opinion, the common assumptions came from a single source. Its purpose is to minimize liability for damage caused and prevent disruption of existing technology.

While the aluminum industry was locking up the state standards on fluorides, they got plenty of help in putting down another unacceptable business risk created by a momentary legal embarrassment. The problem was that the

Bonneville Power Administration had included in its ancient form contracts a remarkably strong prohibition against water pollution. The contract clause was titled "Conservation of Natural Resources" and read as follows: "The Administrator will not be obligated to deliver power pursuant to this contract whenever, in his judgment, plants or operations of the Purchaser would harm or detract from the scenic beauties of the Columbia River Gorge, or the waste products from such plants or operations would harm or destroy the fish or other river and aquatic life or otherwise pollute the waters or drainage basins of the Pacific Northwest."[27]

This lawyer's language gave the administrator life and death authority over industrial polluters in the Pacific Northwest. Asking whether BPA customers generate wastes that "would harm or destroy the fish or other river and aquatic life or otherwise pollute the waters" is to seek the obvious. BPA buyers read like a list of Who's Who of the region's polluters—joining the aluminum plants were the utilities, pulp and paper and chemical industries.

Clearly BPA wasn't about to chop the lines it had built for its customers because of embarrassing legalities. The one occasion it was asked to do so[28] brought the reply that "this is the first such notice that Bonneville has received charging ITT Rayonier with operations which might justify termination of power deliveries."[29] (Polluted water doesn't count as sufficient notice.)

But no industry respectful of its planning responsibilities can tolerate a sword being dangled over its power lifeline, even one wielded by hands as friendly as those of the Bonneville Power Administration. There was a chance, however small, that outsiders could force the administrator to act. Unacceptable risks for the modern corporation are eliminated; the law conforms to the technology.

During 1970, as the aluminum industry wrote the state standards on fluorides, BPA and its customers rewrote the "dangerous" anti-pollution clause. The process consisted of a series of Bonneville drafts being whittled down by enthusiastic advisers. A letter from R. Ken Dyer, manager of the Public Power Council ("A Foundation Program of the Northwest Public Power Association") expressed the widely shared opinion that Bonneville's contract provisions can be influenced by the buyers: "We believe substantial progress has been made on these subjects, and that the documents reflect BPA's consideration of PPC suggestions. However, we believe it is reasonable to insist upon a few additional changes in the General Contract Provisions and the BPA Industrial Sales Policy. . . . We believe it is of vital importance that these last remaining details be finalized in a mutually satisfactory manner."[30]

There was mutual satisfaction with the final contract provisions, especially the anti-pollution clause. The rewrite job makes it virtually impossible for the administrator or anybody else to deny power to a polluting buyer.[31] Profound change without a ripple is the epitome of the efficient technological defense.

An immediate beneficiary of Bonneville's relaxed policies on pollution control was Intalco Aluminum Company, whose plant near Bellingham, Washington, was already one of the largest in the world when its pot lines started up in the fall of 1966. The company has "spared no expense in efforts to control pollution" was the kick-off pledge of Ian MacGregor, president of American Metal Climax and soon to become a member of the National Industrial Pollution Control Council. The company's idea of sparing no expense on water pollution control was to bully state officials into allowing a five-year delay in the installation of a primary treatment system, which finally went into operation late in 1971, just about the time a marked deterioration in water quality was detected over an area in excess of four square miles in the vicinity of the plant outfall.[32] Intalco's notable contribution to careful land use was to divert illegally millions of gallons of effluent from its plant by a ditch to a natural drainage way flowing over a bluff and across state-owned tidelands. The bluff eroded, depositing 300,000 cubic yards of earth on the beach. The company's contribution to air quality was over 800 pounds per day of hydrogen fluoride and 15,000 pounds per day of particulates. These emissions began taking their toll of local cattle in as little time as it takes toxic chemicals to react with biological systems.

Bonneville got a chance to endorse these policies when Intalco showed up in 1971 asking for a contract amendment increasing its firm's power.[33] A less deserving candidate for administrative leniency would be hard to find. Department of the Interior Regional Representative L.B. Day sent a tough memo on the subject to BPA Administrator H.R. Richmond: "Excessive air [pollution] being discharged from this particular plant has come to my attention repeatedly. . . . Until such time as I ascertain the environmental controls that this corporation is making, I recommend withholding consummation of this power sales contract agreement." The Department of the Interior's Bureau of Sport Fisheries was tougher yet: "[S]erious environment[al] degradation has and will continue to occur with plant operation. Air and water pollution may be substantially abated with operation of control devices now under construction. However, we believe that additional treatment and control mechanisms should be installed whenever possible to reduce [environmental] degradation." Air and water pollution control systems were described as "either inadequate or nonexistent."

Tough talk, no action. The views of the Bureau of Sport Fisheries never were forwarded to Richmond, apparently because the staff man who was supposed to do it "was piqued at the Bureau's failure to meet his 'September 1' deadline."[34] Richmond wasn't interested in finding out for himself, either. Intalco quickly promised to meet state water pollution standards and pledged to spend $14 million more to control air pollution. Fittingly, for the corporation Governor Evans welcomed five years earlier as a "truly good neighbor . . . in every respect," it was now time for the corporation's president to affirm that "these actions will show our good intent of becoming responsible industrial citizens of the state."[35] In a matter of days Intalco had its power contract and protection from the official threat that had prompted its momentary commitment to social responsibility.

"To summarize," an agency spokesman told a House subcommittee in December 1971, "BPA has continued to strengthen its environmental contract provisions and monitor compliance through recognized agencies."[36] The explanation for BPA's reluctance to crack down on Intalco? "Specifically," Richmond explained, "we were not informed [by state agencies] of any official complaint having been received relative to Intalco's operations."[37] Extensive, documented damage, a dozen pending lawsuits, a notorious record of intransigency, files full of angry correspondence, and the BPA administrator looks for an "official complaint." Such selectivity confirms the suspicion that the government tends to welcome the role of the trained seal assigned to it by the likes of the aluminum industry.

It is recognized that the lawyer is an advocate, hired to put the interests of his client in the best light. The scientist is someone finer, supposedly scrupulously objective in the search for truth, oblivious to public relations diversions, legal one-sidedness, economic necessities. That science can be bought and sold like a full-page ad or hustled like a lawyer's brief is unacceptable. But the science that looks at the aluminum industry, like the law, suffers a bad case of temporary blindness.

The industry's investments in science and engineering do not differ materially from its investments in bauxite deposits and coal fields. The objective is total control, and it is accomplished by classifying research, channeling funds to friendly hands, stacking advisory committees. The aluminum industry has preferences in science, and they survive concerns about technological abuse remarkably well.

A universally warrantied sanitizer of scientific truth is secrecy. The aluminum industry uses secrecy to make sure uncomfortable truths can't be turned against the technology. It goes without saying that a study paid for by the Aluminum Association will be released if and when it conforms to group notions of propriety:

> The study to which you referred concerning gaseous effluents from aluminum production was completed on schedule but not released. Our reason for withholding this is due to the fact that in our view the study was incomplete. We have since provided additional funds to Battelle Memorial Institute to expand on the scope of this study and expect that the final results will be available within the next two months. As soon as we have received final clearance from Battelle, I will be most happy to provide you with a copy.[38]

It is disappointing but predictable that industry's preferences for classified research turn up in grants to universities. A boiler-plate clause found in a Kaiser Aluminum research contract on the "Measurement of Particle Size Distribution at Tacoma Works of Kaiser Aluminum"[39] begins with an acknowledgment that plans or data prepared by the researcher or disclosed to him are "the property of the owner." The contract obligates the researcher to limit access to employees directly concerned with the performance of the work. Persons gaining access to data are obliged to sign written agreements promising not to use it except as approved by Kaiser. And the researcher also must go to the extreme of notifying in writing "officers and employees having access to any of said information as to the source and confidential nature thereof" and is obligated to restrain "officers and employees from making unauthorized disclosures and use of any said information."

The ostensible purpose is to protect against disclosure of proprietary information that could help a competitor. Conceivably trade secrets exist, even in this industry born not too long ago of a common mother, Alcoa, and operating with a fundamentally unchanging technology for eighty years. But the lawyer never goes wrong in drafting his suppression clauses to include the kitchen sink. A very real reason for swearing secrecy on subjects as sensitive as the "Measurement of Particle Size Distribution at Tacoma Works of Kaiser Aluminum" is to make sure the data doesn't get into the hands of the enemy, notably the public or its anti-pollution authorities. The whistle-blower who would do something so rash as to tell the truth about the effects of emissions from an aluminum smelter would offend carefully contrived legal restraints and professional engineering good manners which habitually elevate loyal service above something so intangible as the public interest.

Since research is a function of money invested, it can

fairly be said that the truth is available to anybody who pays for it. Dr. Oliver Compton of the Department of Horticulture, Oregon State University, has done work on experiments involving fumigation of fruit with fluorine to determine how much causes damage. Portland, Oregon, Attorney Arden Shenker questioned Compton in a courtroom:

> Q. Why didn't you make that study before 1967?
> A. I imagine the money was not available for this particular study.
> Q. Well, speaking of money, you were working at Oregon State University at the time, were you not?
> A. Oh, yes.
> Q. Do you know how much the Harvey Aluminum Company contributed to the project [on] which you were working in money?
> A. I'm not sure exactly.
> Q. Give me an approximation then.
> A. I wouldn't even mention a figure.
> Q. They did make contributions, didn't they?
> A. I understand they did.
> Q. Did you understand them to have been substantial contributions?
> A. Just contributions.
> *The Court:* I presume everything is relative.
> *Mr. Shenker:* I suppose.[40]

Research services on the effects of fluorides on living things are unavailable to some. In 1967 Grant J. Saulie representing Japanese-American vegetable growers hit by the fluorides from the Harvey plant, wrote to request help from the State of Washington.[41] He was told that specialists were available elsewhere: why don't you contact Professor Don Adams at Washington State University who "has ex-

tensive experience with fluoride problems and may be able
to suggest a course of action for your client."[42] A letter
from Saulie to Adams brought this response from the director of Washington State's Engineering Research Division: "The Engineering Research Division is a scientific
investigative body devoted to basic and applied research in
technological areas for the general good of the state. We
do not undertake test work as such nor do we knowingly
engage our efforts for one party in a legal dispute with
other parties. Since you appear to be seeking a court action
for alleged damages," came the sanctimonious expression
of neutrality, "[w]e would not be interested in working on
this problem under these circumstances."[43] A persistent
Saulie was put down harder a year later: "[A] full blown
fluoride   pollution   surveillance   program   requires
meteorologists, fluoride specialists, bio-chemists, agriculture and animal scientists with adequate field laboratories
as well as back-up laboratories. . . . costs to mount such a
program [are] in the area of $75,000."[44]

Investigating fluorides may be a rich man's folly but it
is pursued with enthusiasm at Washington State University's College of Engineering. The college's advisory board
is top-heavy with industry influence and could not be without a man from Alcoa. Trade associations and corporations
are a principal source of the college's research funds.[45]
Intalco bought a seat on this exchange by funding research
into the environmental impact of its plant near Bellingham.
Short on publishing, long on defense of the employer is the
thrust of this academic venture. "Even as scientists," wrote
the dean of the Western Washington Huntley College of
Engineering, "we have experienced difficulties getting information concerning the over 5-year old study on air pollution."[46]

A request for a copy of the contract between Intalco and WSU's College of Engineering brought not the contract, but additional evidence that some academic institutions revel in their role as industrial laboratories. The director of the Engineering Extension Service sent three reprints on fluorides with the following notation: "Some of them are rather technical and I trust you will need a chemist to interpret the meanings. I hope you will use them with discretion."[47] WSU researchers have been exercising discretion for years, typically on the side of the aluminum industry.

The industry invested early and wisely in the science of fluorides. The chief market to be cornered was the Boyce Thompson Institute for Plant Research which was set up by the late Colonel Thompson with a broad charter to "attack any problem of plant or animal life."[48] The only "fixed requirement" is that the research "will promote the welfare of mankind, help stabilize society and the results will be made freely available to the public." Back in 1951 Dr. F.C. Frary of Alcoa got an idea on how to promote the welfare of mankind and "suggested that the Institute could be of great service to industry and agriculture if it would undertake a definitive research program on fluorides."[49]

By 1963 growers in the Pacific Northwest were beginning to get an insight into the service offered. In one courtroom session, Managing Director George L. McNew testified that Boyce Thompson was "a privately endowed nonprofit institution devoted to the public welfare by the late Colonel Thompson."[50] Institute members were said to be experts in air pollution and in other problems affecting agriculture. On cross-examination, a few more details were extracted by Portland, Oregon, Attorney James Morrell:

Q. Dr. McNew, yesterday you told us a little bit about the organization that you represented, the Boyce Thompson Institute. Isn't it a fact that the Boyce Thompson Institute receives contributions from industry for research in industrial fields?

A. We have a number of grants and contracts with the Federal Government—

The Court: No. The question is, Doctor, does private industry make grants to the concern.

The Witness: Yes.

The Court: That is the question

The Witness: Yes

The Court: All right. Proceed.

By Mr. Morrell:

Q. Have you received any grants from the aluminum companies around the country?

A. In a group of 12 or 13—

The Court: No. Doctor, the question is do you receive grants from aluminum companies. Just answer the question, and then if you have an explanation you may give it.

The Witness: The answer to that is Yes. It is one of 12, I believe, different organizations that contribute toward air pollution studies.

By Mr. Morrell:

Q. And is one of the 12 aluminum producing companies?

A. The fertilizers, oil, any number of phosphate fertilizers, get interested in this—the people get interested in this, and others.

Q. So you have received grants from phosphate fertilizer producers; is that correct?

A. Yes.

Q. Isn't it a fact that phosphate fertilizer plants are also large fluoride-emitting plants?

A. Yes.

Q. You have received grants from aluminum companies
as well; is that correct?

A. That is right. They pool their resources with us.

Q. Has Harvey Aluminum contributed in this field?

A. I believe one year or two years, yes. The last two
years, I think it is.

Q. You received grants from Harvey Aluminum; is that
correct?

A. Yes.

Q. Now, actually, a couple of your men came out here to
the Dalles area a couple of years ago, did they not?

A. That is right.

Q. Was that at the request of Harvey Aluminum Company?

A. I believe that is right; yes, sir.

Q. And you came out last Sunday, also at the request of
Harvey Aluminum?

A. That is right.[51]

Seven years later in another courtroom, another ardu-
ous effort was undertaken to find out about Boyce Thompson's promotion of the welfare of mankind. The Institute's
David McLean was cross-examined by Arden Shenker:

Q. Does Harvey Aluminum Company continue to make
its contribution[to the] $200,000 per year that indus-
try contributes to Boyce Thompson Institute?

A. Two hundred thousand dollars per year?

Q. Yes, sir, at least that was what it was in 1963, I assume
it is a lot more now. Do you know whether Harvey's
contribution continues in the same percentage of the
$200,000 annual contribution of the industry for the
non-profit research?

A. No, I don't. I know how the budget for the air pollution program is worked up, in general, and it's not
nearly to that amount. The institute as a whole has 40

or more senior scientists and the air pollution program has but five, so our budget does not include that whole $200,000, there are some programs that are entirely—

Q. Harvey continues to contribute substantially to Boyce Thompson?

A. I wouldn't say "substantially" but they do, as many of the industries, and the phosphate industries, the public health service.

Q. How many of the aluminum industries contribute to Boyce Thompson?

A. There are 14 sponsor industries. These are not all aluminum industries.

Q. Practically all of them?

A. Most of them

Q. The sponsors are the aluminum companies, is that right?

A. Partially, yes.

Q. Who else sponsors the project on which you work besides the aluminum companies?

A. The National Air Pollution Control Administration of the Public Health Service, Health Education and Welfare, and funds from our endowment.

Q. You forgot about the phosphate industry, they—

A. I mean as industrial sponsors, yes.

Q. All right, sir. That has been true all the time you have been working for Boyce Thompson and a considerable time before you began working for Boyce Thompson?

A. Since 1951, I think

Q. How many growers contribute to Boyce Thompson research?

A. No growers.[52]

Over the years, Boyce Thompson mans the skirmish lines in defense of fluorides. Boyce Thompson's Delbert

McCune is ready to write a fluorides criteria document for the Aluminum Association and another for the American Petroleum Institute.[53] Boyce Thompson's Leonard Weinstein serves as an arbitrator in a court case on industry's behalf. McCune and Weinstein show up together to make sure Oregon and Washington adhere to the industrial norm on fluoride standards. Boyce Thompson witnesses frequent courtrooms, invariably on the defense side and invariably on industry's behalf. As "neutral" experts before state agencies and the courts, as authorities to be quoted, they sell a service, and the service helps the Institute and the aluminum industry.

Science strains under twenty years of incest where financial interests, common attitudes and joint ventures intersect. Boyce Thompson has underestimated adverse effects at The Dalles, has shown extraordinary solicitation for control costs, has expressed interest in developing air pollution-resistant plants and chemical spray defenses[54] — a diversionary mythology that obviates crackdowns at the source. It's all part of the twenty-year plan.

Industry-purchased science does not automatically become government policy. To accomplish that, an intermediary is often needed, and none is more efficient than the nation's most prestigious body of objective thought, the National Academy of Sciences. There is, surprisingly, little difference between the science paid for by the Aluminum Association and the science promulgated by the Academy.

Not too long ago the Academy was enlisted by the Air Pollution Control Office of EPA "to provide a scientific basis for APCO to issue an air quality criteria document on airborne fluoride."[55] The criteria document will point the way toward the emission limitations that will be required of the aluminum industry by the federal government.

The nine members of the academy panel on fluorides include familiar names : Dr. Leonard H. Weinstein of the Boyce Thompson Institute; Dr. Frank A. Smith, co-author of the Aluminum Association's publication on the effects of fluorides on human health, and John W. Suttie who wrote "Air Quality Criteria to Protect Livestock from Fluoride Toxicity" for the Aluminum Association. Delbert McCune of Boyce Thompson "served as a special consultant [to the academy panel] and was especially helpful with questions related to the effects of fluorides on vegetation."[56] Suttie, Weinstein and McCune were the trio who testified in support of the Oregon-Washington fluoride standards under the auspices of the Aluminum Association.

Suttie's work for the National Academy of Sciences borrowed heavily from his work for the industry. "Reviews directed specifically toward fluoride toxicity in livestock as an air-pollution problem have been prepared by Suttie,"[57] he wrote anonymously, citing himself. In both publications Suttie insists that "[a]lmost every ailment to which cattle are subject has been claimed by someone to be a sympton of fluoride toxicity."[58] In both publications he downgrades a report on fluorosis in cattle in the Columbia River Valley, which stressed poor reproduction, diarrhea and overgrowth of the hoofs as symptoms of the disease.[59]

What's wrong, one may ask, with the Aluminum Association getting a corner of scientific talent good enough to speak for the Academy? It's preferable to go to the best. And scientists surely do not misrepresent data, whether wearing the hat of the Aluminum Association or the National Academy of Sciences.

The difficulty is that every nuance, every bias counts in a conflict that turns on parts per billion. The National Academy's, i.e., Suttie's, repudiation of the Columbia River Valley study, for example, could be used to discredit that effort if relied upon in the courtroom. Any scientific judgment about permissible standards, moreover, is fraught with value choices about trade-offs society must make. The hard question is whether it asks too much of a researcher to cash a check from industry, on the one hand, and yet be sufficiently independent to bite the hand that feeds him, on the other, if that prescription is in order.

A minimal precaution for sanitizing the National Academy's research panels is full disclosure. Timidly, the Academy has gone so far as to ask a committee member to disclose activities and commitments "others may deem prejudicial to the work of the committee or compromising of his independence of judgment."[60] Who hears about these entangling alliances? "This information will be shared with all committee members and protected, thereafter. Only under unusual circumstances will such information be included in a committee report or otherwise made public, and then, only after consultation with the committee member concerned." A scientist is called upon to echo a judgment that may profoundly affect the nation's economy, technology and environment. But somehow it's an invasion of privacy to ask him to disclose whether he's made a few dollars espousing the views that may become the law of the land.

While forces friendly to aluminum were taking care of the basic science at the National Academy, the industry was keeping a firm lid on the applied science that was under discussion at EPA. It goes without saying that the government needed an industry advisory committee to help in the preparation of its comprehensive study of the pollution control prospects for aluminum. The big producers, including Alcoa, Anaconda, Reynolds and Intalco, pull up a chair at this table. Joe Byrne sits in for Martin Marietta; J.C. Dale and Attorney Don Winson represent the Aluminum

Association. Why EPA needs a trade association lawyer sitting on a technical advisory committee defies explanation. Why the industry needs him is easier to understand, for he is there to make sure nothing appears in the report that can jeopardize the technology of his client.

The industry started one step in front, since EPA's choice of contractor for the study was Singmaster & Breyer, an engineering consulting firm that has been rendering services to aluminum companies for years. In case of doubt about first loyalties, the liaison committee was ready with helpful advice. Don Winson fully understands that no future lawsuit against an aluminum company for air pollution can avoid consideration of the capabilities of control technology and its costs. Casting doubt on the state of the art thus quickly became the committee's chief function:[61] the control cost estimates of the contractor were said to be demonstrably too low; references to equipment or control systems that were applicable but had not been *"tried"* in the industry should be deleted; claims of equipment manufacturers ought to be downplayed; foreign data eliminated; references to trade names of control systems stricken. This coordinated peevishness is designed to make sure the EPA study's definition of the "best technology" reflects what industry is now doing, not what it can be expected to accomplish. There is a difference.

By the end of 1970 even Singmaster & Breyer was losing patience: Some plant operators returned no questionnaires; others left serious gaps including "incomplete information concerning particulate fluoride emissions, carbon and bake plant emissions."[62] More than a year later, with the report nearing completion, the industry deluged the contractor with new data. EPA explained: "This will cause the contractor . . . to rewrite considerable pages in the report as well as redo many graphs and tables. At this late date, the contractor will probably require more money to finish the contract as well as delay the issuing of the final report.''[63]

The strategy worked unfailingly. As of June 1972 the Singmaster & Breyer study had not seen the light of day. Five years of federal authority to do something about fluorides brought neither relief nor a promise of it. Today, as in less turbulent times, the technology of aluminum production is not the people's business. They may pay for it, suffer because of it, clean up after it, pretend to govern it. But the technology's defenders insist upon their own solutions.

The word conspiracy is often used too loosely. It means, simply, an agreement to accomplish unlawful ends; or more broadly, an agreement to accomplish anti-social ends. Conspirators, at law, need not know each other. They need know only that somebody else is going along with the program.

Ask whether the word conspiracy is too strong to describe the domination of economics, politics and science of those who fight under the banner of the aluminum industry. Laws do not pass, science does not come into being unless that industrial sponsor approves. Economic theories are turned upside-down by a system of favoritism that is as elusive as it is massive. The corporate aims of protecting the product and planning for its growth corrupt and overwhelm the institutions that question the inevitability of it all. Influence is not occasional but routine, not accidental but systematic, not modestly successful but thoroughly so. If a technological conspiracy exists, this is it.

8 THE HAZARDS OF WHISTLE-BLOWING

*"And to a world that would be free" the
Humboldt Bay nuclear power plant "will
be the example of free enterprise in a free
America."** *

*We believe that PG&E management per-
sonnel have fulfilled their responsibilities
in a conscientious reliable manner. The
Company has been cited only a few times
for items of noncompliance and these items
have been of a minor nature. There has
been no evidence of irresponsible practices.** *

It was a minor incident, but it was important to Bob
Rowen.[1] Bob worked as a radiation safety officer at Pacific
Gas & Electric Company's Humboldt Bay nuclear power
plant in Eureka, California, and he took his job seriously.
He was supposed to keep a sharp eye out for safety problems at the plant. In August 1969 Bob was helping techni-
cian Raymond Skidmore and supervisor Gail Allen take
smear samples on a shipping cask, which weighs about
eighty tons and is used to carry spent radioactive fuel

*The Hon. John Pastore, quoted in PG&E Life, Nov. 1963, p. 3.
**Report of the Atomic Energy Commission, Safety Evaluation By the
Division of Reactor Licensing, Dkt. No. 50-133, Humboldt Bay Power
Plant Unit No. 3, July 22, 1968.

from Humboldt Bay to a reprocessing facility in New York.

The law respects the risks of radiation. A Department of Transportation regulation says a shipping cask is contaminated if more than 2,200 counts (disintegrations) per minute can be detected on each 100 square centimeters of surface area.[2] But cleaning up shipping casks can be bad for business: high radioactivity means the cask must be scrubbed with alcohol and detergents, another day's rental charge possibly lost.

Allen was in a hurry to move the shipping cask to save the company $70,000, and he knew how to make a shipping cask fit the law. He took smears using a very light touch.[3] Sure enough, his samples averaged 400 disintegrations per minute, well within the limits. But Rowen's samples averaged 2,600 counts per minute. Skidmore's, too, were high. "When [Allen] saw the difference between his smears and mine," said Skidmore, "he made some comment that he knew we wouldn't believe he deliberately got favorable samples." But this supervisor figured the samples were close enough, so he brought Rowen the shipping papers for the cask already filled out for the 2,200 the law requires. Rowen protested, but he signed after changing the 2,200 to 2,600. Then he recorded the incident in the Control Technician Log Book:

> G. Allen asked Rowen to sign the release papers for the spent fuel shipping cask stating the contamination level of the cask to be less than 2200 d/m, when in fact they were greater than 2600 d/m. Further, G. Allen gave Rowen directions to take final smears for determination of release conditions on the top and bottom avoiding the middle areas on all sides of the cask, when just previously, R. Skidmore took smears of the middle areas to find out of limit conditions.
>
> R. Rowen

Putting criticism on paper for Atomic Energy Commission inspectors to read does not win praise from management. The next day Rowen was called before the Plant Engineer Edgar Weeks for a "counseling session."[4] "I reminded [Rowen]," Weeks wrote, "that he had a responsibility to promote harmony, not disrupt it. I reminded him that I was still not satisfied with his job performance and believed there was considerable room for improvement."

The shipping cask incident was the beginning of the end for Bob Rowen. It was followed in February 1970 by a dispute over radiation-contaminated pipe, some pieces of which had been sold. "Rowen was adamant that [the purchasers] be notified of this matter," his supervisor reported, "but we maintained that it would serve no purpose to call them simply to tell them they had no problem."[5] More bad news went into the Rowen file: "Rowen accused me of attempting to cover up the facts, misconstrue and misinterpret the applicable regulations, and loophole seeking tactics. He became angry and irrational; and when he likened me to a Lt. Calley . . . in my actions, I informed him that there was no point in discussing this matter further with him."

Another Rowen indiscretion was recorded in May 1970 when he attempted to raise safety questions at the company safety meeting, something about which he had been warned in the past. He even went so far as to attempt to speak to an AEC inspector. "I had the impression Bob was satisfied with the discussion we had on this subject," Edgar Weeks wrote, "and wouldn't try to see [the AEC inspector] on his own. I advised him that this was, in my opinion, inadvisable." This same man was to say with pride on another occasion: "Our operation is a fishbowl."[6]

Rowen's attempts to help others peep into the nuclear fishbowl at the Humboldt Bay plant offended corporate policy and maligned its nuclear technology. Disruption of corporate harmony must be eliminated, whether it be caused by unsatisfactory laws, hostile administrators or disloyal employees. Rowen was fired. The company cited a history of misconduct. A referee of the California Unemployment Insurance Appeals Board decided the "principal cause" of the discharge was Rowen's extreme safety consciousness: "His efforts in this direction were to some extent a reproof of the more sanguinary attitude of certain of his supervisors. His attempts to bring this matter to the attention of the Atomic Energy Commission and to the attention of fellow employees were also greatly resented."

The company took other steps to rid itself of Rowen's memory: it inspired a police investigation of Rowen and his friends, alleged the existence of a conspiracy to stir up discontent about safety practices within the plant, launched a public relations campaign to dispel community concerns, suppressed information about in-plant safety and wooed the Atomic Energy Commission into a slap-on-the-wrist response. It was just another day for the technological defense.

Thoroughness comes naturally to Pacific Gas & Electric Company, one of the most powerful and profitable privately owned utilities in the world.[7] PG&E owns and operates sixty-five hydroelectric and twelve steam electric generating plants. The energy from these plants is carried through 908 substations, 16,600 circuit miles of transmission lines and 76,100 miles of distribution lines to the company's 2 million customers. Its gas customers are served through 24,200 miles of pipelines. It owns 250,000 acres in California, making it the eighth largest private landholder in the state,[8] behind such notables as the Boise Cascade Corporation [Chap. 4] and Standard Oil of California [Chap.2]. PG&E capital expenditures came close to

$415 million in 1970 and $467 million in 1971, and will reach $2.4 billion for the period 1972 through 1975.

PG&E holds the first license ever granted by the AEC for a privately financed nuclear power plant—at Vallecitos, California.[9] The company was in at the ground floor as a member of one of the original study groups appointed by the AEC to explore the potential of electric generation with nuclear fuels. Today, PG&E is an unquestioned leader among industrial developers of nuclear energy and deserves accolades for accomplishments in geothermal, hydroelectric and natural gas technologies.

Winning corporations extend their planning into the political and economic environment in which they thrive. PG&E shares directors with major land interests like the Kern County Land Company, California Packing Corporation and the DiGiorgio Fruit Corporation,[10] and with major banks like Bank of America, Wells Fargo, Crocker-Citizens, and the Bank of California. Among its top shareholders are Equitable Life, New York Life, Prudential. PG&E is interested in water pollution, so a company man sits on the California Advisory Commission on Marine and Coastal Resources. The company is interested in local politics, so twenty-four executives contribute money to every supervisory campaign in San Francisco. The company is interested in developing good working relationships with important people, so it operates Caribou Lodge, a resort on the Feather River near San Francisco. The company is interested in its image, so it spends millions on public relations each year.

Like other great American corporations, PG&E preaches free enterprise and practices subsidy. It has backed a John Birch Society film given wide distribution[11] and contributes to the Foundation for Economic Education (FEE), a group urging such "reforms" as repeal of the income tax, United States withdrawal from the United Nations, and abolition of public post offices, public education, public roads and public power.[12] PG&E executives send out rhetoric condemning the "advocates of statism"[13] while the corporation hauls in the benefits of statism— hundreds of millions worth of technology for use in the Vallecitos plant and other facilities, token charges for the fifty-year Federal Power Commission licenses on its hydro projects, captured generation from public agencies sold back to the public at a handsome markup, government insurance in the event of a holocaust at one of its nuclear plants.

PG&E's version of free enterprise was manifested during one of the first major conservation struggles in America —the damming of the Hetch Hetchy in Yosemite National Park in the early part of this century.[14] The original idea was to allow the project only if the City of San Francisco generated and distributed low-cost hydro power. But for four decades PG&E has used its political pull in San Francisco to head off full public development, benefiting nicely by grabbing the power from the hydro-generating facilities wholesale, then selling it retail in the city. Selling the public its own power is a plum that runs into tens of millions a year. Secretary of the Interior Harold Ickes once summed it up nicely by defining "to Hetch Hetchy" as "to confuse and confound the public by adroit act and deceptive word in order to turn to private corporate profit a trust set up for the people."[15]

PG&E further sharpened its technological defenses in the battle of Bodega Bay, famous both as the setting for

Alfred Hitchcock's movie *The Birds* and as a preview of modern conflict over power plant siting.[16] The company proved to be a domestic at heart, preferring home-made news and home-made science.

Hal Stroube, who for some time was PG&E's publicity man on nuclear energy issues, once reminisced about the successful counter-attack against negative thinking at Bodega Bay. Thousands "heard our story" through speakers' bureaus and "countless" TV and radio interviews, he said. "In every case, after they heard the facts—when they had their questions answered—they were satisfied, and were *with* us." Stroube credited public relations successes to the company's intensive efforts to "win the confidence" of the press: "We found that newsmen paid *less* attention to the anti's as they found that their stories and accusations and suspicions just didn't jibe with the facts we gave them." He protested because the AEC's choice of words was sometimes a source of difficulty for men like himself whose business it was to make the public understand: "I suggest that those gentlemen [from the AEC] have the *responsibility* as well as the *ability* to [replace the word 'hazards' in the title of the 'Preliminary Hazards Summary Report'] *within a week of returning to Washington.*"[17] Masking high private risks with a low public voice is the company's preference.

PG&E's scientific difficulties at Bodega Head arose because of questions about the rock foundation of the site and the proximity of the proposed reactor to the San Andreas and other fault zones.[18] The company was equal to the challenge: It ignored its consultant's recommendations for further study by structural and soil mechanics engineers and played down his warnings about site instability. The earthquake problem was met by getting the AEC to relax its criterion so Bodega would qualify.[19] This march to siting success was interrupted, not by second thoughts by

PG&E, but by a report of the Geological Survey confirming fears about the gravelly foundation and the consequences of an earthquake.

To this day, PG&E clings closely to its science. The company speaks proudly of environmental impact studies at its plant sites,[20] while critics quote biologists in the Department of the Interior's Fish & Wildlife Service as describing the efforts as "P. R. documents" and "bogus research."[21] But there are ways to control research more dependable than hiring a tame researcher.

PG&E's method is a contract, and the attorney who writes contracts, remember, is intent upon protecting the interests of his client. Major design changes, enforced plant relocation, heavy liabilities for damage inflicted are not in the interests of the client. The practice in California, widespread in other states, is for a state agency to contract with a power company to make pre- and post-operational studies of a proposed site. Under the typical agreement,[22] PG&E secures an express commitment from the State Resources Agency binding it to refrain from opposing PG&E license applications before other agencies. In return, PG&E pays for the study and offers several lawyer-conceived, unenforceable promises to "minimize erosion," to make the installation "aesthetically compatible with its surroundings," to hide the plant facilities from public view "to the extent feasible"[23] and so on. PG&E also "agrees to furnish the Resources Agency with copies of all geologic reports pertaining to the site filed with other governmental agencies."[24] Those not filed with other agencies apparently aren't given to the resources agency.

A pattern emerges as contracts on impact studies are read: PG&E retains the agency (which is friendly from the outset) to do a study in return for a promise not to cause any trouble. The company conducts part of the study itself, specifies hypotheses to be explored, influences, if not controls, publication. To keep this murky chain of command visible, one of PG&E's agreements goes so far as to provide: "All personnel of [the] Department or [PG&E] shall at all times when engaged in any of the activities contemplated hereunder, remain the employee of either the Department or [PG&E] respectively, and shall not for any reason or purpose be considered the general or special employee of the other party to the . . . agreement."[25] Sometimes a clause in the contract makes it easier to tell the difference between the state and the corporation.

The test of science is its accuracy. PG&E's science is only coincidentally designed to be accurate. Above all, it must be harmless to the corporation.

The insulation sold by lawyers and publicists proved useful at Humboldt Bay as it has elsewhere on the PG&E system. The plant located about four miles southwest of Eureka in Humboldt County, California, began operation long before the public had heard of a power crisis or pollution. The *Eureka Times-Standard* came up with 120-point type in red ink to "emphasize the warmth of [the] reception,"[26] and the company reciprocated with attractive pamphlets depicting children playing happily in a school yard under the protective shadow of a power plant stack. The nuclear unit is operated along with two conventional steam generating units.[27] As nuclear plants go, Humboldt Bay is old (full power was first achieved on May 4, 1963), small (65,000 kilowatts), inefficient (operating above the estimated design cost of eight mills per kilowatt hour) and technologically obsolete (boiling water reactor). Eighty or so employees are responsible for the plant's operation, with about twenty primarily concerned with the nuclear unit.

Minor administrative problems at Humboldt Bay, fore-runners of the Bob Rowen incident, were resolved in favor of the technology. In March 1966, the North Coast Regional Water Quality Board, in response to a request from the company, formally upped permissible concentrations of radioactivity in the Humboldt Bay plant's outfall flow.[28] The reason for this administrative generosity—that extensive monitoring turned up no evidence of increasing radioactivity—was still good three years later when the board relieved PG&E of a detailed self-monitoring program and replaced it with a looser regime "deemed adequate" by the Department of Health.[29]

The kind of monitoring "deemed adequate" by the Department of Health is an occasional smile from PG&E. Passing the buck is a familiar pattern in the regulatory world, and when it comes to nuclear power, the buck always seems to return to the utility. The regional water quality board relies upon the Department of Health.[30] Who does the Department of Health look to? Almost exclusively, PG&E. The only action undertaken by the public agency is to analyze duplicate samples once a year for the purpose of verifying the company's analysis.[31]

Routine collection of marine samples and consulting on marine radiobiology would be done, PG&E told the AEC in 1966, by the Humboldt State College Foundation. Humboldt State College students collect the samples which are then sent to the PG&E laboratory for analysis.[32] To make sure nothing goes wrong a lawyer's protective clause appears in PG&E's contract with the Humboldt State College Foundation: "Basic oceanographic data and biological observations gathered during the course of the survey may be used by contractor [the Foundation] for academic purposes only. This shall exclude, however, information regarding the radioactivity of samples collected. Contractor shall disclose no information to third parties concerning the services performed under this contract without express permission from [the] company."[33] This is that unvarnished pursuit of truth known as self-monitoring.

Several years of this type of monitoring of the marine environment has turned up no radiation levels significantly above background. This probably means there is no problem at Humboldt Bay. Of course, gathering reliable data is not the primary aim of PG&E self-monitoring. The primary aim is to protect the technology.

PG&E did run into some serious technological trouble at Humboldt Bay, occasioned by leaking stainless steel fuel cladding that eventually had to be replaced with zircalloy. With radioactivity in the plant's stack gases inching toward the AEC's permitted maximum, it was time to try for a change in the law. Company President S.L. Sibley gave the reasoning: "Authorization [for the increase] is requested by May 1966 because operation of the unit is expected to be affected by the present limits within a few months."[34]

PG&E didn't get authority from the AEC to change the law to accommodate the practice. Children in the school yard are still there and still under fire. *Science* calls the Humboldt Bay reactor the "dirtiest" in the nation.[35] The latest available data (for 1969) show the plant emitted 490,-000 curies of noble and activation gases (thirty times the AEC's proposed limit) and sixty-five curies of halogens and particulates (sixteen times the proposed limit).[36] The technology is in jeopardy but not in limbo.

The single institution that presents high business risks to PG&E is its principal governmental overseer—the Atomic Energy Commission. Lately the AEC has been embroiled in nuclear power plant controversy, first over whether its low-level radiation standards were adequate to protect the general population from risks of cancer, then over the safety of the emergency core cooling systems in commercial reactors. The low-level radiation fight was relieved in 1971, not without official ignominy, when the commission joined its strongest critics[37] by proposing a hundred-fold reduction in off-site radiation standards. The safety and reliability of the plants themselves is a question now being openly contested.

There is a third area of conflict that remains entirely out of sight and mostly out of mind. The issue involves the safety of the 200,000 or so people who presently wear film badges to monitor radiation exposure in AEC-licensed operations[38]—they compose a population under fire that will expand significantly as the number of nuclear power plants in the U.S. increases from twenty in 1971 to 250 by 1990.[39] The drastic reduction in off-site exposures proposed by the AEC has no application to nuclear workers, so they can legally be subjected to radiation a thousand times in excess of the standards soon to be set for the general population. This disparity should at least raise eyebrows, given the concurrence of most geneticists that there is no "threshold" level below which no damage from radiation occurs.[40]

Another disparity that should give pause is that the AEC happens to pursue its task of protecting more people from more radiation while tolerating industrial abuses outlawed in virtually all work establishments. The legal excuse is that the Occupational Safety and Health Act of 1970 left out employees of AEC licensees, for the AEC already had a program to protect workers from on-the-job hazards.

The AEC has confidence in its radiation safety precautions. It points to the record: no major radiation disasters, few proven injuries on the job.* It points to the need for enforcement: virtually none. Under the law a licensee (including an operator of a nuclear power plant) violating a radiation standard can be prosecuted criminally, taken to court and enjoined, stripped of its license or hit with a civil penalty. As of late 1971 *none* of these sanctions had been invoked against a licensee operating a nuclear power plant.[41] Letter writing is the bite of the law.

Congressional hearings document this rosy picture.[42] "This recitation of malfunctions that you gave us," observed Congressman Craig Hosmer (R-Calif.), "at least the way you gave them, sounded about as innocent as a nun's confession. . . . You don't have any lurid ones that you are hiding someplace?"

"No, sir," responded the Commission spokesman.

"Those various noncompliance incidents that you testified about, what causes noncompliance? What is behind it? Is it just inattention? Is it deliberate? Can you tell?" Hosmer persisted.

"I would say most of them are mistakes, just the failure of employees to follow the details of the procedures that they should be following."

"Does management have anything to do with it?" the Congressman asked.

"Certainly this is all part of it," he was told. "Licensee management has to have a very positive program of insisting that all procedures be followed. I think in the large organizations you see the better disciplined and better operated systems."

In the AEC's view, PG&E runs one of the "better disci-

---

*Not usually mentioned is what is perhaps the worst occupational health travesty in the history of the nation: fully 6–1,100 or nearly 20 per cent of the 6000 men who work as underground uranium miners are expected to die of lung cancer from preventable occupational exposures.

plined and better operated systems." The commission has expressed this confidence in many ways. It accommodated its reactor siting criterion on earthquakes to fit the Bodega application. It has praised the "conscientious reliable manner"[43] in which the business of safety is conducted at Humboldt Bay. It has found management to be "extremely responsive" to "constructive criticisms."[44]

Bob Rowen walked into this den of self-satisfaction in April 1971. He had been fired by PG&E for raising safety objections about the Humboldt Bay plant and was determined to tell the commission everything he knew. The Rowen-inspired investigation blossomed into one of the major AEC efforts of the year, taking months to complete. In all, Rowen detailed forty-nine separate instances of unsafe practices and procedures prominent during his employment at Humboldt Bay, many of them established by written evidence.

Rowen told inspectors from the AEC's Division of Compliance about the scrap metal and shipping cask incidents. He told of workers forgetting to wear film badges (which measure exposure). He explained how the devices used to screen employees for radiation before they left the plant had been doctored so the workers could be hustled out. (Careful records of exposure are crucial to the lawyer's world of deciding who gets compensated for low level radiation injuries.[45]) He told of the routine work permits allowing exposures of only five to fifty millirems, which in practice became 2,500 millirems.

Rowen laid bare the inadequacies of PG&E's radiological monitoring tests said to cover "grazing rabbit thyroid glands." The company had confidently outlined the tests for the AEC: "Domestic rabbits are raised at the plant site on a diet mainly of fresh grass to supply the thyroids for analysis." It all sounded quite scientific. "Milk and rabbit thyroids are forwarded to Hazelton Nuclear Science Corporation for iodine-131 analysis. . . . Rabbit thyroids are mounted in a 3-inch by 3-inch diameter plastic container and counted on a 3-inch by 3-inch Na I (Te) crystal."[46] But there were some problems, Rowen explained. Nobody liked to go out in the rain to cut the grass to feed the rabbits. Furthermore, rabbits don't like to eat grass. Eventually, the rabbit pellets purchased to supplement the diet of the "grass-fed" rabbits gradually became the main course. The sophisticated thyroid analysis conducted at the Hazelton Nuclear Science Corporation might as well have been run on rabbits from Timbuctoo.

Rowen exposed the policy of announcing inspections for the fraud that it is. The Humboldt Bay plant engineer once told how tough it is to stand inspection:

> When I find out an inspection is coming and we get a tentative date, I notify the supervisors and I say in the message, be sure your house is in order, fellows. And, I'm sure they get the word out. Just like, if you're driving along and somebody says, there's a black and white car, and you glance down at the speedometer, I mean it's . . . quite frankly, yes, I get the word out to my supervisors to make sure your records are in order. We're going to have an inspection. I do this for several reasons. One is to save time, which is, if you've got everything in order, you can get through with these inspections in two days rather than a better part of a week.[47]

Another reason is to make sure the AEC doesn't find anything that can hurt.

The same engineer, Edgar Weeks, expounded on the wisdom of a plant employee talking to an AEC inspector: "I couldn't stop him from going to see the inspector after work or picking up the phone and call[ing] at any time. He could do it any time he wants to. But I don't advise that kind of action. I think it's unethical, actually."[48] It is a peculiar kind of ethics that condemns protecting oneself and enforcing the law.

But there is insight here about freedom of information in some "fishbowls." However difficult it is to track down the effects of environmental contaminants in the general population, special problems are found inside the plant. Outside, the evidence is available to anyone who looks; the subjects are usually cooperative, independent and communicative. Inside, where exposures are worse by orders of magnitude, the areas investigated are private property, and trespassers are kept out by security guards or controlled by rigid limits on clinical investigations, reviewed always by lawyers worried about liability. Subjects are unwilling or reluctant witnesses, knowing well that acts of disloyalty are the actual, if not the assigned, cause for discharge. When the safety inspector walks through the plant arm in arm with a member of management, down-to-earth confessionals by the men at the lathe are not likely to develop.

Rowen told commission inspectors of the practice of hopscotching the workers around the radioactivity. This is a common prescription for occupational health. Transient employees at Humboldt Bay (like painters) didn't know as much about radiation safety as the others and often got stuck with the worst jobs—handling "hot" tools, wearing dirty clothes, working in areas that were contaminated. Under AEC standards, employees can be subjected to only three rems per quarter or five rems per year.[49] Rowen reports cases "where guys have been put to work beneath the reactor for a special job and received most of their quarterly (three month maximum) in a couple of hours. Of course the company only needs them for that one job, so it doesn't care. And the employee is told he's some kind of hot shot handling a special assignment."[50]

October 28, 1971, was judgment day for PG&E. L. D. Low, director of the AEC's Division of Compliance, wrote to Frederick Searles, company vice president and general counsel, to advise him of *two* items of noncompliance with regulatory requirements—a late report on exposure to radiation on an individual terminating employment (Rowen) and another incident involving unknown exposure of workers to airborne concentrations of radioactive materials. In addition to the "items of noncompliance," the commission identified four "certain other matters" which "warrant your consideration." Among these was a finding that "in at least one instance, one of your employees was discouraged by plant management personnel from talking with an AEC inspector on matters of safety interest."

Having been served with a piece of paper formally called a "notice of violation," it was time for PG&E to write back to say that nothing was wrong in the first place, but that everything would be taken care of anyhow. That happened, and that was that. End of investigation, end of enforcement.

The findings were indelibly recorded in whitewash. The AEC's *modus operandi* seems to be to forget about violations now cleared up, accept the company's version if the evidence is conflicting, ignore the evidence that can't be explained away. The commission badly fumbled Rowen's allegations about manipulated records, harassment of employees, abuses of the policy of announcing inspections. The charge that the company cleans up the plant in anticipation of AEC inspections brought this response from one investigator: "If they've cleaned it up, what's your point?" The charge that PG&E violated radiation limits incorporated in its license was put down decisively: "We do not

routinely cite licensees for exceeding radiation limits spe-
cified in their procedures if those limits are more conservative than limits established in the AEC rules and regulations." The charge that PG&E authorized release of a
contaminated shipping cask was answered as follows:
"PG&E advised that clearance was obtained from the [De-
partment of Transportation] prior to shipment by phone."
PG&E advised the Department of Transportation that it
got telephone clearance *after* the shipment departed.
Before or after, what's the difference? Either way, the law
fits the technology.

PG&E responded to this brush with the law in the tradition of the great corporation in crisis—prevarication,
retaliation, a strong dose of public relations. Typical was
the back of the hand given *Eureka Times-Standard* reporter
John Read who asked the company seventy-one questions
probing the Rowen allegations and practices at the plant.
PG&E wanted the questions in writing and got them in
writing. Two months later came the response—complete
with seven answers. None of the questions about Rowen
was deemed worthy of a reply.

It would be enough, one would think, to deprive a man
of his job and destroy his reputation out of corporate
necessity to suppress information about radiation safety.
Being thorough, PG&E does better than that. Bob Rowen
and some of his co-workers were engaged in nothing less
than industrial sabotage (the company's phrase) by asking
questions about safety. Saboteurs are dealt with summarily.

The company's theory was disclosed in an argument
before an arbitrator on the propriety of firing Rowen and
co-worker, Forrest Williams:

> We believe that the evidence will show that there was a
> common plan and a common design on the part of these

two people . . . —and I might add one more. In fact, in the nomenclature of one of the grievants himself, there were three dissenters in the plant, three people who dissented, who felt that the company's safety program was not adequate, it was unsafe. And they set themselves up to protect, sometimes openly and, I believe the record will demonstrate, sometimes in a more insidious manner to carry this protest not only to the supervisors but to also at the same time degrade or cause the reputation of the supervisors to be downgraded in the eyes of the employees.[51]

In the company lawyer's view, the employees' acts were "tantamount to industrial sabotage and inimical to continuation of their employment."[52]

"If there is any conspiracy involved in this case," Rowen and Williams responded through their lawyer, "it is the conspiracy of certain company personnel to get rid of employees who ask embarrassing questions."[53]

One way to prove a conspiracy is to ask the local police to investigate. However accustomed he was to serving the company, Eureka Police Chief C.E. Emahiser was more than a little surprised when contacted by PG&E about a plot among the power plant employees led by Bob Rowen.[54] Emahiser met with Robert Taylor, PG&E local personnel manager, and talked to "someone" in the general office in San Francisco who told him the incredible details: Plans were afoot to blow up the Humboldt Bay nuclear power plant. No policeman in the country would refrain from acting upon such startling intelligence, and Emahiser did not. He conducted his investigation, and sent his findings to PG&E. By the end of 1971, Emahiser's enthusiasm about the crime of the century had waned considerably. He told John Read, the *Eureka Times-Standard* reporter, that "he had taken the [PG&E] report in good faith, later having the feeling he had been used." He said he "couldn't remember" who gave him the information he put in the report he prepared on Rowen, but admitted it "was no longer in police offices because of the possibility of being leaked to outsiders."

Leaking a police report to Pacific Gas & Electric Company and to nobody else including those named in it, makes the company-town constabulatory look a bit like a corporate Pinkerton. Frank Morgan, the attorney representing Local 1245 of the Electrical Workers, wrote to the local district attorney making the point: "The purpose of this letter is to urge you, in your capacity as District Attorney, to advise the Chief of Police that he can and should permit Mr. Rowen access to the report. It is our opinion (albeit formed without specific knowledge of the report's contents) that refusal to permit Mr. Rowen to read the report as well as whatever communications from PG&E prompted its preparation, raises serious constitutional questions. This is particularly so insofar as the report appears to have been prepared in response to the private inquiry and interests of one citizen of [the] state (PG&E) and was not instigated or motivated by any overriding interest."[55]

An inquiry from Morgan to PG&E drew a surprising response from attorney L. V. Brown:[56] "Chief Emahiser's letter of June 3, 1970, was reviewed by myself and the Company's Security Department. I was of the opinion that the information was of no value to the company and extraneous to the employment of all persons named in the letter. The company has, therefore, destroyed the letter and no part of it has been recorded or contained in any record maintained by Company. Further, for the reasons given above, the information contained in the letter will not be utilized in any manner with respect to any of the persons named therein. I am of the opinion," this PG&E lawyer wrote, "that this action by [the] company should be sufficient reason for you and the individuals named to disregard any further action towards Company." Dressed up as an expression of good faith, this timely file-cleaning protected PG&E from the embarrassment of an almost certain-to-be-successful lawsuit by Rowen and covered up the role PG&E played in the preparation of the report. The practice of shredding documents—perfected by ITT after columnist Jack Anderson's disclosures linking an antitrust settlement to a political contribution—is not unknown in other circles.

Rowen was forced to sue the City of Eureka and Chief Emahiser for the privilege of discovering how he might have been defamed by PG&E. If the report ever surfaces it will provide useful memorabilia on a corporation's frame of relevancy as it undertakes investigations of its critics.*

Because Bob Rowen has courage and persistence and a penchant for collecting pieces of paper along the way, some things will change. His experience points up deficiencies in AEC regulations protecting workers from harassment and intimidation on the job long obscured by happy assumptions about corporate cooperation and helped along by a policy of announcing inspections.** The Rowen case should revive concern about inadequacies in workmen's compensation laws for radiation injuries, which ten years ago gave rise to proposals for a federal compensation act. His experience adds impetus to the conventional, by now almost trite, assumption that the AEC can't simultaneously accomplish both its promotional and enforcement responsibilities.[57] The slap on the wrist given PG&E by its official brother is a slap in the face to a regulatory policy promising heavy fines, injunctions and jail sentences.

Rowen's case also puts disclosure in context. To a cor-

---

*In October 1972 Rowen won access to the report by court order. He is presently considering further legal action.
**As this goes to press in October 1972, the AEC is on the verge of initiating lengthy procedures to upgrade its in-plant safety regulations.

poration like PG&E public information is a dangerous thing, and controlling it a major part of the company's business. Workers are denied information at safety meetings, inspectors deceived when they tour the plant, journalists put off when they ask questions, dissenters fired. From this point of view, it makes no sense to advise a buyer of scrap metal that the material might be contaminated, since the only consequences would be a damaged reputation, loss of future business, or conceivably, legal liability.

PG&E treatment of Rowen is helpful in emphasizing the deficiencies of the laws protecting workers aggrieved about safety questions and the ineffectiveness of the AEC's intercession on behalf of the men working within nuclear power plants. But it's important in another way. PG&E's letter of discharge, undoubtedly reviewed by a lawyer, is but a trifling example of the excommunication of one whose waves rocked the corporate ship. The letter was written, not to Bob Rowen, but to an arbitrator, appeals board referee, grand juror, inspector, journalist, future employer or future reader of this book who might believe what Bob Rowen says. For the record as written by PG&E, Rowen is just another dissident who threatened to beat up his supervisor. He is said to have had a history of misconduct, "including among other things, harassment of the company and its supervisors, insubordination, failure to follow instructions, frequent instances of unsatisfactory job performance and a poor record of attendance." Ask the company about Rowen, and that's what you'll be told. Don't doubt either that the evaluation hurts in the circles where the company spreads its influence; it's supposed to. Rowen got in the way of the technological defense perfected by free enterprise in a free America.

9 SILENT NIGHT

*Engine and airframe manufacturers have indicated that it is not economically feasible to modify our existing transport airplane fleet in order to markedly reduce noise. As a consequence we must look to the future for new models in which noise considerations have played a part in the early design.**

*If you are thinking we are going to retrofit that fleet with new engines and nacelles— forget it. The cost is simply beyond economic reason. The air carriers cannot support it.***

The ceremony had been planned for a long time. It was to be a solemn moment on the steps of the Lincoln Memorial, honoring the craggy-faced Lincoln biographer and poet, Carl Sandburg. President Lyndon B. Johnson was to deliver the main address and present an award. As the

---

*Harvey M. Hubbard, National Advisory Committee for Aeronautics, Langley Field, Va., Airplane and Aircraft Noise, in Proceedings of the Fourth Annual National Noise Abatement Symposium 81 (1953).
**Hon. Secor Browne, Chairman, Civil Aeronautics Board, Speech of Aug. 11, 1970, Before the Administrative Law Section, American Bar Association.

opening speeches began, a low-flying jet on its final approach to Washington's National Airport roared across the sky, drowning out the words and causing people in the audience to cover their ears. An angry President beckoned an aide and told him to phone the airport and divert the flights. It was done. The speeches were delivered without further aerial accompaniment.[1]

Not too long after Lyndon B. Johnson prevailed upon the authorities to send the planes over somebody else's speechmaking, James Madison made a similar plea.[2] But this was not the James Madison who lived at the White House. It was the James Madison who lived at 1106 Gatewood Drive, Alexandria, Virginia. The jets kept coming. James Madison did the moving. In September 1971 he found another home.

Madison got out of the way of a potent industrial force. The airlines and aircraft manufacturers together, Civil Aeronautics Board Chairman Secor Browne is fond of stressing, are the nation's largest employer. The carriers, manufacturers and parts manufacturers are closely knit contributors to high technology. Imperatives that drive the modern industrial state permeate the aerospace community: the end product requires years of planning and development and vast amounts of capital. The challenges to technological management and control are imposing, the successes without parallel, the failures monumental.

The industry is perpetually money-hungry. Incestuous relationships have developed with banks—interlocking directorates, extensive leasing and loan arrangements. A move is afoot to declare illegal the heavy stock holdings in the carriers of the leading banks and insurance companies.[3] There is a hypothesis, not without documentation,[4] that the financial dependence of the airlines makes them mere subsidiaries of their financiers. Next to Pan-Am, the First National City Bank of New York owns more 747's than anybody else.[5] With so many supporters, it is not surprising that the technology seems to have a life of its own: "An industry that had a rational control over its own technology would not introduce the 747 at this time because there is no need for it. It is an airplane at least five or ten years ahead of its time in terms of growth of the market. The plane . . . , in fact, may result in bankruptcies of some airlines, either bankruptcies or mergers."[6]

By conventional standards of free enterprise, there are vast risks in business ventures riding on billion dollar investments in unknown technologies with returns postponed for a decade. But then, conventional standards of free enterprise don't apply to aerospace. Risk reduction by politics has been the rule, long before the Lockheed bailout removed all doubt.

The subsidies roll in—a trust fund fed by fuel taxes to pay for airport development, military equipment available at a fraction of full cost, massive public contributions for research. The CAB's Secor Browne sees the aircraft of the future as being sired by the state: not that the government should design the plane, but it "should step in to help with the down payment, with the progress payments and with the delivery in the form of a guaranteed loan, in the form of accelerated depreciation and finally with an interest structure."[7]

A rash of rate-cutting back in the thirties called for a shot of industrial politics to assure it wouldn't happen again. "If the CAB didn't exist the airlines would have had to invent it and as a matter of historical fact—they did," Browne explained.[8] So the CAB exists—to parcel out routes, grant rate increases, authorize mergers and keep competition under control. Never satisfied, airline executives are prone to view the agency as the chief obstacle to industrial gratification, instead of an extension of corporately created certainty.

The aerospace subsidy most familiar to 9 million Americans is an ear-shattering experience typically described as noise exposure "incompatible with residential living."[9] The people experiencing it are mostly the poor and the blue-collar workers. Probably four-fifths of them have never flown, missing out on the technological benefits to which they incessantly pay homage. They are unhappy watching their homes gradually become unlivable while their property taxes continue to rise.

There is no relief in sight. By 1978 24 million Americans will be suffering from excessive aircraft noise.[10] Pessimistic are the predictions of no less an authority than the Airlines and Aircraft Sub-Council of the National Industrial Pollution Control Council, chaired by Charles C. Tillinghast, Jr., chairman of the board of Trans World Airlines:

> The aircraft and engine manufacturers, recognize, that despite claims for the coming availability of 'quiet engines,' future commercial aircraft are not likely to have significantly quieter engines than the wide-bodied aircraft currently entering service, and overall noise levels at and around airports will show only small improvement over the next 10-15 years as a result of further changes to the engine or nacelle.[11]

The reasons the noise lingers on are two. There is the conventional explanation that the free market brings no competition in noise control, for the benefits accrue not to buyer or seller but to the public at large. There is another part of the story that recognizes major industries with a heavy stake in certain technologies will resist change to the extent of subverting the government to achieve it.

The conventional explanation is a good one. The market has brought a better thrust-weight ratio, improved fuel consumption, higher climbing and crosswind capabilities. It has brought different colored paint, the wide-bodied look, champagne on one flight, leg room on another. But the airlines are no more interested in tacking something unproductive onto their technologies than are the copper smelters or auto makers. Buyers and sellers understand the problem. An executive of American Airlines shrugs his shoulders and looks at the seller: "No noise-reducing retrofit kits of any description whatsoever can be bought today."[12] A Boeing vice president stares back at the buyer: "No amount of regulation can cause a financially imperiled industry to adopt a massive, negative change program. Resistance by the industry is predictable and will be effective."[13] Without a willing seller and buyer, there is no sale.

The market has gone through the motions—and failed. A peek behind the industrial proprietary screen into the performance specifications of, say, the Boeing 747, a few years ago would have disclosed noise level guarantees running from the manufacturer to the airline customer. But even these guarantees were not designed to meet airport noise regulations then in effect.[14] And when the guaranteed specifications were not met, nobody did anything about it because a $25 million airplane is not rejected on delivery as simply as a can of bad tuna fish.

The explanation of a technological conspiracy to resist improvements in noise control is believable, too. The thirty-two commercial air-carriers have a rich tradition in group-thinking through the offices of the Air Transport Association of America. ATA's stated purposes are "to represent the common interests of its member airlines to public and governmental agencies,"[15] and it is in the common interests of the airlines to head off regulatory efforts aimed at the capital equipment. An example of the technological defense at work on a government that ought to know better was the ATA-negotiated, industry-wide "smokeless" jet retrofit program, a farce generally credited with cutting down non-toxic particulates while increasing more noxious constituents such as nitrogen oxides.[16]

Technological conspiracies among the manufacturers convene in groups like the Aerospace Industries Association and the Manufacturers Aircraft Association. When the Justice Department filed suit in March 1972 against twenty manufacturers for conspiring to suppress competition in airplane research and development, the Manufacturers Aircraft Association was duly recognized as a defendant.[17] Government lawyers allege a conspiracy with origins going back to a 1928 patent-sharing agreement among the manufacturers. The conspiracy to suppress improvements in noise control is of more recent vintage.

No acoustical consultant is needed to suggest that jet airplane noise can be controlled in three ways: at the source, by juggling take-off and landing operations (shades of the smelters' "closed-loop" [chap. 3]), or at the receptor (moving him out of the way, furnishing him with earmuffs, fattening the plaster on the walls of his home). Unbiased professional and popular opinion alike no doubt would opt for common sense: if something is noisy, shut it up.

But this hypothetical opinion poll founders on the technological defense which has followed the classic pattern of conspiracy through trade groups, creation of myths that ignore the technology, enforcement of the myths through law and science.

Defensive research got off to a predictable start back in 1959 with the founding of the National Aviation Noise Abatement Council, made up of the airport operators, pilots, airlines and manufacturers.[18] By 1968 the operators had withdrawn, charging the airlines and manufacturers were laying "a smokescreen over the problem of jet noise." Behind the smokescreen would be the operators spending billions to buy out property owners. Next to depart were the pilots who understandably were unhappy with NANAC's profound interest in makeweights like flight operation maneuvers as the key to the noise problem. Not being a member of NANAC, the public never got a chance to walk out. But you can be sure it would have soon discovered that "people oriented" solutions are popular mythology among equipment manufacturers and users: Can the people move? Keep their windows closed? Adjust their sleeping hours? Combat irrational fears?

A policy of studying people is a good way to give the technology a perpetual lease on life, for human responses to noise are peculiarly subjective, immune from generality. Those who invest in technology prefer to be left with a debate so they study the people. A 1971 publication of the Air Transport Association came right to the point: "Of first priority is research on the subjective effects of aircraft noise on people."[19] NIPCC's Airlines & Aircraft Sub-Council also knows what's important: "There is a need for comprehensive, well conducted studies to determine how aircraft noise does, in fact, affect the physiological well-being of human beings, to find out what levels of noise are acceptable."[20] A 1971 speech by Marcy B. Fannon of American Airlines took the "study of the people" approach to its industrial extreme: "Research into human response to aircraft noise is crucial to help establish whether technologically achievable noise reductions are 'meaningful.'"[21] Fannon set priorities: "The most pressing basic research need —both in terms of understanding today's problems and guiding future research—is in the area of human response to aircraft noise. Until a more complete understanding is achieved of what type of community noise is 'acceptable,' judgment as to where the noise research funding should be expended will at best be speculative." This is an appeal to reason and study, and it is an excuse for doing nothing.

The CAB's Secor Browne, an acknowledged favorite of the industry, delivered a series of speeches in 1970 that captured the irony of the differing degrees of urgency that attend research for people and research for profit. In March 1970 he said, "I am not saying that our national fleet must [not] have its noise impact on the community reduced; I merely point out that we ought, rather quietly, to determine what these figures will be and how long rationally must be required to achieve such programs as retrofit."[22] In April he found the data on retrofit to be "incomplete and insufficient,"[23] and in May he protested that "[w]e don't know what we're talking about [on retrofit]."[24] But in June Browne suddenly changed the tune. "I realize that this will mean acquiring and installing a lot of equipment which, relatively soon, could be considered obsolete in view of our technological capability today. But we don't have time for any more research and development. We have barely time to fit the system with the equipment we know how to manufacture at this time."[25]

Why did the caution of May become brashness in June? In May, Browne was talking about a noise retrofit technology that protects people; in June he was talking about an air traffic control technology that brings increased sales and earnings.

Not so strangely, the carriers' emphasis on anything but the technology found its way into federal research priorities. In 1970, the Federal Aviation Administration, for example, proposed to spend approximately a million dollars per year for ten years on aircraft noise evaluation and control programs.[26] (This comes to about 1/5,000 of what operators say it would cost them to buy out homeowners at ten airports.) The FAA's research effort anticipated an "integrated plan,"[27] looking at the source, the transmission path and, sure enough, the receiver. Of the agency's fiscal 1972 request of $3.5 million for research on evironmental quality, about half ($1.8 million) was allocated to "noise suppression," of which half ($.9 million) went to source suppression.[28] Part of this was to be devoted to examining "techniques of noise measurement, data reduction and analysis, plus refinements of yardsticks for evaluation and rating of various levels of aircraft noise." That left a drop in the bucket for what was important: "development of equipment or devices necessary to be installed, attached, or actually built into engines of various designs to suppress that noise which is generated."

The FAA research effort on airplane noise, if it has accomplished little else, has contributed to the technical jargon of the noise testers and to the profits that come from refining the dialect. The "bewildering array of terminology," says one sophisticated reporter, is "complex and confusing even to those well versed in acoustics."[29] So we have decibels (db) to measure sound pressure, perceived noise decibels (PNdb) which take into account subjective responses to each of the octave bands, and effective perceived noise decibels (EPNdb) which add still greater refinement by judging the effects of tone and duration.

Measuring noise has become a business. The short generation that brought jetport grief to tens of millions throughout the world has seen a tiny acoustics firm organized in 1948 grow into Bolt, Beranek and Newman, Incorporated, the U.S. government's principal off-campus laboratory on noise matters. With a technical staff of 300 scientists and engineers and a like number of support personnel, BBN now has offices in a half-dozen U.S. cities.[30] BBN measures noise, recommends insulation materials, predicts the community response. It has measured the noise characteristics of many of the civil jet aircraft in service today and has described noise exposures, present and future, for over thirty civil airports in the country. BBN developed the perceived noise level for rating aircraft noise —which explains the "PNdb" often discussed—and the complex noise exposure forecast (NEF) contours. When the Congress moved toward the enactment of noise control legislation in 1972, investors in BBN saw their stock take a healthy jump.

While researchers were doing such things as refining their symbolism and studying people to make airplanes quieter, the courts were doing their part to make life easy for the technology. In 1962 a United States Supreme Court decision, *Griggs* v. *County of Allegheny*,[31] imposed liability for noise damage on the operators of the airport in Pittsburgh, Pennsylvania. The court said: "Without the 'approach areas' an airport is indeed not operable. [The operator] in designing it had to acquire some private property. Our conclusion is that by constitutional standards it did not acquire enough." The effect of the decision was to take the heat off the airlines and manufacturers and put it on the operator who had the responsibility of moving the people out of the way of the technology by buying property or juggling traffic in a futile attempt to appease complainants.

Thus it was that the aerospace industry's preference for cosmetics that ignored the equipment worked its way into the dogma on tackling airport noise: preferential runways, holding patterns, turns after take-offs, delayed extension of the landing flaps. "Keep'em High" is the FAA's recent contribution to this line of learning. Climb steeply at full throttle to relieve the people downstream is one idea. No, says another school of thought, reduce thrust and climb gradually to help the people close in. Keep shifting the traffic to stay one jump ahead of the complaints. Cut the throttle when flying over the noise monitoring station, but make up the difference over somebody else. This jungle of non-regulation, non-enforcement and non-relief met the specifications of the manufacturers.

For the most part, it was enough for the operators, too. Although developers kept building near the airport (in some cases with federal financing), those who ran the airports for several years after *Griggs* escaped heavy liability. The reasons were the usual ones of damages not being high enough to attract the lawyers and the technology being too mysterious for all but the most determined. Thus it was that throughout the 1960's only one person of the hundreds of thousands suffering from the noise at Chicago's O'Hare International Airport saw fit to file suit (unsuccessfully, as it turned out).[32] By 1966 combined judgments against the operators on behalf of citizens came to less than half a million dollars, and as late as 1971 were just over $1 million.[33] A single judgment for the grand total of $12,500 had been entered against a manufacturer—Lockheed.[34] Who is to say that studying the people did not bring high dividends?

In 1968 two seemingly unrelated events took place in the conflict over jet noise. A Tennessee farmer, 68-year-old Walter King, was arrested for shooting at low-flying aircraft because the planes were disturbing his chickens.[35] And the Congress passed a law giving the FAA authority to control noise on the present fleet of jet airplanes.[36] As it turned out, both incidents had comparable effects on reducing noise. The difference was that King was summarily dealt with, for his was a common crime, not a technological crime.

"Of all the thousands of government agencies, it would seem almost impossible to rate one as the worst,"[37] said a trade journal for the electronics industries. But it assigned the honor to the FAA for its work on the air traffic control problem. That the agency deserves distinction is affirmed again by its regulation of jet noise.

The predicament of the FAA and its administrator, John Shaffer, was acute as a result of the passage of the 1968 law: It was caught between its two client groups, the airport operators and the airlines. One response to the protests would be to require retrofitting for noise control on the current fleet, notably the DC-8's and 707's, but the airlines were quick to put down that indiscrete interference with their present technology. Another would be to buy out the homeowners, but that commitment, running into tens of billions, didn't appeal to the operators. Put in this squeeze, the FAA pulled a Houdini: helped the airlines avoid retrofitting, helped the operators defend their lawsuits. The only loser was the public.

With the Supreme Court having put the operators on the hook, the best way the FAA could get them off was to make it more difficult for citizens to sue. This was accomplished by muddying up the standards for measuring airport noise and erecting procedural obstacles to those who brought suit.

Back in 1967, Bolt, Beranek & Newman did some work for the FAA on standards for developing a noise exposure forecast (NEF) for airport environments.[38] Basically, the NEF procedures provided a means for predicting the impact of noise on people (at least on those who complain) and on land use. It was developed, in the tradition of unmitigated complexity, utilizing a number of different operations (take-offs, landings, ground runups) by different aircraft. The result was recorded on an overlay of an airport map to depict graphically the noise radiating over surrounding areas from the airport runways. NEF 30 translated into seriously affected residential uses; NEF 40 recommended no residential usage under any circumstances; less than 30 anticipated no serious problems.

Since 1967, BBN has produced NEF maps for over thirty civil airports in the country starting with JFK in New York, Los Angeles International and O'Hare. As the volumes accumulated, the FAA began to take steps to avoid being consumed by its creation. The agency, for example, approved an expansion of the Portland International Airport by diking and filling a lengthy stretch of the Columbia River without so much as acknowledging the NEF forecast study in the Department of Transportation's review of the proposed airport extension.[39]

For it was soon discovered that there was a very practicable problem with the NEF's. Bolt, Beranek & Newman, despite its record for obscurity, had come up with an extremely useful tool for the wrong party. The problem was that an angry citizen could look to see where he lived on the NEF map, and he wasn't very happy about it if he discovered that the leading noise consulting firm suggested that the place he lived was better suited for a bowling alley or a warehouse. Worse, some of the angry citizens began to hire lawyers to make the same point to a judge.

When the science is being used to embarrass the technology, the time is ripe to change the science. A memo of December 18, 1968, leaked from the files of the Port of Portland, tells an interesting story:[40]

At this point, Mr. Songstad [of the FAA] requested that the conversation be off the record. He advised that there were some problems with the NEF method of measuring forecasted noise levels at airports and that there was a great deal of concern and discussion between the FAA and Bolt, Beranek and Newman. He attributed a great deal of this concern to the furor existing in Los Angeles over aircraft noise and the fact that when the NEF information became public in Los Angeles that the incidence of complaints and suits had more than doubled.

Bolt, Beranek and Newman and the FAA are attempting to find a better way of portraying the results of the NEF studies. He could not give any definite date as to when the problem might be resolved, but said that he could not foresee any hope that it would be before the end of the year. . . .

This problem was not to be ironed out before the end of 1968 nor the end of 1969 nor 1970.

Nor, as it turned out, 1971. After years of doing nothing but talking to Bolt, Beranek & Newman and the other interests, the FAA began circulating a draft order on the adoption of the NEF methodology early in 1971. It was packed with qualifications about how imprecise it was, and how unusable in law suits. It pointed out the danger of telling somebody he lived in uninhabitable territory: "Interpretations based upon predicted human response are sometimes accused of being too suggestive in the sense that people often tend to respond in the manner they believe they are supposed to respond."

Notwithstanding this effort to play down the usefulness of the NEF contours, airport operators were uneasy. Clifton A. Moore, general manager of the Los Angeles Department of Airports, expressed his anxiety at the 1971 Aviation/Space Writers Annual Meeting in Wichita, Kansas.

"As an intermediary between the interests," said Moore, "we are the meat in the sandwich." The word was out that the FAA was considering adoption of the NEF noise footprints, and that would be curtains for Los Angeles: The severely impacted NEF 30 zone contains 150,000 homes stretching 9 1/2 miles east of the airport; the NEF 40 disaster area has 65,000 homes on more than 9,000 acres. To buy out 65,000 homes would cost over $3 billion. The alternative? Slash operations by 80 per cent, declared Moore.

A June 1971 memo of the Airport Operators Council International shuddered at the prospect of the NEF contours becoming a federal standard for measuring aircraft noise:

> Presently existing NEF studies have already helped to inflame public opinion, and to focus public pressure upon the efforts of some to restrict improperly the air transport system of the United States. The NEF studies are being sought as valuable plaintiff handbooks for noise litigation. Plaintiff attorneys have submitted the studies into evidence, and at least one judge has accepted the studies as a yardstick for measuring noise liability at public airports. . . .
>
> Aside from the fact that NEF contours have stirred up litigation, they have encouraged lawsuits and complaints in areas of the community which did not formerly constitute problem areas. Plaintiff attorneys and some city planners are relying upon the NEF contours to recommend wholly impracticable land usage in the vicinity of airports. . . .

The operators demanded that the FAA take "no unilateral action" by issuing the proposed order "until the entire NEF methodology and policy have been reviewed and corrected." As a last resort, they would demand more study: "Should the FAA decide to pursue issuance of an NEF order, the AOCI respectfully requests the opportunity to continue discussions with the FAA in analyzing and verifying the NEF methodology through further research."

The FAA did better than that. Influence was not to be denied. At the four-day October 1971 meeting of the Airport Operators Council International, some good news was reported by Bert J. Lockwood, assistant general manager of the Los Angeles International Airport. The FAA officials "indicated they can't seem to develop a standard with which they can obtain the concurrence" of the contending groups, and "they want to turn over the responsibility to industry." He added, "We have a verbal commitment from them that they will let us do it."[41] In response to an unsightly headline in the New York Times—"FAA to Let Industry Help Rewrite Noise Rules,"[42] Administrator John Shaffer quickly denied that his agency was prostrate before the special interests: there would be routine consultation, not abject surrender.[43]

The FAA's collapse brought rich returns in the spring of 1972 when a court hearing complaints about jet noise from National Airport in Washington, D.C., found that the NEF contours were useful only as a planning device, not as a noise standard.[44] (After all, the FAA never said otherwise.) The finding was gratifying to every operator in the country, not excluding the FAA, which happens to run National Airport. The operators and their trade association tail should continue to wag the FAA dog as the leisurely search for standards to measure airport noise proceeds. Two non-negotiable criteria guide the effort: standards must not "over describe" the operators' version of the noise problem, and they must be useless in lawsuits.

Another technique the FAA uses to help itself and the operators hold off the citizens is to unleash a bag of lawyer's tricks designed to prevent lawsuits from being tried on the merits. Michael Berger, a Los Angeles attorney representing property owners in jet noise cases, explains the practices in "Games the FAA Plays":

> Game Number 1 approaches, if not breaches, the borders of unethical legal practice. It is simplicity itself. When the FAA is sued in a United States District Court outside of Washington, D.C., the FAA tells the U.S. District Court that jurisdiction resides solely in the U.S. District Court in Washington, D.C. When someone sues the FAA about airport noise in the U.S. District Court in Washington, D.C., the FAA tells the U.S. District Court in Washington, D.C. that jurisdiction rests with the U.S. District Court in which the airport is located.[45]

District Judge William Timbers reacted to the FAA's brand of law practice as it extracted itself from a controversy between East Haven and New Haven, Connecticut, over the location of an airport:

> Although the Court's hands are tied as far as providing the relief here demanded against the Administrator, the Court would be derelict if it failed to comment on the conduct of the Administrator during the pendency of this action. . . . The Administrator is charged with serving the "public interest." The people who live near expanding airports in this jet age are no less a part of the public than those who fly in the planes. The Court expresses no opinion as to the merits of plaintiffs' claims; but it does believe it is within the Court's competence to comment on the Administrator's apparent desire to avoid the issue rather than to take the initiative and meet it head on.[46]

With the FAA out of the case, East Haven and New Haven fought all the way to the Connecticut Supreme Court which ordered New Haven to cease expansion of its airport into or over East Haven without its approval.[47] Displeased with the result, the FAA returned to the hustings with its own lawsuit. Having dismissed itself originally on the ground that it should have been sued in the District of Columbia, not Connecticut, where did the FAA file suit? In Connecticut, of course.[48]

Just as it is difficult to find a court in which to file the papers, it is equally difficult to find someone responsible. Berger explains:

> Game number 2 is when a citizen makes a formal complaint for an administrative hearing before the FAA to control the unendurable noise about jet airports, the FAA formally and officially declares that control of airport noise is wholly a local concern of the operator of the airport. But, when an aroused citizen sues the operator of the local airport or an aroused neighboring municipality enacts legislation to ease the problem the FAA comes before the court and says the control of airport noise is solely and exclusively within the jurisdiction of the FAA.[49]

For the record the FAA insists its noise certification powers detract not at all from the airport operator's responsibility for noise control:

> It should be emphasized that nothing is intended to substitute federal judgment for that of the airport proprietor in the determination of the noise levels, noise measurement, or noise evaluation techniques that are most responsive to the particular and unique problems facing each airport proprietor.[50]

Sure enough, when the City of Santa Monica, California, asked the FAA for some noise control regulations, it was told the issue was a matter of local concern.[51]

The solution seems to be for the proprietor to ban jets, or to impose curfews or traffic restrictions. But "local control" is a rationale only for federal abdication, it is not an excuse for local enforcement. While the FAA offers airport owners aid and comfort in defending lawsuits, it offers the opposite when they step out of line to enforce harsh traffic restriction. The legal muzzle is the grant agreement tied to FAA funds given local operators. For example, when San Diego's Board of Airport Commissioners opted for a curfew to help out local property owners, they got trouble. Berger explained:

> Immediately upon publication of the Commissioners' request, the [FAA] informed them that any such restrictions would violate their commitments under their Federal Aid to Airports grant agreements which required them to operate the airport without restriction as to hours. After many discussions with FAA officials, it was determined that the proposed regulation should not be implemented.[52]

The few traffic restrictions that slip past the FAA are immediately set upon by the carriers. The Port of New York Authority's attempts to ban jet aircrafts from using one runway at La Guardia were met by Eastern Airline's claim that federal law forbade such an "interference" with commerce.[53] Acceptance of Eastern's argument would have prevented the operators from resorting to even traffic controls to govern the jets they are legally obligated to keep quiet under court decisions like *Griggs.*

Although the courts have withheld this nationwide free

pass from the carriers, they have said that communities who don't operate airports can't impose flight restrictions.[54] This explains the operators' inclination to buy peace with their own constituents by dispensing the jets over somebody else: Los Angeles traffic over Inglewood, Santa Monica traffic over Los Angeles, New York City traffic over Hempstead and Cedarhurst.

In addition to making it difficult to sue the operators and nearly impossible to sue the carriers, the FAA has found still another way to protect the technology, and it has done it with a flair that is a near perfect parody of all that is wrong with the administrative process. The agency has gone through the motions of deciding whether to require a noise control retrofit of today's jet fleet. The motion is distracting, but it's not leading to any decision that will solve the noise problem.

As long ago as 1966, the National Aeronautics and Space Administration began studying the possibilities of reducing noise from the JT3D engine, a principal noise-maker on the current fleet of 707's and DC-8's. In 1967 contracts were let to Boeing and McDonnell Douglas to determine the practicability of acoustically treating the DC-8 and 707 engine nacelles to reduce noise. The tests conducted were sophisticated and thorough, culminating in successful test flights of aircraft with treated nacelles. By late 1969 the work was completed with surprisingly optimistic conclusions. John G. Lowrey, a staff scientist at NASA's Langley Research Center, summed it up: "[S]ubstantial noise reduction is possible, even in big, screaming Boeing 707's. A sound absorbing material in the engine mountings of these four-jetters cuts landing sound to one-quarter of its present volume. Takeoff noise, which is louder, can be lowered significantly by combining sound absorption and a reduction in engine thrust."[55]

With the technology looking attractive, there remained the question of economics. The FAA put the problem to the Rohr Corporation and got answers in 1970.[56] Significant noise reductions could be realized at costs ranging from \$306,881 for a 727–200 to \$783,453 for the DC-8-61. Cost to the entire U.S. airline industry would be about \$600 million, and operating cost increases could be offset by a fare increase of sixty cents per \$100 in 1975, dropping to eight cents per \$100 in 1982. Rohr assumed the small rise in fares would have little or no effect on demand and would yield increased revenues, which is exactly what the airlines assume every time they ask for a hike in fares.

Evidence of a workable technology at tolerable costs was tempting enough to lure the operators into public disagreement with the carriers. The November 1970 general membership meeting of the Airport Operators Council International adopted a resolution urging the FAA to proceed with a retrofit on the basis of the Rohr study.[57] To the operators, the hundreds of millions needed to repair the existing fleet didn't look like much alongside the billions needed to relocate an army of airport sufferers.

It's rare that a particular technological change in the public interest appears so compelling. The technology and economics looked good; the hurts were genuine and widespread; respectable political support was assembling. There was but a single missing ingredient—a law-making authority with sufficient integrity to close the circle.

The FAA acted out the dictates of its industry not with a clear capitulation but a slinking off that left expectations slowly dying. The big motion on retrofit took the form of an "Advance Notice of Proposed Rulemaking" in November 1970.[58] (The ostensible reason for publishing an advance notice instead of a proposed rule is that the agency doesn't even know enough about the problem to identify tentative courses of action. The bureaucratic reason is that such proposals can't back you into a corner.) The notice raised enough questions to last the lifetime of a 707: The NASA program "did not develop a modification design or hardware of certification quality that could meet the requirements of economic reasonableness or technological practicability." But nobody requested this of NASA. As for the Rohr economic study, it was "an analytical investigation only. No hardware was developed during this study."[59] Since it was the FAA that designed the Rohr study, it is a permissible inference that the agency wanted "an analytical investigation only," without hardware. The FAA wanted "more study," and that's exactly what it got.

The advance notice drew much comment hardly surprising in content.[60] A second-grader: "I hope you will put mufflers in all of the jets. My teacher yells when 707 jets come over us. . . . I cannot stand it one more day." An optimist: "My husband and I were very happy to learn . . . that we have finally located the correct department to complain about the noise and disturbance of the jet planes." A pessimist: "I feel all levels of government have let us down, and I am bitter. . . . Financially, we are ruined. That is what noise from jets has done to us." An insomniac: I am "constantly awakened between two and three in the morning." An engineer outside the industry: "[T]here is technology now available that will enable these rules to be met at reasonable cost." An airport operator: "We must conclude that the FAA at the national level has accomplished little to alleviate the aircraft noise problem. . . ."

Nor were there surprises from the industry's group-thought defenders: "[I]t is the AIA [Aerospace Industries Association] view that the necessary studies and information required to reach . . . decisions are presently not in hand." The Air Transport Association concluded: "[I]t is our carefully considered position that there should not be

a noise retrofit requirement for currently certificated turbofan and turbojet aircraft. Until the value to the public of
a retrofit program has been demonstrated and proven to be
economically reasonable and technically feasible, such a
program would be meaningless."

Drawing on this advice the FAA's John Shaffer wound
down the retrofit issue in the classic do-nothing style of
administrative decision-making. In October 1971 he said a
proposed rule on retrofitting the 727's and 737's and DC-
9's would be released "imminently."[61] By the following
February he let slip that the October rule (still not publicly
disclosed) had become "less stringent" than previously announced.[62] In May Shaffer told the Aerospace Industries
Association it would cost "considerably more than one million each to retrofit either a DC-8 or 707. . . . Considering
the size of the fleet, admirable as it may be, I just don't
believe our airlines can absorb such costs nor do I personally believe such a program would be, in the long term, in
the best interest of this nation."[63] Not in the best interests
of the airlines, a retrofit was not in the best interests of the
nation. The fourth anniversary of the 1968 statute giving
the FAA authority to promulgate rules on retrofit came and
went with the administrator sleeping quietly.

In time, even gaping vacuums are gradually filled. The
Department of Transportation's Office of Noise Abatement, under the direction of Charles Foster, has invaded
the jet noise arena pursuant to a legal mandate not at all
clear. Retrofit alternatives will get a thorough going over
in Foster's office. Some time in 1973 an announcement will
be made. A charitable judgment is that it is doubtful the law
will be able to overtake a technology given a four-year
breather by government regulators. There is no doubt at
all that the industry will repeat its advice of twenty years

ago that noise control will come only from new models designed for the future, if then.

Few advocates of corporate responsibility would suggest that the airlines and manufacturers should undertake a massive retrofit program without governmental guidance. Their assigned role is to defend the technology with pleas of further study, threats of bankruptcy, understatements of the noise problem. The disappointment is that this industrial bias is welcomed as state policy. The solution is only partly a new administrator at the FAA or retrofit responsibility shifted elsewhere.* In the end, the aim should be a government that listens to its industries without parroting them.

---

*Late in 1972 the Congress approved legislation that would give EPA limited advisory responsibilities concurrently with the FAA to control jet noise. *See Cong. Rec.,* Oct. 18, 1972, pp. 18638–43.

10 CORPORATE COUNTRY

I have long dreamed of buying an island owned by no nation, and of establishing the World Headquarters of the Dow Company on the truly neutral ground of such an island, beholden to no nation or society. *

Admission of the Country of Dow to the United Nations would mark a culmination of the imperatives of technology. The needs of the corporation are well understood: an integrated series of operations requires time, capital and hordes of specialists. A legal entity must exist to collect on the investment, and that entity is a corporation. Its goals are equally well understood: live and grow, raise capital, use specialized manpower and, as we have seen, protect the investment.

Of the shorthand explanations of corporate behavior, I prefer the security theory: minimizing risks is the dominant aim. Risks are eliminated by reaching into the political process and grabbing a government loan or subsidy, by staving off a regulatory initative or blurring the rules. The technology often can be made secure at the expense of the people it hurts.

Extension of the industrial planning process into the

*Carl A. Gersticker, chairman of the board, the Dow Chemical Company, in "Structure of the Corporation," pp. 9–10, prepared for the White House Conference on the Industrial World Ahead, Feb. 7–9, 1972.

affairs of government brings with it a suspicious rhetoric. It is a rhetoric that plays down the conflict between the corporation and the state. Read the words of B. R. Dorsey, president of the Gulf Oil Corporation: "Business has a responsibility to society that transcends the traditional business purpose of making money. . . . [M]aximum financial gain, the historical number one object of business, today drops to second place whenever it conflicts with the well-being of society. The first responsibility of business, then, is to operate for the well-being of society."[1]

While Dorsey so attests, his company makes an anonymous and illegal contribution to beat down an attempt by some people in California to divert gas tax monies for rapid transit use [Chap. 2].

The evidence, I believe, proves the traditional business purpose of making money still predominates. The new polluting technologies of throw-away containers, chemicals and detergents bring higher profits; increased sales and earnings steadfastly guide Procter & Gamble, American Cyanamid, Kennecott and the others. It is evident that any corporation respectful of the market place tends to resist unproductive outlays for pollution control or safety engineering, especially if extensive process change is required.

The profit maximization principle surely is as acute as it ever was in what the economist might call the microeconomic sphere—the Humboldt Bay plant of Pacific Gas & Electric Company, a Boise Cascade development, a Harvey Aluminum or ASARCO smelter. It is here that "unauthorized" activity flourishes: cutting corners on quality control, falsifying documents, intimidating inspectors, exceeding standards. On the assembly line, the glowing pollution control pronouncements from corporate headquarters founder on the reality of performance standards based upon increased earnings per share. Reward him if he gets away with socially irresponsible—but profitable—practices, fire him if he fails is the prevalent paradox. No, there hasn't been much slackening of pressure on the modern manager for current earnings performance. There may be demands to clean up the procedure, but sacrificing earning power to do so is not recommended.

Count me among the skeptics of the theory that corporations can serve simultaneously as profit maximizers and as reliable engineers of social progress. Beneficence bestowed can be withdrawn when the good-will objective of the moment disappears. Scant is the evidence that corporate altruism can begin to scratch the surface of society's stickier problems of race, poverty or pollution. When pressed about criteria of social performance, the corporation and its lawyers point only to the law. Far better is it that social obligations be prescribed by law than be dependent upon the vaporous writ of the corporate promise.

Worse, the corporation that thinks like a nation tends to pre-empt or head off governmental action and undercut the role of the state. Keep America Beautiful's insistent claim that litter is a people problem and the pesticide industry's commitment to writing labels are good examples of technological myths serving to defuse meaningful social controls. Moreover, when corporations set out to do good, they rarely go alone, either because it's competitively unwise to be the only one wasting money or because it's competitively risky to allow someone in the business to get a jump on new technologies. Among the groups mentioned in these pages whose founders would claim the loftiest motives are Keep America Beautiful, the National Center for Resource Recovery, the Smelter Control Research Association, the Joint Task Force on Eutrophication, the Aluminum Industry Liaison Committee, the Air Transport Association. All are—or were—involved, one way or another, in lobbying, research and public relations. All have an anti-competitive potential that can be—or was—exploited to suppress competition, defend damaging technologies, stifle improvements, pre-empt governmental conduct. All qualify as technological conspiracies.

Prescribing a remedy for bringing to heel the power of the corporation and its technology has intrigued more than a few. No one has found the formula.

Nationalization is one recurring suggestion. I'm inclined to brush it off with a reference to the words of I. F. Stone: "The Soviet Union today is like a huge company town."[2] If there is hope in replacing several ponderous bureaucracies with one, I don't see it. The histories of the Bonneville Power Administration, the Federal Aviation Administration or the Pesticides Regulation Division give little indication that their successors deserve supremacy over the energy, aviation and pesticides policies of the nation. Our corporations today are supposed to be efficient, our governments humane; combine them, and you have a state that is inefficient and inhumane.

The corporate responsibility movement is another effort to curb big business power. I see nothing wrong in theory or practice with attempting to enforce the usual rules of public accountability against groups that walk, quack and swim like governments. It is in vogue for corporate management to report it is "listening" to its critics, after swamping them in proxy battles. But the Council on Economic Priorities tells us that no shareholder has ever won a social-issue proxy fight.[3] And in May 1972, the shareholders of Warner-Lambert, a leading pharmaceutical house, rejected a proposal to require the company to provide physicians in foreign lands with the same warnings about its medicines it provides physicians in the United States.[4] The forty-five to one margin of the vote may have been a fair reflection of the sentiments of that crowd (whoever they are), but it is hardly a strong affirmation of the health of the corporate responsibility movement.

Despite (or perhaps because of) such goings-on, Robert Heilbroner insists that corporations have social responsibilities beyond maximizing profits for the stockholders. He gives instances: "For if corporations in fact sought to maximize the profits of their stockholders, we would find General Motors lowering the price of its cars enough to drive Chrysler and even Ford to the wall; IBM underselling its puny competition; General Electric driving Westinghouse out of the market. All of this would be entirely legitimate and perfectly consistent with profit-maximizing, but it would of course be generally viewed as an exercise of supreme corporate *irresponsibility* [emphasis in original]."[5]

Heilbroner is wrong. For General Motors to destroy Chrysler would not be an exercise of corporate irresponsibility, it would be an exercise of corporate stupidity. The reason it would be stupid is that the Justice Department, however pliable it may be, would kick up a fuss. Even General Motors confronts business risks, and the red flag would go up well before Chrysler went under. Chrysler would be saved, not by the conscience of General Motors, but by an antitrust law made credible by the enormity of the abuse.

Such examples persuade me that the best prescription for calling the corporation and its technology to account is to head off efforts to subvert the government. For the most part our laws are acceptable; they collapse only in the administration, and then under heavy pressure. The corporation's pronounced preference for bending the state around the technology reinforces the need to insist upon a bright line between the two; make the state fully accountable to the public and you reform the corporation.

Easily the most potent measure in recent years for making the technology responsible to the people has been the National Environmental Policy Act[6] which is designed to enforce broad disclosures prior to major federal actions impacting the environment. This interruption of the technological imperative was aimed not at the corporation, but at the state. The government was given no sweeping new powers over technologies, but was obliged to explain its decision-making to the people. This reform of government, some business executives would say, makes it virtually impossible to build a new power plant, airport or highway, or to develop new sources of raw materials. Others see it as a major step toward making the technologies pause to consider the public need.

Full disclosure is the pervasive guardian of the bright line between the government and its corporations, and the protection the public should insist upon.[7] And full disclosure is being sought—by shareholders advancing proxy proposals (albeit unsuccessfully) that would force disclosure about pollution suits or business activities overseas, by investors objecting to closed-door meetings between company officials and select financial analysts, by legislators seeking to assess technologies before the federal funds begin to flow or to better economic reporting that would cast light on the performance of conglomerates, by employees questioning the risks to which they are exposed, by the general public asking about rate increases, tax breaks, environmental degradation, minority hiring. Every chapter in this book is a brief for disclosure and an explanation of resistance to it.

The highest priority must be given to the disclosure of campaign contributions and expenditures, for this well-traveled avenue of influence is a perpetual source of hand-wringing. The failures of the litter initiative in Washington State [Chap. 1] and the gas tax proposition in California

[Chap. 2] tell something of the impact of money on, not the politician, but the issue. Rigid conflict of interest and asset disclosure should become a routine part of public life. It is commendable that the National Academy of Sciences respects the need to report potential conflicts on its study panels but deplorable that the academy stamps "classified" on this information.

Continuing efforts are needed to force disclosure of the activities of thousands of groups functioning as a fourth branch of government—the advisory committee.[8] This path of influence must be well lighted. Strict accountability and disclosure should be required of the National Industrial Pollution Control Council, the Joint Task Force on Eutrophication, the Primary Nonferrous Smelting Industry Liaison Committee, to mention but a few examples. My hope is that the movement to reform advisory committees envelops the trade associations to require full disclosure of research and lobbying activities and publication of verbatim transcripts of meetings. These special governments, convened to defend technologies, should be treated as such.

Perhaps the most serious institutional imbalance in recent times is the perceptible shift of power from the Congress to the White House. The authority lost is hard to reclaim, for the growing White House bureaucracy stands mute behind doctrines of executive privilege and exceptions to the freedom of information act. The power that belongs to the Peter Flanigans is an autocratic power and a dangerous one, for it is officially invisible. It is time for the Congress to reopen closed doors before they are rusted shut by precedent.

In addition to disclosure, other devices are available to make the state responsible to the public. Fewer special interest subsidies and more special interest taxes (like effluent charges) is not a new idea. Nor is the suggestion that cutting down on administrative discretion may help cut back on administrative irresponsibility. The slap on the wrist meted out to the smelters by local officials, to PG&E by the Atomic Energy Commission, to the oil companies by the courts is evidence that severe economic retaliation is incompatible with a large corporation's plans for growth and stability. Making the penalties mandatory, divesting administrators of authority to excuse the offense is one way to avoid unhealthy compromise. Giving citizens the power to sue to correct an offense is another way to strengthen public resolve.

A serious proposal that seeks to tackle abusive corporate power directly is the Industrial Reorganization Act,[9] proposed by Senator Philip Hart (D-Mich.) after years of study by the Antitrust and Monopoly Subcommittee. The act would establish an Industrial Reorganization Commission (with a fixed term of existence) to devise means of eliminating economic concentration and would set up a special court to handle cases resulting from the commission's work. Top priority industries would include chemical, electrical equipment, energy, motor vehicle and nonferrous metals. A conspicuous feature of this proposal that will be denounced as radical and unacceptable is that it makes few changes in what has long been the "law" of the land, for it concentrates, instead, on devising a mechanism that would help the state achieve its professed objective of curbing monopoly power and the technological abuses that accompany it.

A state setting rules to believed can do much to make the technology sensitive to the public interest. Barry Commoner offers one vision of the changes in productive technologies needed to bring the economic system into harmony with the eco-system:

[S]ystems to return sewage and garbage directly to the soil; the replacement of many synthetic materials by natural ones; the reversal of the present trend to retire land from cultivation and to elevate the yield per acre by heavy fertilization; replacement of synthetic pesticides, as rapidly as possible, by biological ones; the discouragement of power-consuming industries; the development of land transport that operates with maximum fuel efficiency at low combustion temperatures and with minimal land use; essentially complete containment and reclamation of wastes from combustion processes, smelting and chemical operations (smokestacks must become rarities); essentially complete recycling of all reuseable metal, glass, and paper products; ecologically sound planning to govern land use including urban areas.[10]

That this vision comes upon hard times more often than not in these pages is an acknowledgment of the strength of our dominant technologies and the powers that move them. But the technology does not live without the concurrence of the government. And the state of the union is the responsibility of its citizens. So, in the end, the problem is a people problem.

NOTES

Introduction

1. *The Closing Circle* (New York: Knopf, 1971), pp.284–5.
2. *See* JEC print, "The Economics of Federal Subsidy Programs," 92d Cong., 1st Sess., 1972.
3. The recipient of the jail sentence is Mr. Hank Adams, an Indian fishing-rights demonstrator, who recently was involved in the "Trail of Broken Treaties" negotiations taking place in Washington, D.C., late in 1972. The builder of dams is the Corps of Engineers whose contributions to reducing the salmon population in the Columbia and Snake Rivers are documented by the Pacific Northwest River Basins Commission, in *Status of Columbia River Salmon and Steelhead Trout,* May, 1972.
4. For some background on NIPCC, *see* Rodgers, "The NationalIndustrial Pollution Control Council: Advise or Collude," 13 *Bost. Coll. Ind. & Comm. L. Rev.* 719 (1972).

Chapter One

1. The computations are those of Gary Wm. Fenchuk, "The Economics of Banning Throwaway Beverage Containers," Wharton Graduate School, April 10, 1972, p.4.
2. The facts about KAB are extracted from various publications of that organization.
3. EPA, "Initiating a National Effort to Improve Solid Waste Management," 1971, p.23.
4. "A Time for Constructive Progress—Not Wheel-Spinning," speech before the Los Angeles Rotary Club, Jan. 15, 1971, p.4 (emphasis in original).
5. *See Wall Street Journal* (Western ed.), Nov. 2, 1970, p.6, col. 2.

6. Bureau of Solid Waste Management, *The Role of Packaging in Solid Waste Management: 1966 to 1976,* 1969, p.60.

7. *Canner/Packer,* March 1971, p.23.

8. June 1971, p.21 (speaking of both the ban-the-bottle proposals and the Federal Trade Commission's attack on the bottle franchising system).

9. Crusade for Cleaner Environment, "Do it Yourself Ecology."

10. *Hearings to Prohibit Certain No-Deposit, No-Return Containers,* Before House Subcommittee on Public Health and Welfare, 91st Cong., 2d Sess., 1970, pp.18–19 (testimony of W. Roger Strelow, HEW). The Council on Environmental Quality in an unpublished report projects cost savings to consumers of 25 per cent and savings to municipalities of $125 million on refuse collection if bans on non-returnables are generally adopted.

11. "Litter Prevention . . . A First Step to Improve the Environment," p.2.

12. The $5 billion figure comes from National Center for Resource Recovery, Inc., Bull. No. 2, Jan.-Feb. 1972, p.3.

13. On the general subject of the economics, *see Hearings on the Economics of Recycling Waste Materials,* Before the Senate Subcommittee on Fiscal Policy, 92d Cong., 1st Sess., 1971.

14. Council on Environmental Quality, *First Ann. Rep.,* 1970, p.117.

15. *Ibid.*

16. Fenchuk, note 1 *supra,* p.17.

17. Data in text was compiled by the Crusade for a Cleaner Environment and is verifiable elsewhere.

18. Letter from J.P.R. Molette, Owens-Illinois Glass Container Division to Peter Chokola, March 27, 1969.

19. Letter to the author, July 29, 1971.

20. A discussion of the Washington State campaign has been published by the author under the title "Ecology De-

nied: The Unmaking of a Majority," *The Washington Monthly*, Feb. 1971.

21. Ch. 307, 1971 Wash. Extraord. Sess., approved by the people in the 1972 general election; California's McCarthy-Welsh Act, ch. 1548, 1970 Sess., reflects the Model's philosophy.

22. Summary Minutes, Oct. 14, 1970, p.3.

23. NIPCC, Minutes of Beverage Sub-Council, June 23, 1970, p.4.

24. KAB, "Number of Trash Receptacles on State Highways."

25. *See Hearings on Solid Waste Management Act of 1972*, Before the Senate Subcommittee on the Environment, 92d Cong., 2d Sess., 1972 [hereinafter cited as *1972 Solid Waste Hearings*]. For a useful discussion, *see* Solow, "The Economist's Approach to Pollution and Its Control," 173 *Science* 495 (1971).

26. Reported in Statement of Contributions and Expenditures in Connection with Initiative No. 40 to A. Ludlow Kramer, Washington Secretary of State, from Irving E. Stimpson, on behalf of the Washington Committee to Stop Litter, Dec. 30, 1970.

27. *Seattle Post-Intelligencer*, Oct. 14, 1970.

28. *See* 37 Fed. Reg. 3644 (1972).

29. Testimony of Hugh Folk, in *1972 Solid Waste Hearings*, pp. 298–301. The Folk testimony contains an enlightening discussion of three leading studies on the employment effects of mandatory deposit legislation, including an industry-financed study by the Midwest Research Institute predicting economic losses of $10.2 billion in the beverage container manufacturing industries.

30. Letter from Sherman R. Huffine to Mr. & Mrs. Slade Gorton, Oct. 26, 1970.

31. Letter from Don M. Lee, Olympia public relations

manager to Robert Keller, Oct. 5, 1970.

32. Rev. Code Wash. § 29.79.490(6) (1965).

33. "Scope," *Softdrinks,* Dec. 1970. These representations arguably evidence an illegal agreement to fix prices and a lawsuit is pending to test the point. *See Rodgers* v. *Federal Trade Commission,* Civ. No. 9612 (W.D. Wash. 1971) (the author is plaintiff). The action was dismissed by the District Court, and a notice of appeal has been filed.

34. *See New York Times,* Nov. 5, 1970.

35. *New York Times,* March 24, 1971, p.25.

36. Letter from Mrs. Irene Mylan, recycling chairman, Salem Chapter of Oregon Environmental Council to Mr. Rich Chambers, Apr. 15, 1971. Mr. Chambers was a leader in the citizens' movement to enact Oregon's deposit law.

37. *Ibid.*

38. Reported in Adams, "A Recycling Nut Answers the Backlashers," *Compost Science,* July-Aug. 1971, p.31.

39. Nov. 8, 1970.

40. Council on Economic Priorities, Vol. 2, No. 3, Sept-Oct. 1971, p.8.

41. National Center for Resource Recovery, Inc. press release, "Resource Recovery Emphasized in Organizational Name Change," Sept. 7, 1971.

42. Minutes of Ad Hoc Subcommittee, Aug. 5, 1970.

43. July 31, 1971.

44. *Id.,* p.56.

45. Note 4, *supra.*

46. NIPCC, Minutes of Glass and Plastics Sub-Council, Jan. 11, 1971.

47. "Everything You Always Wanted to Know About Garbage (But Were Afraid to Ask)," address before 1970 Newspaper Food Editors Conference, Sept. 21, 1970. The Environmental Protection Agency apparently agrees for it has funded only one study to develop a disposable package.

See Summaries of Solid Waste Research and Training Grants-1970, 1971, p.17.

48. Reported in National Canners Association, "Research Information," June 1, 1971. (Study sponsored by GCMI at Drexel Institute of Technology).

49. *See Wall Street Journal* (Western ed.), July 1, 1971, p.24, col. 4.

50. Reported in the *New York Times,* Oct. 27, 1971.

51. Titled "Litter Can't Be Put Off 'Til Later," Sept. 15, 1971.

52. *New York Times,* Oct. 27, 1971.

53. Letter from Deputy Director H. Lanier Hickman to Ellis L. Yochelson, Jan. 10, 1972.

54. Before the Packaging Education Foundation, Inc., Atlantic City, N.J., Nov. 17, 1971.

55. *Hearings to Prohibit Certain No-Deposit, No-Return Containers,* Before the House Subcommittee on Public Health & Welfare, 91st Cong., 2d Sess., 1970, p.24.

56. Statement of Samuel Hale, Jr., deputy assistant administrator, solid waste management programs, *1972 Solid Waste Hearings,* p.229.

57. Note 4, *supra.*

58. *Seattle Times,* Aug. 30, 1971, p.7, col. 4.

Chapter Two

1. The account is based on Skow, "Incident on I-90," *Saturday Evening Post,* Dec. 1968, p.64.

2. On the general subject of the relocation problem arising out of urban renewal and highway programs, *see* D.R. Mandelker, *Managing Our Urban Environment* (Indianapolis, Kansas City, New York: Bobbs-Merrill, 2d ed., 1971), pp.821–46.

3. Whalen, "The American Highway," *Saturday Evening Post*, Dec. 1968, p.22.

4. Oct. 1969, p.2.

5. *Fortune's List of the 500 Largest Industrials*, May 1972, p.190.

6. *Asphalt*, Jan. 1970; *American Road Builder*, March 1971, p.19 (remarks of Rep. John Blatnik).

7. Reported in document titled, "Proposed Defendants and Co-conspirators," reprinted in *Congressional Record*, May 18, 1971, H4063, H4064 (an internal Justice Department document recommending criminal prosecutions in the "smog conspiracy" case).

8. *Id.*, p.4067.

9. *United States* v. *Automobile Mfrs. Ass'n.*, 1969 Trade Cas. ¶ 79907.

10. *See National Observer*, April 15, 1972, p.13, col. 5.

11. For the particulars of a costly, inefficient auto accident compensation system, *see* Department of Transportation, *Motor Vehicle Crash Losses and Their Compensation in the United States*, 1971.

12. A conservative estimate indicates savings of well over $2 billion annually with a 50 per cent reduction in air pollution in urban centers. *See* Lave and Seskin, "Air Pollution and Human Health," 169 *Science* 723 (1970). A study finds a statistically significant association between ambient air concentrations of carbon monoxide and increased mortality in Los Angeles County. Hexter and Goldsmith, "Carbon Monoxide: Association of Community Air Pollution with Mortality," 173 *Science* 265 (1971). Carbon monoxide comes from automobiles.

13. *See* Nader, "A Citizen's Guide to the American Economy," *New York Review of Books*, Sept. 2, 1971, p.14.

14. Reported in California Air Resources Bd. Bull., July-Aug. 1970.

15. One urban consultant told a Congressional subcommittee that uncompensated social costs from federal highway and urban renewal programs came to about $200 million annually. *See Hearings on Economic Analysis and the Efficiency of Government,* Before the Joint Economic Committee, 91st Cong., 1969, p.285.

16. Reported in R.A. Buel, *Dead End: The Automobile in Mass Transportation* (Englewood Cliffs, N.J.: Prentice-Hall, 1972), p.60, based on Rapoport, "Los Angeles Has a Cough," *Esquire,* July 1970.

17. Sept. 9, 1970, editorial in *Los Angeles Times.*

18. *Compare Hearings on Federal Highway Act of 1970 and Miscellaneous Bills,* Before the Senate Subcommittee on Roads, 91st Cong., 2d Sess., 1970, p.486, *with* Secretary of the Treasury, "Fifteenth Ann. Rep. on Highway Trust Fund", 1971, p.1.

19. "Fifteenth Ann. Rep. on Highway Trust Fund," 1971, p.9.

20. J. Burby, *The Great American Motion Sickness* (Boston, Toronto: Little, Brown, 1971), p.299.

21. M. Weidenbaum, "Budget 'Uncontrollability' As An Obstacle to Improving the Allocation of Government Resources," in Joint Economic Committee, *The Analysis and Evaluation of Public Expenditures: The PPB System,* vol. 1, 91st Cong., 1st Sess., 1969, pp.357, 360.

22. 107 *Congressional Record* 2014 (1961) (Hon. Tom Pelley).

23. For details, *see* J. Burby, note 20 *supra,* pp.225–33.

24. Senate Committee on Public Works press release, Nov. 5, 1971.

25. Speech to the American Transit Association, Sept. 23, 1971, quoted in *The Concrete Opposition,* Dec. 1971, p.2.

26. Burby, note 20 *supra,* p.296.

27. Simmons, "The Freeway Establishment," *Cry California*, Spring, 1968.

28. *Ibid.*

29. *American Road Builder*, Nov. 1961, p.4.

30. 82 Stat. 830.

31. Internal Memorandum of Aug. 2, 1971, leaked by the Highway Action Coalition.

32. Another internal document, also leaked by the Highway Action Coalition.

33. The incident is reported in the *Seattle Post-Intelligencer*, Dec. 9, 1971, p. A 13.

34. Opinion Research Corporation, "Public Attitudes Toward Highway Transportation," foreword.

35. Highway Users Federation for Safety and Mobility press release, Aug. 30, 1971.

36. Petree, "The Whole Story," address at the Annual Meeting of the California State Chamber of Commerce, Jan. 15, 1970, p.5.

37. *Id.*, p.7.

38. An authoritative publication on trust fund revenues is Cope, "Trends in Highway Taxation in the United States," 1963 (updated and modified by the U.S. Department of Transportation).

39. California Senate Select Committee on Rapid Transit, "Public Transit in California," 1971, p.71.

40. *Oakland Tribune*, Oct. 12, 1970, p.E-3.

41. *San Francisco Chronicle*, Oct. 30, 1970, p.2.

42. Note 27, *supra.*

43. *Los Angeles Times*, Dec. 27, 1970, p.1, col. 1.

44. *Ibid.*

45. *Ibid.*

46. *Ibid.*

47. Quoted in Buel, *Dead End: The Automobile in Mass Transportation* (Englewood Cliffs, N.J.: Prentice-Hall, 1972,) pp.133–134.

48. *See San Francisco Examiner & Chronicle,* Dec. 12, 1971.

49. Note 43, *supra.*

50. Press Release, Jan. 22, 1971.

51. Letter from Neil Petree to Marvin Braude, Jan. 29, 1971.

52. Letter from Marvin Braude to author, Apr. 5, 1972.

53. Letter to author, June 21, 1971.

54. R. Fellmeth, 2 *Land and Power in California,* (Washington: Center for Study of Responsive Law, tent. ed. 1971), p. VII-15.

55. Quoted in an unidentified newspaper clipping supplied by Senator Mills' office, in possession of author.

56. Statement of the California Study Group of Ralph Nader's Center for the Study of Responsive Law, Oct. 26, 1971.

57. Reported in *Sacramento Bee,* Oct. 16, 1970. These were early rounds in a national campaign to democratize the auto clubs. *See Wall Street Journal* (Western ed.), Aug. 27, 1971, p.1, col. 1; *National Observer,* Aug. 16, 1971, p.1, col. 1.

58. *Pierce* v. *Standard Oil,* No. 989057 (Super. Ct. Cal. 1970).

59. This suit was dropped after the election for lack of funds. The volunteer attorneys handling the case decided against continuing when it appeared it would be virtually impossible to have the election voided without evidence based on an expensive, statistically valid post-election survey showing that a substantial number of voters were persuaded to vote against the proposition by the deceptive ads. Letter from Thomas H. Crawford to author, Aug. 15, 1972.

60. Assorted clippings supplied by persons involved in the campaign, in possession of author.

61. Reported in *The Concrete Opposition,* Mar. 1972, p.2. As

of this writing, Mobil is now to be recorded in favor of diversion of trust fund monies for rapid transit purposes.

62. Letter to author, Aug. 18, 1971.

63. *Brown* v. *Superior Court*, 96 Cal. Rptr. 584 (1971) (holding that statutory differences requiring greater disclosure in ballot measure election than in candidate election were not invalid legislative classifications).

64. Calif. Election Code §11890.

65. 1970 net income for Mobil was $482,707,000, *see* Ann Rep., p.29; for Gulf, $550,000,000 *see* Ann. Rep., p.24; and for Standard Oil of California, $454,817,000, *see* Ann. Rep., p.3.

66. *United States* v. *National City Lines*, 186 F. 2d 562 (7th Cir. 1951).

67. Published in *Passenger Transport*, Dec. 3, 1963.

68. Metro Summary Report, "A Transit Plan for the Metropolitan Area, Seattle and King County," 1972, p.26.

69. Quoted in R. Heilbroner, *In the Name of Profit* (Garden City, N.Y.: Doubleday, 1972), p.33.

70. 84 Stat. 962 (1970). Fiscal 1971 appropriations came to about $600 million, up from $435 million in 1970. *See Business Week*, Sept. 18, 1971, p.21.

71. *Hearings on Airport/Airways Development*, Before the Senate Subcommittee on Aviation, 91st Cong., 1st Sess., pt.2, 1969, p.957.

Chapter Three

1. ASARCO, "El Paso Smelter Environmental Lead Problem," March 27, 1972.

2. Quoted in the *El Paso Times*, May 13, 1972.

3. *See Congressional Record*, May 18, 1972, p. H4770 (report of Rep. Ken Hechler (D.-W. Va.)).

4. *See Congressional Record,* May 22, 1972, pp. H4751–72. The legislation was vetoed by President Nixon.

5. Reported in Semrau, "Sulfur Oxides Control and Metallurgical Technology," *J. Metals,* Mar. 1971, p.1.

6. *American Smelting and Refining Co.* v. *Godfrey,* 158 Fed. 225 (8th Cir. 1907).

7. The study is reported in the Minutes of the National Industrial Pollution Control Council's Mining and Non-Ferrous Metals Sub-Council, Sept. 24, 1970.

8. The decree is reprinted in the *Report of the Selby Smelter Commission,* U.S. Bur. Mines Bull. 98, 1915, p.3.

9. *See* "Poisoned Pastures," *California's Health,* July-Aug., 1970, p.1.; California Department of Public Health, "Study of Benicia Area Horse Deaths: Interim Report," May 1, 1970. American Smelting and Refining Co.'s lead smelter is identified as the "most likely source of the lead contamination problem." *Id.* at 6.

10. The decree is reprinted in the *Report of the Anaconda Smelter Smoke Commission Covering the Period May 1, 1911 to October 1, 1920,* pp.13–15.

11. *Georgia* v. *Tennessee Copper Co.,* 206 U.S. 230 (1907), 237 U.S. 474 (1915) (motion to enter a final decree), 237 U.S. 678 (1915) (decree), 240 U.S. 650 (1916).

12. *See* Rodgers, "Tacoma's Tall Stack" *The Nation,* May 11, 1970, p.553.

13. Quoted in *id.*

14. Council on Environmental Quality, "The President's 1971 Environmental Program," 1971, p.26.

15. Hearings Before Washington State Pollution Control Appeals Board, ASARCO Appeal, May, 1971, vol. 5, pp.17–32 (testimony of Dr. David Discher, director, University of Washington's Department of Environmental Health and Safety) [hereinafter cited as Washington Hearings].

16. Quoted in Bureau of National Affairs, *Occupational Safety & Health Reporter: Current Report,* 1972, p.839.

17. *Ibid.*

18. Based on conversations with Frank Ainsa Jr., an attorney for the City of El Paso.

19. Quoted in note 8, *supra,* p.14.

20. Washington Hearings, vol. 7, pp.47, 57.

21. Quoted in Environmental Protection Agency, "Helena Valley, Montana, Area Environmental Pollution Study: Summary," Jan. 1972, p.2.

22. Reported in *El Paso Times,* Apr. 5, 1972.

23. Affidavit of Lee C. Travis, American Smelting & Refining Co., *Fisher* v. *American Smelting & Refining Co.,* No. 70 Civ. 729 (S.D.N.Y. 1970). The Company claims improved performance in more recent statements.

24. 42 U.S.C. §1857b.

25. Minutes of Primary Non-Ferrous Smelting Industry Advisory Committee, in possession of author.

26. *Ibid.*

27. Arthur G. McKee & Co., *Systems Study for Control of Emissions: Primary Non-Ferrous Smelting Industry,* June 1969, p. VIII A-3.

28. Testimony of Dr. C. B. Meyer, in Regard to the Application for Variance of American Smelting & Refining Co., Puget Sound Air Pollution Control Board, Tacoma, Wash., March 12, 1970, p.3.

29. Note 27, *supra.*

30. U.S. Dept. HEW, "Tall Stacks, Various Atmospheric Phenomena, and Related Aspects," NAPCA Pub. No. APTD 69–12, May 1969.

31. *See* Nicholson, "Cominco's Air Pollution Control Practice," in *Symposium on Air Pollution Management Practices,* 66th Nat'l Meeting, Am'n Inst. Chem. Eng., Portland, Oregon, Aug. 1969.

32. 18 U.S.C. § 207.

33. S. Doc. No. 91–65, 91st Cong., 2d Sess., 1970, p.32.

34. Statement of J.M. Henderson, before Puget Sound Air Pollution Control Board, July 10, 1970, p.9.

35. Statement of Charles Barber, *id.*, p.5.

36. *Id.*, pp.1–2.

37. Memorandum to American Smelting & Refining Co. on Legality of NAPCA's Establishment of Emission Control Standards for Nonferrous Smelters, submitted to NAPCA, July 23, 1970.

38. June 29, 1970.

39. *Ibid.*

40. Reported in Memorandum from NAPCA's Edward Tuerk, special assistant for program operations, to William Megonnell, NAPCA's assistant commissioner for standards and compliance, July 20, 1970.

41. U.S. Dept. HEW, "Suggested Emission Limits for Equivalent Sulfur from Existing Primary Nonferrous Smelters," rev. ed., Aug. 1970.

42. Remarks of July 6, 1970, reproduced in the Sub-Council minutes, July 6, 1970.

43. Note 42, *supra.*

44. *Hearings on Advisory Committees,* Before Senate Subcommittee on Intergovernmental Relations, 92nd Cong., 1st Sess., 1971, pp.413–14.

45. Remarks of Apr. 9, 1970, p.8.

46. "Environment Problems Facing the Extractive Industries," Before the Mining and Metallurgical Society of America, Denver, Colorado, Feb. 17, 1970.

47. The quotations and factual statements that follow are taken from the Minutes, NIPCC's Mining and Non-Ferrous Metals Sub-council, Mar. 8, 1971.

48. The report is Fluor Utah Engineers & Constructors,

Inc., "The Impact of Air Pollution Abatement on the Copper Industry," 1971.

49. 36 Fed. Reg. 6680, 6683 (1971).

50. 36 Fed. Reg. 15486, 15496 (1971).

51. Petition by the Anaconda Company to the Montana State Board of Health for Reconsideration of Certain Regulatory Standards, Sept. 17, 1971; letter from Stanley M. Lane, manager, East Helena Plant, to Mrs. John C. Sheehy, chairman, Montana State Board of Health, Oct. 20, 1971; Petition for Reconsideration and Modification of Arizona Emission and Ambient Standards for Sulfur Dioxide to Mrs. Elaine McFarland, Arizona State Board of Health, Oct. 20, 1971 (filed by all owners and operators of copper smelters in Arizona).

52. Reply brief of American Smelting & Refining Co., Nov. 1, 1971.

53. Dated Sept. 9, 1971.

54. Statement concerning petition by Anaconda Company to reduce control requirements for copper smelters, Dec. 15, 1971.

55. Dec. 20, 1971.

56. Rough draft, dated Jan. 6, 1972.

57. Section 110 (2) (3), 84 Stat. at 1680.

58. NAPCA Memo titled "Technology and Economics of Sulfur Oxide Control in the Nonferrous Smelting Industry," Aug. 18, 1970.

59. Letter from John A. Green to Mrs. John Sheehy, Jan. 6, 1972.

Chapter Four

1. The incident described is based almost verbatim on an account in T. Coffman, "The Boise Cascade Story,"

Honolulu Star-Bulletin, Feb. 17–21, 1970. Coffman quotes the company's sales magazine.

2. Cases No. 71–419, 72–21, signed Mar. 1, 1972.

3. The quotations are taken from an undated account in the *Coast Press,* in possession of author.

4. The Boise story has been published by the author under the title "Boise Cascade: The One That Didn't Get Away," *The Washington Monthly,* Nov. 1972, p.43.

5. *See* McDonald, "Bob Hansberger Shows How to Grow Without Becoming a Conglomerate," *Fortune,* Oct. 1969, p.134; *Fortune* 500 List, May 1970, p.186.

6. McDonald, note 5, *supra.*

7. *Paper Profits* (New York: 1970), p. B-2.

8. Boise Cascade Corp., 1969 Ann. Rep., p.9.

9. *Los Angeles Times,* Sept. 20, 1970.

10. Berliner, "Plague on the Land," *Cry California,* Summer 1970, pp.1, 5.

11. Aug. 29, 1970, p.75.

12. Examples are taken from the complaint in *People* v. *Boise Cascade Recreation Communities Corp.,* Civ. No. 127–902 (Cal. Super. Ct. 1971).

13. Note 10, *supra,* p.7.

14. Hearings on Nettleton Project, before Kitsap County Washington Planning Commission, Mar. 31, 1970, p.65 (testimony of Harold Berliner). [Hereinafter cited as Nettleton Hearings.]

15. The quotations are extracted from the transcript of the Nettleton Hearings, Mar. 31, 1970.

16. Nettleton Hearings, Oct. 29, 1970, p.58.

17. Amended par. 17, Nettleton Project.

18. R. Fellmeth, 1 *Land and Power in California* (Washington: Center for Study of Responsive Law, tent. ed. 1971), p. IV-26.

19. Gierking, *The Organization of Governmental Relations for a*

Large-Scale Corporation: A Case Study of the Boise Cascade Corporation, 1970, p.34 (unpublished thesis).

20. *Id.,* p.43.
21. *See New York Times,* Sept. 14, 1970.
22. For details, *see Honolulu Star-Bulletin,* Feb. 21, 1970, p. E-1.
23. S. B. No. 259, reintroduced in the fifth legislature, 1969.
24. Address before the Los Angeles Society of Financial Analysts, Jan. 27, 1972.
25. *Ibid.*
26. Address before the New York Society of Security Analysts, Apr. 11, 1972.
27. Reported in *National Observer,* June 10, 1972, p.15.
28. Reported in *Honolulu Star-Bulletin,* Feb. 18, 1970, p.1.
29. The figures on rates of development come from R. Fellmeth, note 18, *supra,* pp. IV-4–6.
30. *People* v. *Boise Cascade Recreation Communities Corp.,* Civ. No. 127–902 (Cal. Super. Ct. 1971).
31. *See Wall Street Journal* (Western ed.), Jan. 27, 1972, p.6, col. 2.
32. Note 30, *supra,* State's Notice and Motion for Protective Order and Points and Authorities and Declaration in Support Thereof, Ex. A.
33. Note 30, *supra,* Ex. N.
34. *Id.,* Declaration of L. Neil Gendel, Deputy Attorney General, p.5.
35. *Id.,* Ex. 01.
36. *Id.,* Ex. 015, p.6, memo from Bruce Walker to Don Marek, Boise Cascade Recreation Communities Group, Oct. 9, 1970.
37. (Western ed.), Dec. 29, 1971, p.10, col. 1.
38. *See Wall Street Journal* (Western ed.), Dec. 24, 1970, p.1, col. 2.
39. *Ibid.*

40. *San Francisco Chronicle*, Mar. 29, 1972, § B, p.2.
41. *See Wall Street Journal* (Western ed.), May 8, 1972, p.26, col. 2.
42. *Tribune Pub. Co.* v. *Boise Cascade Corp.*, No. 753625 (June 22, 1972, Wash. King County Super. Ct.).
43. *Wall Street Journal* (Western ed.), July 14, 1972, p.2, col. 4.

Chapter Five

1. "Pesticides and the Environment," 17 *Bio-Science* 613, 615–16 (1967).
2. Quoted in F. Graham, *Since Silent Spring* (Boston: Houghton Mifflin, 1970), p.49.
3. Jan. 1971, pp.6–7.
4. *Ibid.*
5. For general background, *see* National Agricultural Chemicals Association Speaker's Kit, "Facts on Pesticides"; H. Wellford, *Sowing the Wind* (New York: Grossman, 1972) [hereinafter cited as Wellford].
6. J. Backman, *The Economics of the Chemical Industry* (Washington: Manufacturing Chemists Association, 1970), p.60. [hereinafter cited as Backman].
7. Van Rumker, Guest and Upholt, 20 *Bio-Science* 1004 (1970). Dow's Julius Johnson estimates that one new pesticide emerges from each ten thousand tested and that time from discovery to market ranges from eight to ten years at a cost of $10 million or more. "Safety in the Development of Herbicides," presented to the California Weed Conference, Jan. 19, 1971.
8. Backman, pp.196–97.
9. B. Commoner, *The Closing Circle* (New York: Knopf, 1971), p.173.
10. For details, *see Hearings on Deficiencies in Administration of*

Federal Insecticide, Fungicide and Rodenticide Act, Before a Sub-committee of the House Committee on Gov't Operations, 91st Cong., 1st. Sess., 1969; House Committee on Gov't Operations, *Deficiencies in Administration of the Federal Insecticide, Fungicide & Rodenticide Act,* H. Rep. No. 637, 91st Cong., 1st Sess., 1969 [hereinafter cited as Deficiencies Report].

11. 26 Stat. 331.
12. 7 U.S.C. §§ 135–135k (1964).
13. *Canner/Packer,* Mar. 1971.
14. *Ag. Chem.,* Jan. 1970.
15. Washington State University Cooperative Extension Service, *1969 Washington State Chemical Insect Control Handbook,* p.6. (recent revisions of the handbook have eliminated this embarrassment).
16. R. Davidson, *Peril on the Job* (Washington: Public Affairs Press, 1972), p.136.
17. *Id.,* p.63.
18. Note 10, *supra.*
19. Deficiencies Report, p.17.
20. "Safety in the Development of Herbicides," before the California Weed Conference, Jan. 19, 1971, p.8.
21. 7 U.S.C. § 135b (c) (1964).
22. H. Wellford, *Sowing the Wind* (Washington: Center for Study of Responsive Law, tent. ed. 1971), pp. XV–7, 8.
23. Deficiencies Report, p.65.
24. *Id.,* p.70.
25. *Id.,* pp.59–62.
26. The incident is reported in Novick, "The Burden of Proof," *Environment,* Oct. 1970, p.16.
27. Cavender, "The Big Pesticide Battle," *Top Operator,* Mar. 1970, p.31.
28. Deficiencies Report, pp.56–59.
29. Backman, p.42.

30. *Environment,* Apr. 1970, p.22.

31. "The Agricultural Chemical Salesman," reprinted in *NACA News & Pest. Rev.,* Dec. 1966, p.7.

32. *See* President's Science Advisory Comm., *Restoring the Quality of Our Environment,* 1965, p.291. The 50 per cent figure is commonly mentioned although it is obviously disputed by pesticide interests and their supporters.

33. For details on NACA's public relations activities, *see* Harmer, "Merchants of Death," *Environmental Quality,* July 1972, p.21.

34. Davidson, *op. cit. supra,* pp.15, 72–73, 146–48, 184–85.

35. Revised July 1965.

36. *Hearings on Federal Pesticide, Control Act of 1971,* Before House Committee on Agriculture, 92nd Cong., 1st Sess., 1971, p.404.

37. "Pesticide Industry Profile Study," May 1971, p.18, compiled by Ernst & Ernst, Trade Ass'n Dept., Washington D.C.

38. For details, *see* articles in *Science,* reprinted in *Hearings on Advisory Committees,* Before the Senate Subcommittee on Intergovernmental Relations, 92d Cong., 1st Sess., 1971, pp.770–75; *Wellford,* pp.195–218; T. Whiteside, *The Withering Rain; America's Herbicidal Folly* (New York: E. P. Dutton, 1971).

39. For details, *see Hearings on Federal Environmental Pesticide Control Act,* Before Senate Subcommittee on Agricultural Research and General Legislation, 92d Cong., 2d Sess., 1972, pp.317–48.

40. Deficiencies Report, p.66.

41. *Ibid.*

42. A report on Zavon's response to the interim findings appears in Oil, Chemical & Atomic Workers Union News, Sept. 1970.

43. Wellford, note 22, *supra,* p. VIII-13.

44. DDT Hearings before Washington State Director of Agriculture, Oct. 1969.

45. Deficiencies Report, p.36.

46. Letter to James Nathan Miller, Oct. 7, 1969.

47. *See Chemical & Engineering News,* Aug. 11, 1969.

48. Reported in *Agrichemical Age,* Feb. 1971, p.10.

49. Wellford, p.333.

50. *Environmental Defense Fund* v. *DHEW,* 428 F.2d 1083 (D.C. Cir. 1970).

51. *Environmental Defense Fund* v. *Hardin,* 428 F.2d 1093 (D.C. Cir. 1970).

52. *Environmental Defense Fund* v. *Ruckelshaus,* 439 F.2d 590 (D.C. Cir. 1970). A fourth decision in 1971, like decisions two and three, ordered Ruckelshaus to explain his reasoning on the question of suspending DDT as an "imminent hazard" in light of a new report. *Environmental Defense Fund* v. *Environmental Protection Agency,* No. 71–1256 (D.C. Cir. 1971) (order of Sept. 22).

Chapter Six

1. U.S. Dept. of HEW press release, Sept. 15, 1971, p.2.

2. Unofficial transcript of press conference, Sept. 16, 1971.

3. *Seattle Post-Intelligencer,* Sept, 28, 1971, p.C-12.

4. Sept. 25, 1971, p.144.

5. National Industrial Pollution Control Council, "Report of the Detergents Sub-Council," Oct. 1970, p.7. (giving data for 1969).

6. *Ibid.*

7. Facts about P & G are based principally on *New York Times,* Feb. 28, 1971, § 3, p.1., col. 3.

8. *Hearings on Water Pollution,* Before Senate Subcommittee on Air and Water Pollution, 91st Cong., 2d Sess., pt. 3,

p.1223 (testimony of Senator Gaylord Nelson (D.-Wis.) (discussing the 1970 budget for research on eutrophication).

9. *See* Leading National Advertisers, Inc., *National Advertising Investments,* 1970, p.5.

10. *Ibid.,* pp.31, 79, 107. The percentage content of phosphates in Biz was reported by the Federal Water Quality Administration in tests on 23 leading laundry products. *See* Bureau of National Affairs, Inc., *Environment Reporter: Current Developments,* May 8, 1970, pp.27–8. Percentages will have changed since then.

11. p.3.

12. Statement in Opposition to Proposed FTC Rule on Detergents, June 23, 1971, p.4.

13. *The National Observer,* Feb. 1, 1971, p.1, col. 4. Procter & Gamble says this fellow never was the project engineer and certainly doesn't know what he's talking about.

14. *In re Lever Brothers Corp.* (N.Y. Sup. Ct. Mar. 2, 1971); *In re Colgate-Palmolive Co.* (N.Y. Sup. Ct. Mar. 2, 1971).

15. *See Wall Street Journal* (Western ed.), Mar. 4, 1971, p.6, col. 2.

16. *See* HEW news release, Aug. 3, 1971.

17. Bureau of National Affairs, Inc., *Trade Reg. & Antitrust Rep.,* Aug. 31, 1971, p.14.

18. *Clean Air & Water News,* Dec. 23, 1971, p.782.

19. *Wall Street Journal* (Western ed.), Jan. 13, 1972, p.13.

20. *See* House Rep. 92–918, 92d Cong., 2d Sess., 1972, pp.55–6.

21. *See, e.g., Hearings on Phosphates in Detergents and the Eutrophication of America's waters,* Before House Conservation and Natural Resources Subcommittee, 91st Cong., 1st Sess., 1969 [hereinafter cited as 1969 Detergent Hearings]; *Hearings on Phosphates and Phosphate Substitutes in Detergents,* Before House Conservation and natural Resources Sub-

committee, 92d Cong., 1st Sess., 1971 [hereinafter cited as 1971 Detergent Hearings]; W.T. Edmondson, "Nutrients and Phytoplankton in Lake Washington," 1 *Nutrients and Eutrophication Special Symposia* (American Society of Limnology and Oceanography, 1972), p.197.

22. 1969 Detergent Hearings, p.6; Report, note 20, *supra*, p.77.

23. "Where We Stand," p.2, speech before 1971 annual meeting of the Soap & Detergent Association (emphasis in original).

24. 1969 Detergent Hearings, p.57 (emphasis in original).

25. *Id.*, p.93 (statement of Frank Healey, Lever Bros.)

26. USDI press release, Aug. 4, 1967.

27. Letter from Charles M. Rogers, director of public information, FWQA, to author, Oct. 4, 1970.

28. JTF Minutes, Oct. 22, 1968.

29. *Ibid.*

30. *See* G. Lamb and C. Shields, *Trade Association Law and Practice* (Boston: Little, Brown, 1971), p.178.

31. Except where otherwise indicated, quotations in text are taken from JTF Minutes, on file with author.

32. Statement before Federal Trade Commission, June 16, 1971.

33. Minutes of Nov. 1, 1968.

34. Minutes of Oct. 22, 1968.

35. Minutes of Sept. 24, 1968.

36. 1969 Detergent Hearings, p.3.

37. "The Facts About Today's Detergents," p.8.

38. Letter of June 13, 1969.

39. Dec. 7, 1967.

40. 1969 Detergent Hearings, p.68.

41. Facts appear in a letter from Robert A. Sweeney, director, Great Lakes Laboratory, to Assemblyman Larry Lane, New York State Assembly, Apr. 30, 1971.

42. *Ibid.*

43. Department of Commerce, Transcript of Press Conference, p.9.

44. Exec. Order 11007 (1962).

45. Rukeyser, "Fact and Foam in the Row Over Phosphates," *Fortune,* Jan. 1972.

46. SDA press release, "Detergent Manufacturers to Label Phosphate Products," Nov. 9, 1970.

47. D. Zwick and M. Benstock, *Water Wasteland* (New York: Grossman, 1971), p.80.

48. Facts in text are taken from a Jack Anderson column titled "Soap Suds Lobby Fights," *Seattle Post-Intelligencer,* Apr. 8, 1972.

49. For the background on the Okun testimony, *see* 1971 Detergent Hearings, pp.439–50. For criticisms of it, *see* House Report, note 20, *supra* pp.72–77.

50. Statement of Apr. 26, 1971, p.4 (reprinted and distributed by Procter & Gamble).

51. Statement of Apr. 26, 1971.

52. *Ibid.*

53. *Ibid.*

54. Senate Commerce Committee, Committee print: "Advice to Consumers on Laundry Detergents," A Report by the Hon. William Spong (D.-Va.), 92d Cong., 1st Sess., 1971.

55. 1971 Detergent Hearings, p.206.

56. For early background, *see* Senate Committee on Public Works, Committee print: "Toxicological and Environmental Implications on the use of Nitrilotriacetic Acid as a Detergent Builder," 91st Cong., 2d Sess., 1970.

57. Unpublished memo to commission from Detergent Task Force, May 18, 1972, p.4, quoting John E. Kinney, a witness at the FTC's hearings.

58. For details, *see* letter from the Hon. Henry S. Reuss

(D.-Wis.), to Miles Kirkpatrick, chairman, FTC., Oct. 11, 1972.

59. Proctor & Gamble press release, Sept. 15, 1971.

Chapter Seven

1. The quotations and other details of the incident come from *Meyer* v. *Harvey Aluminum Inc.,* Tr. on Appeal, vol. 2, pp.390–99 (Ore. Hood River Cir. Ct. 1970).

2. Facts in this paragraph come from H. Stein, *A Casebook on Public Administration and Policy Development* (New York: Harcourt, Brace, 1952), p.313 (chapter titled "The Disposal of the Aluminum Plants") [hereinafter cited as Stein].

3. *United States* v. *Aluminum Co.,* 148 F. 2d 416 (2d Cir. 1945).

4. Stein, p.318.

5. 91 F. Supp. 333 (S.D.N.Y. 1950).

6. *See* Office of Emergency Preparedness, "Stockpile Report to the Congress," June 30, 1971. Disposal of the stockpile "surplus" to the major producers has been going on for several years, *see* letter to author from Bob Ross, assistant commissioner, Office of Stockpile Disposal, General Services Administration, Feb. 2, 1972, but the concept is secure and the aluminum industry the beneficiary.

7. Bonneville Power Administration, *Pacific Northwest Economic Base Study for Power Markets: Aluminum* (1967), Vol. 11, part 7B, pp.139–40.

8. *Reynolds Metals Co.* v. *Lampert,* 324 F. 2d 465, 466 (9th Cir. 1963).

9. These groups filed *amicus curiae* briefs in *Reynolds Metals Co.* v. *Lampert,* note 8 *supra.*

10. Reported in P. Keeton and R. F. Keeton, *Cases and Materials on Torts* (St. Paul: West, 1971), p.377, quoting a newspaper account.

11. *See Seattle Times*, July 10, 1964.

12. *See Seattle Times*, Jan. 23, 1969.

13. D. Coughlin, "Here's How Whatcom County Won Smelter," reprinted in *Seattle Times*, July 9, 1964.

14. For details on Harvey's origins, *see Seattle Times*, Sept. 20, 1955; *id.*, Sept. 21, 1955; *id.*, Jan. 21, 1953.

15. Quoted in *Seattle Times*, Sept. 20, 1955.

16. *Ibid.*

17. *Ibid.* (quoting Mobilization Director Arthur S. Flemming).

18. *Id.*, Sept. 21, 1955.

19. Quoted in *Seattle Times*, Nov. 13, 1970.

20. *Seattle Times*, Mar. 2, 1967.

21. *Smith* v. *Skagit County*, 75 Wash. 2d 715 (1969).

22. The Association recommends that the yearly average fluoride content of forage consumed by cattle should not exceed forty parts per million, with higher values for shorter periods, and suggests the following ambient air standards in parts per billion for gaseous fluorides:

> 4.5 ppb for 12 consecutive hours
> 3.5 ppb for 24 consecutive hours
> 2 ppb for 1 calendar week
> 1 ppb for 1 calendar month.

23. Notes 25, 26 *infra*. As long ago as 1955, the National Academy of Sciences was stipulating a safe level of flourine for dairy cattle to be only 30 parts per million. *See Report on Animal Nutrition: The Fluorosis Problem in Livestock Production*, Pub. 381.

24. "Air Quality Criteria to Protect Livestock from Fluoride Toxicity" by Dr. W.J. Suttie, University of Wisconsin; "Establishment of Air Quality Criteria, With Reference to the Effects of Atmospheric Fluorine on Vegetation" by Delbert C. McCune, Ph.D., Boyce Thompson Institute for Plant Research; and "Air Quality Criteria and the Effects

of Fluorides on Man" by Dr. Harold C. Hodge and Dr. Frank A. Smith, University of Rochester School of Medicine and Dentistry.

25. Letter from A. Clyde Hill to Peter W. Hildebrandt, Feb. 20, 1970.

26. Letter to Ralph Longacre, Feb. 23, 1970.

27. For an illustration, *See* Ex. E. 18, in Bonneville Contract No. 14–03–69319, executed May 2, 1967, by BPA and Rayonier Incorporated (ITT-owned).

28. *See* letter from author, on behalf of the Environmental Defense Fund, to Henry R. Richmond, BPA administrator, Jan. 19, 1971.

29. *See* letter from H.R. Richmond to author, Jan. 25, 1971.

30. Letter to Hector Durocher, BPA, Sept. 21, 1970.

31. Now the administrator is obligated to afford the purchaser a "reasonable opportunity to correct any [polluting] condition," before curtailing the delivery of energy. Nor can he cut off the power before a "final determination, including all rights of appeal or other administrative or judicial review," has been made that the purchaser is in violation of pollution control laws. This phrase eliminates decisively the administrator's authority to influence the polluting power user, for a "final determination" is virtually unknown in the history of pollution control.

32. Letter from Thor Tollefson, director, Washington Department of Fisheries, to John Biggs, director, Washington Department of Ecology, Dec. 3, 1971.

33. For a discussion of the Intalco contract renewal, *see Report on Protecting America's Estuaries: Puget Sound and the Straits of Georgia and Juan de Fuca*, H. Rep. No. 92–1401, 92d Cong., 2d Sess., 1972, pp.46–9.

34. *Id.*, p.48.

35. Letter from Robert Ferrie to the Department of the Interior regional representative, Sept. 30, 1971.

36. *Hearings on Protecting America's Estuaries: Puget Sound and the Straits of Georgia and Juan De Fuca,* Before the House Subcommittee on Conservation and Natural Resources, 92d Cong., 2d Sess., 1971, p.400.

37. Memorandum from BPA administrator H.R. Richmond to acting field representative Emmett Willard, Nov. 24, 1971.

38. Letter from J.C. Dale to author, Jan. 21, 1972.

39. The clause is titled "Protection of Proprietary and Confidential Information" and appears in a grant contract from Kaiser Aluminum & Chemical Corp., on file at the University of Washington, Office of Grants and Contract Research. This particular clause is inoperative at the University of Washington as inconsistent with university regulations.

40. *Meyer* v. *Harvey Aluminum Co.,* Tr. on Appeal, Vol. 7, p.1273 (Ore. Hood River Cir. Ct. 1970).

41. Letter from Grant J. Saulie to State of Washington Supervisor of Public Health, Welfare and Education, Feb. 6, 1967.

42. Letter from Peter H. Hildebrandt, technical director, Air Quality and Radiation Control Section, Feb. 20, 1967.

43. Letter from E. W. Greenfield to Grant J. Saulie, Mar. 1, 1967.

44. Letter from E.W. Greenfield, May 8, 1968.

45. For a full report on the research division's activities, *see Quest: Annual Report Issue,* Oct. 1971, pp.14–15 (published by the WSU College of Engineering).

46. Letter from Gene W. Miller to author, Jan. 7, 1972.

47. Letter from William H. Knight to author, Jan. 24, 1972.

48. "The Boyce Thompson Institute for Plant Research," undated.
49. "Studies on Atmospheric Fluorides at Boyce Thompson Institute," undated.
50. *Renkin* v. *Harvey Aluminum, Inc.*, Tr., Vol. 5, p.666, 226 F. Supp. 169 (D. Ore. 1961).
51. *Id.* at 666–68.
52. *Meyer* v. *Harvey Aluminum, Inc.*, No. 6402, Tr. on Appeal, Vol. 8, pp.1535–36 (Or. Hood River Cir. Ct. 1970).
53. "On the Establishment of Air Quality Criteria, With Reference to the Effects of Atmospheric Fluorine on Vegetation," Mono #69–3, Feb. 1969.
54. L. H. Weinstein and D. C. McCune, "Implications of Air Pollution for Plant Life," 144 *Proceedings of the American Philosophical Society* 18, 20–21 (1970).
55. National Academy of Sciences, *Biological Effects of Atmospheric Pollutants: Fluorides* (1971), p. ix.
56. *Id.*, Acknowledgments.
57. Note 55, *supra*, p.134.
58. Note 55, *supra*, p.151, repeated virtually verbatim in "Air Quality Criteria to Protect Livestock from Fluoride Toxicity," p.6.
59. D. H. Udall and K. P. Keller, *Cornell Veterinarian* 159–84 (1952).
60. Statement on potential sources of bias, Philip Handler, president, National Academy of Sciences, Aug. 29, 1971.
61. The contentions that follow are taken from a paper titled "Corrections and Comments by Primary Aluminum Industry Liaison Committee," Dec. 27, 1971, and a memo on Trip Report on Aluminum Committee Meeting in San Francisco from Reid Iverson, Metallurgical Section, to Stanley T. Cuffe, Chief of APCO's Industrial Studies Branch, Jan. 24, 1972.

62. Liaison Committee Minutes, Dec. 2, 1970.

63. Memo on Trip Report, note 61, *supra.*

Chapter Eight

1. An account of the Rowen-PG & E incident appears in a twenty-part series by John Read in the *Eureka Times-Standard,* beginning June 18, 1972.

2. 49 CFR § 173.397 (1972).

3. Report of Raymond R. Skidmore to International Brotherhood of Electrical Workers, Local 1245 Shop Steward, Aug. 6, 1969.

4. E. D. Weeks, "Confidential Memorandum: Counseling of R. Rowen on 8/7/69," Aug. 8, 1969.

5. Confidential memorandum on radiation incident of Feb. 18, 1970, signed by J. Boots.

6. State of California, Unemployment Insurance Appeals Board, *In the matter of Robert J. Rowen,* Case No. SF-1319, Tr. p.50 (1971) [hereinafter cited as Transcript].

7. Information in paragraph is taken from Pacific Gas & Electric Co. Prospectus, Oct. 28, 1971, *passim.*

8. Reported in R. Fellmeth, *Power and Land in California* (Washington: Center for Study of Responsive Law, tent. ed. 1971), p.1–17 [hereinafter cited as Fellmeth].

9. Facts are taken from PG & E, "Electricity from Atomic Energy," undated.

10. Fellmeth, p.I-37.

11. L. Metcalf & V. Reinemer, *Overcharge* (New York: David McKay, 1967), p.199.

12. *Id.,* p.191.

13. Norman R. Sutherland, "A Progress Report on Nuclear Electric Power," 1956.

14. For details, *see* the series of articles in the *San Francisco*

Guardian by Peter Petrakis, reprinted in *Congressional Record,* May 18, 1972, pp. E 5431–5433.

15. Quoted in *id., p.* E 5432.

16. For full accounts, *see* J. Holdren & P. Herrera, *Energy* (San Francisco: Sierra Club, 1971), pp.191–203; Pesonen, "A Visit to the Atomic Park," undated.

17. "Public Acceptance of Nuclear Power," speech before the Los Angeles Section of the American Nuclear Society, printed in the Society's Proceedings on Nuclear Power Reactor Siting, Feb. 16–18, 1965, p.247 (emphasis in original).

18. For background, *see* Mattison and Daly, "Bodega: The Reactor, The Site, the Hazard," *Nuclear Information,* vol. VI, no. 5, Apr. 1964. A company version of the Bodega Head controversy appears in Moutz, "Siting of Nuclear Power Plants on the West Coast," in Proceedings, note 17, *supra.*

19. *See* Pesonen, note 16, *supra.* The earthquake criterion appears in 10 CFR § 100.10 (c) (1) (1971).

20. Some of the work is discussed in Adams, "Thermal Power, Aquatic Life and Kilowatts on the Pacific Coast," 31 *Proceedings of the American Power Conference* (1968).

21. *Fellmeth,* pp. IV-120, 123.

22. For sample agreements, *see* Pacific Gas & Electric Co., "Summary of Ecological Studies and Agreements between California Resources Agency and Pacific Gas & Electric Company for Thermal Power Plants," March 1969.

23. Diablo Agreement, paragraph 3, 5.

24. Diablo Agreement, paragraph 11. For an example of suppressed geological data affecting Portland General Electric's Trojan Plant on the Columbia River, *see Wall Street Journal* (Western ed.), Jan. 26, 1972, p.1.

25. Pittsburgh Agreement, paragraph 3.

26. Stroube, note 17, *supra.*

27. For a technical description of the plant and its operat-

ing record, *see* AEC, *Small Nuclear Power Plants,* vol. 1, 1966, pp.172–191.

28. Letter from David C. Joseph, executive officer, to PG & E, Apr. 8, 1966; Findings of Fact, Mar. 30, 1966.

29. Letter from Keith S. Dunbar to Paul Mathew, PG & E, Feb. 28, 1969; Findings of Fact, Feb. 27, 1969.

30. Letter from John R. Hannum, assistant civil engineer, California Regional Water Quality Control Board—North Coast Region, to author, Oct. 29, 1971.

31. Letter from Amasa C. Cornish, California Dept. of Public Health, Bureau of Radiological Health, to author, Sept. 10, 1971. EPA also checks up on the analysis.

32. Letter from James A. Gast, professor of oceanography, to author, Feb. 2, 1972.

33. Humboldt State College Foundation, Contract No. Eng. 8–68, July 8, 1969, p.4, paragraph 3.6.

34. Quoted in S. Novick, *The Careless Atom* (Boston: Houghton Mifflin, 1969), p.115.

35. R. Gillette, "Reactor Emissions: AEC Guidelines Move Toward Critics Position," *Science* 172: 1216 (1971).

36. Data supplied by Atomic Energy Commission.

37. *See* J. Gofman & A. Tamplin, *Poisoned Power: The Case Against Nuclear Power Plants* (Emmaus, Pa.: Rodale Press, 1971).

38. Letter from Peter A. Morris, director, AEC's Division of Reactor Licensing, to author, Oct. 20, 1971.

39. EPA, "Questions and Answers About Nuclear Power Plants," July 1971.

40. *See* Keyes and Howarth, "Approaches to Liability for Remote Causes," 56 *Iowa L. Rev.* 531, 542 (1971).

41. Note 38, *supra.*

42. *Hearings on Licensing and Regulation of Nuclear Reactors,* Before the Joint Committee on Atomic Energy, 90th Cong., 2d Sess., 1967, pp.223–33.

43. Safety Evaluation by the Division of Reactor Licensing, DKT No. 50-133, Humboldt Bay Power Plant Unit No. 3, July 22, 1968.

44. "PG & E Annual Management Meeting with AEC Region V Compliance Personnel," prepared by James G. Carrol, PG & E, Sept. 14, 1970, quoting AEC personnel.

45. Of forty-nine delayed injury cases in which there were either incomplete or no radiation records introduced in evidence, there were forty denials and only nine awards. Eason, "Workmen's Compensation for the Radiation Worker—The Role of the Atomic Energy Commission," 1970 *ABA Section of Ins., Negl. & Com. Law* 136, 146.

46. Letter from PG & E Senior Vice President and General Counsel, to R.L. Doan, AEC's Division of Reactor Licensing, Aug. 22, 1966.

47. Transcript, p.94.

48. *Id.*, p.86.

49. As an annual average over a lifetime after age 18. PG & E standards limit exposure to five rems per year. The difference is meaningless since the AEC does not cite licenses for exceeding standards more stringent than the commission's.

50. Quoted in Rapoport, "Oops!. . . . The Story of Nuclear Power Plants," *Ramparts*, Mar. 1972, pp.49, 53.

51. Transcript of Arbitration, *In re Local 1245, IBEW, and PG & E*, Arb. Cas. Nos. 35, 36, p.144.

52. Brief for Respondent, Feb. 9, 1971, p.25.

53. Brief for Complainant, p.2.

54. For details of this incident, *see Eureka Times-Standard*, Dec. 23, 1971, p.1., col. 1.

55. Letter from Frank D. Morgan, to William F. Ferroggiario, Eureka district attorney, Jan. 18, 1971.

56. Letter to Frank D. Morgan, Apr. 23, 1971.

57. For a recent, forceful criticism of the AEC, *see* H.P.

Metzger, *The Atomic Establishment* (New York: Simon and Schuster, 1972).

Chapter Nine

1. Extracted with a few changes from Stewart, "Noise, A Jet-Age Health Hazard," *Trial,* Feb.-Mar. 1969, p.53.
2. Description of the Madison testimony is found in Plaintiff's Pre-Trial Statement, p.8, *Virginians for Dulles* v. *Volpe,* Civ. No. 507–70-A (E.D.Va. 1971).
3. Complaint of Aviation Consumer Action Project, CAB DKT. No. 24593 (July 6, 1972).
4. *Ibid.*
5. D. Leinsdorf, *Citibank* (Washington: Center for Study of Responsive Law, tent. ed. 1971), page 248.
6. Blaine Cook, T.W.A. senior vice president, quoted in *Saturday Review,* Jan. 3, 1970, p.31.
7. Speech of Dec. 2, 1971.
8. Speech of Oct. 29, 1970, p.10.
9. EPA, *The Social Impact of Noise,* 1971, p.3 (referring to both aircraft and highway noise levels).
10. EPA, *Economic Effects of Noise,* 1971, p.21.
11. "Airports and the Community," Feb. 1972, p.17.
12. Marcy B. Fannon, director of specification development, American Airlines, in Transportation Assoc. of America, *Proceedings on Policy Guidelines for Transport Technology,* Sept. 22, 1971, pp.12–13.
13. J.E. Steiner, quoted in *Aviation Week & Space Technology,* Feb. 14, 1972.
14. In 1958 the Port of New York Authority set limits for Jet take-off noise of 112 perceived noise decibels. *See* Lesser, "The Air Noise Problem: Federal Power but Local Liability," 3 *Urban Law.* 175, 198 (1971). Specifications in

subsequent 747 contracts anticipated exceeding 112 PNdb.

15. Quoted in *Township of Hanover* v. *Town of Morristown*, DKT. No. C3172–68 (N.J. Super. Ct., Jan. 10, 1972).

16. For details, *see* Kaplow, "A Report on Jet Pollution," 1972 (a publication of the Aviation Consumer Action Project).

17. *United States* v. *Manufacturers Aircraft Association, Inc.*, Civ. No. 72–1307 (S.D.N.Y. 1972).

18. The background on NANAC is borrowed from R. Baron, *The Tyranny of Noise* (New York: St. Martin's, 1970), p.171.

19. "The Airlines View of Needed R & D Applications Engineering Efforts for Civil Aviation," June 1971, p.27.

20. "Airports and the Community," p.11.

21. In Transportation Association of America, *Proceedings on Policy Guidelines for Transport Technology*, Sept. 22, 1971, p.12.

22. Before the American Airlines Board of Directors and Freight System Advisory Board, Mar. 17, 1970.

23. Before the SAE Air Transportation luncheon, Apr. 22, 1970.

24. Speech of May 1, 1970.

25. Speech of June 19, 1970.

26. *See National Aviation System Ten Year Plan: 1971–80*, 1970, pp.133–134.

27. Sperry, "Noise Abatement Program, FY 71–72," p.4.

28. EPA, *Summary Report on Noise Programs in the Federal Government*, 1971, incorporating FAA Congressional submission, pp.353 *et seq.*

29. EPA, *Summary Report on Noise*, 1971, p.8.

30. BBN letters, titled "Organization and Services," "Activities in the Field of Aircraft Noise."

31. 369 U.S. 84, 90 (1962).

32. *See* Northeastern Illinois Planning Commission, *Met-*

ropolitan Aircraft Noise Abatement Policy Study, O'Hare International Airport, Chicago, Ill., July 1971, p.3.

33. *See* Christopher, "Legal Aspects of Aircraft Noise and Sonic Boom in the United States," *SAE-DOT Conference on Aircraft and the Evnironment,* Feb., 1971, pp.46, 51.

34. Reported in T. Berland, *The Fight for Quiet* (Englewood Cliffs, N.J.: Prentice-Hall, 1970), p.284, citing another authority.

35. The incident is reported in Berger, "Nobody Loves an Airport," 43 *So. Calif. L. Rev.* 631, 789 (1970).

36. 49 U.S.C. § 1431 (b) (4). The law also vests power to impose noise control requirements on future aircraft.

37. Quoted in J. Burby, *The Great American Motion Sickness* (Boston, Toronto: Little, Brown, 1971), p.200.

38. D.E. Bishop and R.D. Horonjeff, "Procedures for Developing Noise Exposure Forecast Areas for Aircraft Flight Operations," Aug. 1969.

39. Plaintiff's Trial Brief, p.59, *Petterson* V. *Resor,* Civ. No. 71–283 (D. Ore. April 3, 1972).

40. *Id.,* p.69.

41. Quoted in *New York Times,* Oct. 12, 1971, p.1., col. 6.

42. *Ibid.*

43. *New York Times,* Oct. 14, 1971, p.89, col. 5.

44. *Virginians for Dulles* v. *Volpe,* 4 ERC 1232 (E.D. Va. 1972).

45. Undated publication. For an article making similar points, *see* Berger, "You Know I Can't Hear You When the Planes Are Flying," 4 *Urban Law.* 1 (1972).

46. *Town of East Haven* v. *Eastern Airlines, Inc.,* 282 F. Supp. 507, 512–513 (D. Conn. 1968).

47. *East Haven* v. *New Haven,* 159 Conn. 453 (1970).

48. *See* "Games the FAA Plays," note 45, *supra.*

49. *Id.,* p.7.

50. 34 Fed. Reg. 18358 (1969).

51. *In re Dreifus,* FAA Regulatory DKT. No 9071 (1969).
52. "Games the FAA Plays," note 45, *supra*, p.7.
53. *Port of New York Authority* v. *Eastern Airlines, Inc.* 259F. Supp. 142 (E.D.N.Y. 1966).
54. *E.g., Lockheed Air Terminal, Inc.* v. *City of Burbank,* 457 F.2d 667 (9th Cir. 1972).
55. Quoted in Danforth, "Mercury's Children in the Urban Trap: Community Planning and Federal Regulation of the Jet Noise Source," 3 *Urban Law.* 206, 223–24n.67 (1971).
56. "Economic Impact of Implementing Acoustically Treated Nacelle and Duct Configurations Applicable to Low Bypass Turbofan Engines," FAA No-70–11, July 1970.
57. Resolution No. 5, adopted by U.S. members only.
58. 35 Fed. Reg. 16980 (Nov. 4, 1970).
59. *Id.,* pp.16981–82.
60. Examples are taken from the FAA files, DKT No. 10664, Notice 70–44, "Civil Airplane Noise Reduction Retrofit Requirements."
61. *New York Times,* Oct. 14, 1971, p.89, col. 5.
62. *New York Times,* Feb. 15, 1972, p.54, col. 1.
63. Before the Aerospace Industry Association's 28th Annual Conference, May 18, 1972.

Chapter Ten

1. Quoted in *Bus. & Society,* Aug. 25, 1970, p.3.
2. Quoted in M. Mintz & J. Cohen, *America, Inc.* (New York: Dial Press, 1971), p.376.
3. *Minding the Corporate Conscience,* vol. 3, no. 1.
4. Reported in *Washington Post,* May 3, 1972, p.A-3.
5. *In the Name of Profit* (New York: Doubleday, 1972), p.239.
6. Pub. Law 91–190, Jan. 1, 1970.
7. For recent documentation of the pervasive reach of cor-

porate and government secrecy, *see, Hearings on the Role of Giant Corporations,* Before the Senate Select Committee on Small Business, 92d Cong., 1st Sess., 1971. On the subject of federal incorporation as a means of curbing monopoly power and attendant secrecy, *see* "Symposium on Federal Chartering of Corporations," 61 *Georgetown L.J.* 71 (1972).

8. *See,* in this connection, Rodgers, "The National Industrial Pollution Control Council: Advice or Collude," 13 *Bost. Coll. Ind, & Comm. L. Rev.* 719 (1972). Congress, in 1972, enacted legislation that goes part way toward enforcing accountability of advisory committees. Federal Advisory Committee Act, Pub. Law 92–463, Oct. 6, 1972.

9. *See* 118 *Congressional Record* S11491, July 24, 1972.

10. *The Closing Circle* (New York: Knopf, 1971), pp. 283–4.

INDEX

Adams, Donald, 170, 178
Adams, John, 179
Advertising, 3–4
 by detergent manufacturers, 139
 by highway industry, 35, 45, 47
 in land development, 100–103
Advertising Council of America, xvii, 4
Aerospace Industries Association, 220, 236
Aerospace subsidy, 218
Agrichemical Age, 113
Agriculture Department, Pesticides Regulation Division, 115, 119, 121, 129, 132, 244
Aircraft noise, 215–238
 FAA research in, 223–224
Air pollution, McKee Report on, 64–66
Air Pollution Control Office, EPA, 184
Airport Operators Council International, 229–230, 235
Air Transport Association of America, 219, 221, 243
Aldrin, 121
Algae, phosphorus and, 146, 150
Allen, Gail, 191–192
Allen, Sidney P., 103
Allied Chemical Corp., 143
Aluminum, first production of, 162
Aluminum alloys, smelting of, 160–188
Aluminum Association, xv, 5, 168–171, 176, 185–188
Aluminum Company of America (Alcoa), 12, 22, 74, 162, 165, 170, 177, 180, 186
Aluminum industry
 air pollution by, 169–170
 Fluorides and, 169–171
Aluminum Industry Liaison Committee, 243
American Airlines, Inc., 219, 221
American Bar Association, 77

American Can Company, 4, 7, 12, 22
American Cyanamid Company, 242
American Metal Climax, Inc., 74, 165, 168, 173
American Mining Congress, xv, 70, 72, 76, 79, 81, 83
American Road Builders Association, 31, 34–35
American Smelting and Refining Company (ASARCO), ix, 54–84, 242
American Sulfur Institute, 66
Anaconda Copper Company, 56–57, 64, 76, 81, 186
Anchor-Hocking Glass Company, 22
Anderson, Arthur, 105
Anderson, Jack, 211
Anheuser-Busch Company, 22
Anti-litter ads, 3–4
Anti-litter laws, 5
Argenbright, Lee, 68
Arizona State Board of Health, 69, 82
Arsenic, in smelting operations, 54, 59
ASARCO; *see* American Smelting and Refining Company
Asphalt magazine, 30
Aspinwall, Wayne, 56
Association of National Advertisers, x-xi, 139
Association of Oregon Industries, 165
Atomic Energy Commission, 193–195, 197, 201, 205–208, 248
Automobile
 accidents with, 31
 Highway Trust Fund and, 32–33
 pollution from, 30–32, 37
Automobile Club of Southern California, 39, 43–44
Automobile industry, public relations and advertising in, 35–36
Automobile Manufacturers Association, 30

Azodrin, 121

Bank of America, 40, 195
Bank of California, 195
Ban-the-can measures, 7
Barber, Charles, 53, 59, 62, 70, 72, 79
Barron's, 130
Bauxite ore, 162
Beer cans and bottles, return of, 3, 7–8
Benstock, Marcy, viii
Berger, Michael, 231, 233
Berliner, Harold, 90
Better Homes and Gardens, 125
Big lie, in political campaigns, 42–43
Blatt, Fred, 161
Bodega Bay, Calif., 196
Boeing Company, 17–18, 219, 234
Boeing 747 jet, 217, 219
Boiling water reactor, 199–200
Boise Cascade Recreation Communities Group, 87–108, 194, 242
Bolt, Beranek and Newman, Inc., 223, 226–228
Bonneville Power Administration, viii, 163–167, 172–173, 244
Borchardt, Jack A., 155–156
Borgwart, John, 106
Bottles, recycling of, 2–27
Boyce Thompson Institute for Plant Research, viii, 180–185
Braude, Marvin, 42
Brenner, T. E., 144, 148
Brinkley, Parke, 129
British Royal Commission on Noxious Vapors, 56–57
Bronson, John, 46
Brookhauser, Arch, 44
Brown, Edmund G., Jr., 47–48
Brown, L. V., 210
Browne, Secor, 215–217, 222
Bueltman, Charles, 144, 147–149
Bureau of Public Roads, 34
Bureau of Solid Waste Management, 4, 25

Bureau of Sports and Fisheries, Interior Department, 174
Bus equipment, mass transit and, 49–50
Business Week, 22, 91, 137
Byrne, Joe, 170, 186

California
    Proposition 18 in, 38, 40–44, 47, 49
    smog in, 38
    State Public Works Committee in, 34–35
    University of, x, 122
California Advisory Commission on Marine and Coastal Resources, 195
California Agricultural Teachers Association, 122
California Freeway Support Committee, 39–40
California Highway Commission, 38
California Medical Association, 38
Californians Against Road and Tax Trap, 48
Californians for Modern Highways, 39
California Packing Corp., 195
California Spray Chemical Corp., 111 n.
California State Automobile Association, 39
California State Employees' Association, 39
California Taxpayers' Association, 39
California Unemployment Insurance Appeals Board, 194
California Weed Conference, 120
Calkins, David, 80
Campaign contributions, disclosure of, 246
Can manufacturers, stake of, 7–8
Carbonated Beverage Container Manufacturers' Association, 21
"Careful use" policy, on insecticides, 116
Carey, Dave, 95

Caribou Lodge project, 195
Carnow, Bertram, 54
Carson, Rachel, 112, 130
Cavanaugh Communities, 91
Chappie, Eugene, 97
Chemagro, Inc., 127
Chemical industry
 propaganda for, 124–126
 research and development in, 125
 salesmen in, 121–124
 trade secrets in, 126
Chemical pesticides; *see* Pesticides
Cheney, Richard, 21
Chicago Tribune, 125
Chlorinated hydrocarbons, damage
 from, 130
Chokola, Peter, 9, 22
Chrysler Corp., 30, 245
Civil Aeronautics Board, 216–217,
 222
Clean Air Act, 63, 71, 73, 77–78,
 82–83
Closed-loop emission control sys-
 tem, 78
Coca-Cola Company, 4, 15, 22
Cohen, Howard, 132–133
Cohen, Jerry, viii
Colgate-Palmolive Company, 138–
 141, 143, 154
Collier, Randolph, 34, 39
Colson, Charles, 154
Columbia River salmon case, xvi
Columbia River Valley, fluorosis in,
 185
Cominco copper smelter, British Co-
 lumbia, 68
Commerce Department, U.S., xviii,
 77–78, 149; *see also* National
 Industrial Pollution Control
 Council
Commoner, Barry, vii-viii, 248–249
Congress, U.S., highway legislation
 in, 32–35, 50
Connecticut, land sales in, 102
Containers, as refuse, 2–27
Continental Can Company, Inc., 12,
 15, 22

"Controlled use" dogma, in pesti-
 cide use, 116–118
Coors, Adolf, Company, 22
Copper smelting, pollution from,
 53–84
Corestox, Inc., 122–123
Cornell University, 151, 155
Corporate Country
 crime in, xiii-xiv
 propaganda in, xi, 124–126
 three techniques of, vii-viii, xviii
Corporation
 as profit maximizer, 243
 social responsibilities of, 245
Corps of Engineers, U.S. Army, xvi
Council of Economic Advisors, 55
Council on Economic Priorities, 89
Council on Environmental Quality,
 137, 157
"Counterintuitive behavior," phos-
 phate content and, 142
Covington & Burley law firm, 72
Cralley, L. V., 170
Crime, in Corporate Country, xiii-
 xiv
Crocker Citizens National Bank, 40,
 195
Crompton, Oliver, 178
Curia, Joe, 87–88
Currie, Neil J., 34

Dale, J. C., 170, 186
Day, L. B., 174
DDT
 ban on, 131
 government research on, 114
 political losses in, xi
 problems of, 110–133
DDVP Pest Strip, 119–121, 128
Defense Production Authority, 166
Detergent manufacturers, advertis-
 ing expenditures of, 139
Detergents, phosphate-containing,
 135–158
Developments magazine, 99
Dickson, Fred W., 4, 16
Dieldrin, 121

Diesel buses, mass transit and, 49
Di Giorgio Fruit Corp., 195
Di Luzio, Frank, 143
Disposal system, cost-free, 8–9
Dominick, David, 24
"Dooley, Mr.," vi, xix
Dorsey, B. R., 242
Dow Chemical Company, 114, 120, 127, 241
Ducktown, Tenn., smelter at, 58, 67–68
Dunne, Finley Peter ("Mr. Dooley"), vi, xix
Du Pont de Nemours, E. I., Company, Inc., 114
Dyer, Ken, 173

Eco-Action, 38
Edwards, Charles, 136
Ehrlichman, John, 168
Electricity, in aluminum production, 161–164
El Paso, Texas, lead poisoning in, 54–55, 59, 84
Emahiser, C. E., 209–210
Engler, Robert, viii
Entomology, insecticide sales and, 123–124
Environmental Protection Agency (EPA), 24, 53, 57, 71, 78–82, 131–133, 140, 144, 152, 157, 170, 184–187
Equitable Life Assurance Company, 195
Esposito, John, viii
Eureka Times-Standard, 199, 208–209
Eutrophication
  Joint Task Force for, 143
  phosphorus and, 149–150
Evans, Dan, 19, 167, 175

Fairhaven College, Washington State, 13
Fannon, Marcy B., 221–222
Favoritism, influence and, 188
Federal Aviation Administration, 223, 225–238, 244

Federal Insecticide, Fungicide and Rodenticide Act (FIFRA), 115, 121, 131–132
Federal Power Commission, 196
Federal Trade Commission, x–xi, 140, 144, 153–158
Federal Water Pollution Control Administration, 144–145
Federal Water Quality Administration, 135
Fellmeth, Robert, 43
Fery, John, 104
Field, Mervin, 39
FIFRA; *see* Federal Insecticide, Fungicide and Rodenticide Act
Finch, Robert, 131
First Amendment, xi
First National City Bank, 217
Fish and Wildlife Service, 198
Fitzsimmons, K. R., 121
Flanigan, Peter M., 53 n., 57, 82, 84, 154, 247
Fluor, Simon, 78
Fluorosis, in Columbia River Valley, 185
Fluor Utah firm, 78
FMC Corp., 127, 143, 150
Food and Drug Administration, 17, 136, 140
Ford Motor Company, 30
Fortune magazine, 89, 125
Foster, Charles, 237
Foundation for Economic Education, 196
Frary, F. C., 180
Fraud, in land development, 100–101, 103, 105–106
Freud, Sigmund, 112
Fuel tax, 37

GAC properties, Florida, viii, 91
Galbraith, John Kenneth, viii, 114
Garcia, Alberto, 54
Gelcher, Joseph, 44, 46
Gendel, Neil, 102
General Development Corp., 91

General Electric Company, 245
General Foods Corp., 22
General Mining Law (1872), 56
General Motors Corp., xvii, 30, 49, 245
General Services Administration, 167
Georgia-Pacific Corp., 12, 165
Gersticker, Carl A., 241 n.
Gibbons, John, 35
Gibbs, Bill, 88
Giegy Chemical Company, 117
Glass Bottle Blowers Association, 14–15
Glass Container Manufacturers Institute, 5, 21
Good Housekeeping, 150
Gordon, Clarence, 53–54
Gorton, Slade, 19
Great Lakes, eutrophication of, 148
Green, John, 82
Griggs v. County of Allegheny, 224, 234
Grossman, Barry, 77
Gulf Oil Company, 30, 41, 47–48, 242
Hamilton, Walter, 77
Hand, Learned, 162
Hansberger, Robert, 89, 103–104, 107
Hansberry, Roy T., 121
Hardin, Clifford, 131
Hardison, E. Domingo, 44, 46
Harlow, Bryce, 138, 154
Hart, Philip, 248
Hartley, Fred, 41
Harvey Aluminum Company, 161, 165–166, 178–179, 182, 242
Hatfield, Robert, 40
Hayes, Wayland, 130
Hazard, Ellison L., 15–16
Hazleton Nuclear Science Corp., 204–205
Health, Education, and Welfare Department, 128, 183
Heck, Walter, 171

Hecla Mining Company, 74
Heilbroner, Robert, viii, 245
Hennessey, Alice, 104
Herbicides, defects caused by, 127
Hercules, Inc., 126–127
Hertel, Edward K., 135 n.
Hetch Hetchy Dam, 196
Heublein Company, 22
Hickel, Walter, 136, 147
Highway
    accidents and, 31
    oil companies and, 44–49
    problems involving, 28–50
Highway Research Board, National Academy of Sciences, 5
Highway transportation, public attitude on, 36
Highway Trust Fund, 32–34, 37, 50
Highway Users Federation, xvii, 31, 35–36
Hildebrandt, Jerry, 169
Hildebrandt, Pete, 170
Hill, A. C., 170
Hitchcock, Alfred, 197
Holloman, J. Herbert, 31
Home communities, development of, 90–98
Homeowner's association, 98
Hooker Chemical Corp., 143
Horizon Corp., 91, 99–100
Horworth, Ross, 87
Hosmer, Craig, 203
Houghton Mifflin Company, 112
House Interior Committee, 56
House Public Works Committee, 33
Houthakker, Hendrik, 55–56, 72–73, 77
Howmet Corp., 165
Hubbard, Harvey M., 215
Humble Oil and Refining Company, 41
Humboldt Bay nuclear power plant, 191–212, 242
Humboldt County, Calif., 199
Humboldt State College Foundation, 200

Illinois, University of, 18, 54
Illinois Soft Drink Association, 5
Incline Village, Calif., 90, 95
Industrial Reorganization Act, 248
Industrial Reorganization Commission, 248
Industrial Water Engineering, 144
Industry for a Quality Environment, 10
Industry Task Force for DDT, 111
Influence
  favoritism and, 188
  technology and, ix-x
Initiative 256, Washington State litter program, 13–20
Insecticide, Fungicide and Rodenticide Act (FIFRA), 115, 121, 131–132
Insecticide Act of 1910, 115
Insecticides, labeling of, 115–116
Intalco Aluminum Corp., 165, 173, 179, 186
Interior Department, U.S., 148, 174, 198
International Business Machines Corp., 245
International Joint Commission on Lake Erie Pollution, 135
International Minerals and Chemicals Company, 74
International Paper Company, 22
International Telephone & Telegraph Corp., vii, 91, 211
Interstate System, growth of, 29
ITT Ragonier, Inc., 172

Jackson, Henry, 72
Jet aircraft noise, 215–238
John Birch Society, 196
John Day Dam, 164
Johnson, Bob, 94–95
Johnson, Gummy, 13
Johnson, Julius, 120
Johnson, Lyndon B., 215–216
Joint Economic Committee, xii
Joint Legislative Transportation Committee, 36

Joint Task Force on Eutrophication, xvii, 143–149, 243, 247
Justice Department, U.S., 9, 77, 119, 144, 146, 162, 220, 245

Kaiser Aluminum & Chemical Company (Kaiser Industries Corp.), 5, 12, 162–163, 176–177
Keep America Beautiful, Inc., 3–8, 12, 20–21, 27, 243
Keep America Beautiful Act, 13; *see also* Initiative 256
Keller, Robert, 13, 19
Kendall, Donald M., 5, 11, 16, 22–23, 26
Kennecott Copper Corp., 56, 64, 73–74, 76, 78, 81, 242
Kern County Land Company, 195
Kilcoyne, Mary P., 144, 148
King, Walter, 225–226
Kitsap County, Washington, 94
Klamath River Ranches project, Calif., 105
Kluczynski, John, 33
Knowland, William, 38
Kraft paper mill, Louisana, 90
Kramer, M. J. and Associates, 45, 47
Kroger, Inc., 22

Lagomarsino, Robert, 97
Lake Erie pollution, Joint Commission on, 135
Lake-of-the-Pines project, 92, 95, 100–101
Land development
  fraudulent sales in, 101, 105–106
  misleading advertising in, 100–103
Land sales, tactics in, 98–100
Land use planning, 34, 92–93
Lead arsenate, sale of, 115
Lead chamber process, 58
Lead poisoning, 54–56
League of California Cities, 38
League of Women Voters, 38
Leary, John S., Jr., 120

Lever Brothers Company, 137–138, 140, 143, 146, 150, 154
Litter
  mythology of, 6–7
  as "people problem," 3–7, 11
Litter Trust Fund, 12
Lobbies, influence of, ix–x
Lockheed Aircraft Corp., vii, xii, 216, 225
Lockwood, Bert J., 230
Lombardi, Vince, 99
Lone Star Cement Corp., 74
Longview Fibre Company, 12
Los Angeles, smog in, 32
Los Angeles Times, 40
Lotspuch, Edgar H., 135 n., 156
Lucky Stores, Inc., 22
Lundborg, Louis, 40

McClaren, Richard, 77
McComb, John, 41
McCown, George, 104
McCune, Delbert, 169–170, 184–185
McDonnell Douglas Corp., 234
McDowell, John R., 106
MacGregor, Ian, 173
McKee, Arthur G. & Company, 63
McKee Report, 64–69, 73–75
McLean, David, 182
McLean, Louis A., 111–113, 129–130
McNew, George L., 180–182
Madison, James, 216
Manufacturers Aircraft Association, 220
Manufacturing Chemists Association, 148
Magnuson, Warren, 163
Marcor, Inc., 22
Martin, Paul and Verla, 164–165
Martin Marietta Corp., 161, 164, 186
Maryland Real Estate Commission, 88
Massachusetts Institute of Technology, 31
Mass transit, factors in, 48–49
May, William F., 4, 7, 22

Mead Packaging Company, 22
Megonnell, William, 73
Mellon Institute, ix
Mellon National Bank, 41
Meyer, C. B., 66
Michigan, University of, 155
Mickle, D. Grant, 36
Middleton, John, 70, 77
Miller, Otto, 41
Milliken, Frank, 73–74, 76
Mills, James, 38, 43, 111 n., 116
Mills, W. L., 96–97
Mining and Minerals Policy Act (1972), 56
Mining Sub-Council, NIPCC, 73–75, 77
Mintz, Morton, viii
Mobil Oil Corp., 30, 48
Model Litter Control Law, 10, 12, 14
Monsanto Company, 22, 114, 125, 143, 146
Montana, University of, 53–54
Montana State Board of Health, 57, 71, 82
Montrose Chemical Corp., 130–131
Moore, Clifton A., 229
Morgan, Frank, 210
Morgens, Howard J., 138, 152, 156, 158
Morrell, James, 180–182
Morris, W. K., 48
Morrison, Harry, 43
Mosiman, Donald, 82

NACA; see National Agricultural Chemicals Association
NACA News and Pesticide Review, 128
Nader, Ralph, viii
Nader Reports
  on Power and Land in California, 43
  on water pollution, 152–153
National Academy of Sciences, 5–6, 11, 185–186, 247
National Aerial Applications Association, 116

National Aeronautics and Space Administration, 234, 236
National Agricultural Chemicals Association, 111–112, 116, 123–125
National Air Pollution Control Administration, 63–64, 84, 170, 183
National Aviation Noise Abatement Council, 221
National Can Corp., 12
National Canners Association, 7, 116
National Center for Resource Recovery, Inc., 25–26, 243
National Center for Solid Waste Disposal, 22
National Council of State Clubs, 5
National Industrial Pollution Control Council (NIPCC), xviii, 7, 11, 16, 23, 73, 76–78, 89, 138, 149–150, 152, 168, 173, 218, 221, 247
National Master Transportation Program, 48
National Plant Food Institute, 148
National Public Service Organization for the Prevention of Litter, 3–4
National Soft Drink Association, xv, 9–10
NEF (noise exposure forecast), 226–230
Nelson, Ken, 64, 77–78, 83
New Mexico, land sales in, 100–101
Newspaper Enterprise Association, 125
New York Life Insurance Company, 195
New York State College of Human Ecology, 151
New York Times, 48, 138, 230
NIPCC; *see* National Industrial Pollution Control Council
Nitrolotriacetic acid, 157
Nixon, Richard M., 138
Noise, measurement of, 223–224
Noise control, 218–219
 FAA and, 232–233

Noise exposure forecast (NEF), 227
Noise pollution, 215–238
Non-returnable bottles, problems of, 7–22
North Coast Regional Water Quality Board, 200
Northwest Aluminum Company, 167
NTA (nitrolotriacetic acid), 157
Nuclear radiation, dangers of, 191–212

Occupational Safety and Health Act (1920), 202
Ocean Pines development project, 87–108
Office of Consumer Affairs, 22
Office of Interstate Land Sales Registration, 106–107
Office of Noise Abatement, Transportation Department, 237–238
Okun, Daniel, 155
O'Melveny and Myers law firm, 97
Onorato, Robert, 101
Opinion Research Corp., 36
Oregon, aluminum industry in, 165–166
Oregon State University, 161, 178
Overton, J. Allen, 70–71
Owens, James, 72, 77
Owens-Illinois Glass Company, 9, 21–22

Pacific Gas & Electric Company, 191–212, 242, 248
Pan American World Airways, Inc., 217
Pastore, John, 191 n.
Patterson, E. Scott, 142
Pennsylvania State University, 147–148
Pepsico, Inc., 5, 11, 15–16, 21–22
Pesticides
 first use of, 113–114
 misuse of, 110–133
Pesticides Regulation Division, Agriculture Department, 115, 119, 121, 129, 132, 244

Petree, Neil, 39, 42
Phelps Dodge Corp., 56, 64, 76, 81
Phosphate detergents, 135–158
Phosphorus
  algae and, 146, 150
  effect of on water, 141, 151
Pierson, Ball & Dow law firm, 154
Pittsburgh Reduction Company, 162
Place, John, 53 n., 57, 81
Political influence, origins of, ix-x
Politics, technological mythology and, xvii
Pollution laws, violations of, xiii-xiv
Pollution subsidy, pesticides and, 114; see also Air pollution; Water pollution
Poppic, George, 122–123
Post, A. Alan, 38
Prentiss, L. W., 35
Primary Nonferrous Smelting Industry Liaison Committee, xvii, 64, 247
Procter & Gamble Company, 22, 138–140, 143, 152, 154–158, 242
Propaganda, technology and, x, 12
Property, condemnation of for highways, 29
Property Owners' Tax Association of California, 39
Proposition 18, California, 38–44, 47, 49
Prudential Insurance Company, 195
Public Health Service, U.S., 129, 183
Public Power Council, 173
Public relations campaigns, xi
Puget Sound Air Pollution Control Agency, 71
Puget Sound Board, 69
Purchase, Mary E., 151, 155

Queale, William, 44

Radiation, nuclear, 191–212
Ranch Calaveras project, California, 104
Randolph, Jennings, 34

Read, John, 208–209
Reader's Digest, 129
Reagan, Ronald, 38, 97
Real estate
  profits in, 90–91
  sales tactics in, 98–100
Recreational land development, see Land development
Recreational products, sale of, 90
Regaldo, Rubin, 54
Returnable bottles, planned withdrawal of, 9
Reuss, Henry, 146
Reynolds, David P., 25
Reynolds Metals Company, 12, 22, 24–25, 162, 164, 186
Richards, Ray, 94–95
Richmond, H. R., 174–175
Rivers and Harbors Act (1899), xiii
Road Tax Trap, 39, 44–48
Roche, James, 49
Rohr, Corp., 235
Rokow, Stanley M., 32
Rosenblatt, Robert, 40–41
Ross, John, 62
Rowen, Bob, 191–194, 200, 204–208, 210–212
Ruckleshaus, William, 25, 81–82, 131, 137, 154
Ruder and Finn, Inc., 21

Salesmen, in chemical industry, 122–124
Sales psychology, in land development, 98–100
San Andreas fault, 197
Sanchez, Manuel, 54
Sandburg, Carl, 215
San Francisco Chronicle, 103
Santa Barbara oil spill, x, 41
Saulie, Grant J., 178
Schell, Norman E., 80
Schulein, Joe, 161
Secrecy, scientific truth and, 176
Selby Smelter Commission, 60

Senior Scholastic magazine, 125
Sewage, phosphorus in, 141
Shaffer, John, 226, 230, 237
Shareholders, full disclosure for, 246
Shasta Beverages Company, 13
Shell Chemical Company, 117, 119–121, 128
Shell Oil Company, 119–121, 128
Shell Pest Strip, 119–121, 128
Shenker, Arden, 182–183
Sibley, S. L., 201
Sierra Club, 38, 47, 113
Silent Spring (Carson), 112, 129
Singmaster & Breyer consulting firm, 187–188
Skidmore, Raymond, 191–192
Skirvin, Fred, 169
Smaus, Torri, 104
Smelter Control Research Association, 75–77, 243
Smeltertown, Texas, 54, 61
Smelting
    closed-loop emission control system for, 79
    household damage from, 60–61
    problems of, 52–84
    soil damage from, 61–62
Smith, Adam, xvii
Smog
    automobile and, 31–32
    in California, 32, 38
Soap & Detergent Association, xi, xv, 141–143, 148–152, 154, 158
Sobelman, Max, 130
Sodium tripolyphosphate, 153
Soft-drink bottles, return of, 3, 7–22
Softdrinks magazine, 7–8, 11, 19–20
Soviet Union, 244
Spencer, Donald, 128–130
SST financing, xii
Standard Oil Company of California, 47–48, 91, 194
Standard Oil Company of Indiana, 30
Standard Oil Company of New Jersey, 30
Stans, Maurice, xviii, 81–82, 152

Steinfeld, Jesse, 136
Stone, I. F., 244
Stroube, Hal, 197
Stroup, Richard, 61
Stumph, Terry L., 66–67, 71, 81
Stumph Report, 67–69, 73
Sulfur dioxide, problems of in smelting, 53–58, 66, 70, 75
Super Giant Stores, 22
Supermarkets, bottle and container problems in, 7
Supreme Court, U.S., 226
Suttie, W. J., 169–170, 185
Swan, David, 72, 74, 76, 78

Tax Trap Committee, 44–48
Taylor, Robert, 209
Technological conspiracy, xiv–xv
Technological criminality, xiii–xiv
Technological mythology, xvi–xix, 6
Technological subsidy, xii–xiii
Technology
    discipline and, x
    endurance of, vii
    political influence and, ix
    propaganda and, x, 12
Tennessee Valley Authority, viii, 148
TEPP, organophosphate compound, 117
Terry, Romaine, 29
Testin, Robert, 24
Texaco, Inc., 30
Thompson, Col. Boyce, 180
Tillinghast, Charles C., Jr., 218
Timan, Joseph, 99–100
Timbers, William, 231
Torrington, Conn., real estate deals in, 102
Totem and Taboo (Freud), 112
Trade secrets, in chemical industry, 126
Train, Russell, 137, 157
Transportation Department, U.S., 237
Trans World Airlines, Inc., 218

Trohan, Walter, 125
Trucks, excise tax on, 34
Tuberculosis and Respiratory Diseases Association of California, 32, 38, 40, 47
Tuerk, Edward, 72
Turner, Francis, 34
Turner, James, viii
2,4,5–T herbicide, 127

Udall, Stewart, 143, 145
Union Carbide Corp., 114
Union Oil Company, 41
United Nations, 196, 241
United States Land, Inc., 101
United States Steel Corp., 22, 30
Unruh, Jesse, 38
Urban Mass Transportation Assistance Act (1970), 49–50
Ushijima, John T., 97
U.S. Plywood-Champion Papers, Inc., 22
Utah, University of, 75, 170–171
Utah Construction & Mining Company, 74

Van Den Bosch, Robert, 122
Vaughn, John, 40
Velsicol Chemical Corp., 111–112, 129–130

Wall Street Journal, 105
Walsh, George William, 81–82
Warner-Lambert Pharmaceutical Company, 244
Warster, Charles, 129
"Washday miracle," detergents and, 134–158
Washington Business Institute, 12–13, 17
Washington Committee to Stop Litter, 14

Washington Soft Drink Association, 12
Washington State
  and Initiative 256, 13–20
  litter problem in, 10–13
Washington State University, 179
Water pollution
  Nader report on, 152–153
  phosphates and, 141–158
Water Quality Administration, 135
Water Resources Scientific Information Center, 145
Weeks, Edgar, 193, 205
Weinberger, Leon, 144, 147–148
Weinstein, Leonard H., 169–170, 184–185
Wellford, Harrison, viii
Wells Fargo Company, 195
Western Oil and Gas Association, x, 43
Western Washington Huntley College of Engineering, 179–180
Westinghouse Electric Corp., 245
Weyerhaeuser Company, 12, 91, 165
Whitaker, John, 82, 132, 154
White-Stevens, Robert, 130
Williams, Forrest, 208–209
Winson, Don, 186
Wisconsin, University of, 147
Woodridge Lake-Ravenswood Estates, Connecticut, 90, 102
World War II
  aluminum industry in, 162
  pesticides and, 114

Yorty, Sam, 38
Yosemite National Park, 196
Youth groups, anti-litter projects for, 4

Zavon, Mitchell, 121, 128
Zwick, David, viii